Carte Blanche
The Stories Behind the Stories

To Dear Lisa + Russell

Just something small.
Enjoy Reading it

Carte Blanche
The Stories Behind the Stories

Jessica Pitchford

Love + Hugs.
Mum + Dad.

Jonathan Ball Publishers
Johannesburg & Cape Town

2013.

First published in 2013 by
JONATHAN BALL PUBLISHERS
PO Box 6836
Roggebaai
8012

Reprinted once in 2013

Paperbook ISBN 978-1-86842-561-7
ebook ISBN 978-1-86842-562-4

*Every effort has been made to trace copyright holders and to obtain their permission
for the use of copyright material. The publishers apologise for any errors or
omissions and would be grateful to be notified of any corrections that should be
incorporated in future editions of this book.*

All photographs supplied by *Carte Blanche* unless otherwise specified.
Photographs of *Carte Blanche* presenters and staff by Ivan Naude.

Zapiro cartoons reproduced by permission of Zaprock Productions.

Cover design and photo section by MR Design, Cape Town
Typeset by Triple M Design, Johannesburg
Set in 10,75/15pt Rotis Serif Std
Printed and bound by Paarl Media, Paarl

Twitter: www.twitter.com/JonathanBallPub
Facebook: www.facebook.com/pages/Jonathan-Ball-Publishers/298034457992
Blog: http://jonathanball.bookslive.co.za/

contents

foreword

Ruda Landman

When *Carte Blanche* started in August 1988, South Africa was in the opening stages of the roller-coaster ride which, over the next decade, would change the world we live in almost beyond recognition. At the risk of being seriously soppy, I want to misquote Wordsworth's famous lines on the French Revolution: 'Bliss was it in that dawn to be alive/ But to be a journalist was very heaven!' And *Carte Blanche* provided a platform like no other, free of any political or social agenda.

We could introduce our (then mainly white) audience to the new (usually black) faces in their world. In the process we got to know them ourselves, in my case often with astonishment as my preconceived ideas came tumbling down, shattered by the laughter of Archbishop Tutu or the quiet grace of a nurse in Alexandra.

The country was burning – we were there. People made peace, like one courageous man in Johannesburg's warring hostels – we were there. Whether it was the dismantling of the group areas, mixed marriages, gays finding the space to speak out, farms given back to people who had been forcibly removed ... we sought out those in the middle of the drama and told their stories. As the country grew and the stories changed, we just kept right on doing it. We travelled into Africa, to Israel, to China, among so many others. Always it was a learning journey.

My years at *Carte Blanche* expanded my horizons beyond anything I could have dreamed of. They taught me to get out of my box, let go of my comfortable assumptions, really listen to whoever the story confronted me with – and then confront the viewers with the same.

My colleagues are still doing it. *Carte Blanche* still lives up to its name: anything goes, no holy cows, always the unexpected. I wish them every success for the many years ahead.

Derek Watts

If there is another programme like *Carte Blanche* in the world, I haven't found it. This isn't a case of blowing our own trumpet or a comparison with the benchmark investigative journalism of America's *60 Minutes*, our broadcast partner in the formative years. It is more about the staggering variety of topics dealt with on the show, which, in one Sunday, can take you from a horrifying farm murder to jelly wrestling, with a riveting medical breakthrough and the revelations of a sporting hero fallen from grace thrown in for good measure!

The French expression '*carte blanche*', with its connotation of 'anything goes', probably got us started along that magical path. That freedom is the reason why I have never been bored in a quarter-century of reporting. Indeed, if you are tired of *Carte Blanche*, you are tired of life!

What is the reason for the show's success? M-Net's bravery in pushing the broadcast boundaries? The initial vision of song and dance supremo Bill Faure? The succession of executive producers, who each put their own spin on the show? The dedicated team of producers, presenters, researchers, editors and cameramen who have contributed so much over the years? The answer probably lies in the combination of all that home-grown talent.

All I know is that *Carte Blanche* has touched many thousands of lives, and we have a very special bond with our viewers. And that makes me extremely proud to have been a part of the *Carte Blanche* phenomenon.

George Mazarakis

In over 33 years as a broadcaster, I have never brought anything to air on my own. Broadcasting is a collective effort. As viewers, we never, ever sit in front of a screen and watch a show that has been made by one person. It simply isn't possible.

The sense of TEAM that is *Carte Blanche* is, to my mind, the one aspect that makes the show what it is. *Carte Blanche* is not the kind of show one can easily box into a genre; it is not simply a current affairs show, or a magazine show, or an entertainment show, or an investigative show, while being all of those things at once. It has many different elements, and these are defined by the personalities who get involved in the making of the show. In a sense, *Carte Blanche* takes on their characters and becomes different people on different days. And it grows, and it ages, and it rejuvenates itself, as those elements change and new characters grind their stamp on it.

Carte Blanche is a show with many faces. Not just those of the presenters who thrust microphones into people's faces, but also those of the camera operators who craft its visual sense, and who become its vehicles of narrative, of the editors and sound crews who create its texture, of the researchers who ferret out the details, and of its lawyers and editorial team, who massage the content into palatability, both legal and otherwise.

This book is about that process and those individuals. It will introduce you to the people behind the stories, and, more importantly perhaps, it will give you an insight into how and why stories are made, and what happens along the way.

In this information-dense age, when anyone can access material that hitherto was the rarefied preserve of the governing elite, we reveal what we ourselves once considered confidential 'trade secrets'. There are no secrets to the hard slog of investigative journalism. We no longer need to 'protect' our techniques. In fact, we need to be transparent and open about what we do and why we do it, if we want to own the right to challenge, with the same principles, those who govern us.

However, Jessica Pitchford's book is not an academic textbook on how to make television stories; it is rather, simply, a celebration of 25 years of storytelling. She has spoken to the people who made those stories, and they in turn have done all the searching their memories or dusty notes will allow. It is not an academic history either, so don't expect endless cross-references or annotated footnotes. This is, after all, a human story, full of human judgments and their concomitant flaws.

Jessica Pitchford is probably the finest managing editor I have ever had the pleasure of working with, though let me hasten to add that she is the finest of a fine (if sometimes sensitive) bunch. We were at university together in the early 1980s and found ourselves working together at the beginning of our careers and then picking up again as we matured into management roles. I trust her judgment and no-nonsense approach to journalistic and ethical issues implicitly.

It was therefore very natural to ask her to write this tribute to 25 years of what has really been a remarkable journey. It would have been that for any show in any country, but South Africa is a dynamic space in which to practise the craft of storytelling. Few countries can rival its turbulent recent history: the injustice of racial privilege, social and political strife on an epic scale, the redistribution of political power, the persistence of poverty and inequality and finally the rise of a new ruling elite. As a journalist, could I possibly ask for more fertile territory?

The country, by the same token, has often relied on *Carte Blanche* as a trusted authority on the state of affairs. Many South Africans who have grown up with the programme regard it as a trustworthy voice that gives them the real story on a Sunday night. *Carte Blanche* has shaped the viewer's understanding of our recent history.

The team you are about to meet is a remarkable one. Together they have won 157 awards. They have influenced government, changed laws and sparked popular debate. Their vital contribution to the world in which they live makes them exceptional. Commitment is the key word. These are people who take their mission seriously.

They never hesitate to attempt the impossible.

In a fight, these are the people I would want to have on my side. They are the true stars of the show, and I feel very privileged to have had the opportunity to lead them.

Viva *Carte Blanche*!!!

acknowledgements

The writing of this book involved many months of viewing dusty old tapes unearthed from a warehouse by Kathy Ferreira and Vincent Butje. The process helped paint a picture of *Carte Blanche* in the years before computers and digital media. It also involved reviving the fading memories of the producers, presenters, researchers and cameramen intimately involved with the show over the past 25 years. Not all of them feature in this book, but that in no way diminishes their contribution to a programme that was, at some stage, an all-consuming part of their lives. And I would not have been able to write it without plundering their memories, scripts and associated articles. The task was made easier by the input of editor Alfred LeMaitre, whose one-line email advice often made all the difference, and by the gentle encouragement of commissioning editor Ingeborg Pelser, whose frequent phone calls – 'How's the writing?' – made it a little less lonely. I am also grateful to Billie O'Hara, who uncomplainingly ploughed through the chapters before anyone else, and to George Mazarakis, with whom the buck stops and whose sage counsel to 'just blame me' I am in danger of overusing.

Jessica Pitchford
July 2013

the early years 1

Caller: 'I am the Second Coming of Jesus Christ ... I want to put this on record ... my current name is Jesus Govender ... in a way I am the walking truth ... I want to share these milestones with *Carte Blanche*, not to save myself, but all of mankind.'

Carte Blanche *journalist Susan Comrie*: 'So, what's the story – do you want a profile piece on yourself?'

Caller: 'Well, it's time the proper truth was told.'

Susan: 'Can you tell me in 30 seconds?'

Caller: 'I was an average Chatsworth teenager ... went to work in London and got involved with some colleagues who contacted MI5 about stuff I was doing ... they said "Listen, we are going to follow this guy and use psychological warfare on him" ... then the agents practically chased me out of the country ... when I got back to South Africa ... they followed me here, put hidden cameras on me, my house, my car ...'

Susan: 'Why would MI5 be following you?'

Caller: 'To scare me, to mess me up, you know ... '

Susan: 'For what? I'm sure MI5 have better things to do with their time.'

Caller (shouting): 'You are being quite cocky and arrogant! I thought *Carte Blanche* was all about the truth! Do you speak on behalf of *Carte Blanche*? The programme I grew up with that always told the truth is saying it doesn't know what's going on? And I didn't for one minute think that *Carte Blanche* was an organisation that oppressed people! I thought that *Carte Blanche* was there to ensure the smooth running of democracy in South Africa and the world! You are oppressing me!'

Not the average caller to the offices of South Africa's longest-running current affairs television show, but an indication of how some have come to view the programme, without which Sunday evenings just wouldn't be the same. These days, social media has to some extent overtaken the steady stream of phone calls to the show's Randburg offices, complaining about anything from a faulty vacuum cleaner to an errant spouse. Twitter has revealed a new breed of viewers, as tuned into their phones as they are to their tellies:

@palesat2: Hearing the @carteblanchetv jingle is a sign the weekend is realllly done!! *sigh*

@Chwayitisa: Because if it's Sunday, you know you're watching @carteblanchetv.

@maqaks:_I love it when @carteblanchetv exposes the white folks ... hahahaha.

@melinds123: I can already feel that awful 'tomorrow is Monday feeling' creeping up on me! *plays @carteblanchetv music*

@cindyroyle: Shudder at the thought of what this country would be if we didn't have @carteblanchetv – #CarteblancheforPresident VIVA ;)

@sugarplumholly: @carteblanchetv love the show, I feel like I only watch it for the 'bad news' – love the truth to expose lies and corruption.

Love it or loathe it, *Carte Blanche* has become a Sunday night ritual. And while some still call it 'emigration hour', and get that back-to-boarding-school feeling when the familiar jingle beckons, the brand 'Carte Blanche' is a powerful one. The same music, the same presenter, the same logo and the same time slot for 25 years have made the show an institution and, along with quality journalism, the Sunday hour between 7pm and 8pm has become the most expensive real estate on South African television.

Someone who's been associated with the programme since the early 1990s is Billie O'Hara, the first line of defence, the 'listen-hear lady'. The *Carte Blanche* website describes her as the link between 'us and our viewing audience'. And, in turn, it's her link to the world. In her seventies, with a voice slightly husky from years of smoking, 'Mr O' Hara', as she's often mistakenly called, has watched the show's reinventions over the years from a firmly entrenched place on the sidelines. She's seen managers, presenters, producers and researchers come and go from jobs that are rewarding, exhilarating and downright stressful. Although there are callers who irritate her beyond belief (the ones who begin their calls with 'listen here, lady', or who phone to report that the bicycle they ordered on special arrived without a bell), *Carte Blanche* is what she calls 'her oxygen'. She knows, 30 seconds into a conversation, that this call is never going to lead to an on-air story, yet she'll rush into the newsroom hoping someone will be able to help poor Alfred from Ventersdorp who has waited 16 years for an RDP house, or have advice for a mother setting off to find her drug-addicted son in Hillbrow, or for a prisoner phoning from a call box at Pollsmoor with the familiar refrain, 'I didn't do it.'

Granny Billie probably knows more about the nation's car, insurance and medical problems than the average mechanic, broker or nurse, and feels she knows the *Carte Blanche* 'looker' – as one caller eloquently described himself – like the back of her hand.

And that's how it all began in those black-and-white days of August 1988. Subscribers to pay-TV channel M-Net, started by newspaper group Naspers in 1986, needed an alternative news source to what the SABC was dishing up. M-Net approached Louis Moller, the original owner of Combined Artistic Productions (CAP) – the company that still produces the show – to come up with a bilingual, no-holds-barred, weekly eye-opener. Moller brought on board Bill Faure, regarded by many as the most dynamic South African TV director of his day. Ruda Landman remembers Faure as a colourful and intense personality – as camp as they come, long before gay was OK – and capable of creating the magic that M-Net was after. He would walk into a room, throw ideas into the air like burning silver balls, then disappear in his beloved Rolls-Royce, leaving everyone to catch and make sense of them. Moller, now the owner of the Barnyard Theatres, gets misty-eyed when he remembers Faure's 'arrogant, fearless talent'

3

and untimely demise. William C Faure may have been the son of a conservative blue-collar worker, but he showed scant respect for the laws of the time. He was still riding the wave of international acclaim from the TV miniseries *Shaka Zulu* when Moller asked him to help start a show modelled on CBS's *60 Minutes*, which used the then-unique style of reporter-centred investigations, hidden cameras and 'gotcha' visits.

M-Net had been on air for just two years and was starting to make a profit. Its licence restricted it from broadcasting news, then the sole domain of the SABC and fiercely controlled by the government of the time. But it wanted a local production that was different and daring. And that's what it got.

Everyone involved at the time says the same thing: that the aim was to push the envelope, to be inventive and innovative. Sperm collected in a champagne glass from a man of colour for the insemination of a white woman was outrageous in apartheid South Africa, and the name 'Carte Blanche', chosen by M-Net viewers, implied having the freedom to do what you liked when you liked. It was not done in the South Africa of 1988.

In the very first broadcast, on a garish blue and yellow striped set, Ruda Landman said: 'Carte Blanche: *alles is moontlik se die woorde-boek, en dit gaan nie net ons naam wees nie, maar ons leuse vir die program ...*'

Topless tanning in Cape Town, jelly wrestling, male escorts, the curious tale of the man who imagined he had a green light shining from his forehead, erectile dysfunction and a mother and daughter abducted by aliens. They were all to become part of a genre never before seen on South African television. Ex-SABC news presenter Ruda Landman had no hesitation when Faure phoned to ask if she'd like to be part of this brave new venture.

One of the early stories seems basic by 21st-century standards – a day in the life of a township resident. Alexandra was an area white Johannesburgers couldn't avoid seeing, because of its proximity to Sandton, but one that few had visited. Ruda and co-presenter Derek Watts and their crew set off for Alex and did the unthinkable – spent time with black people in their backyards. Ruda got to grips with the life of a nurse at a local clinic; Derek checked out the bucket system, visited a street barber, ate chicken feet and had a drink at a shebeen. It was a story that defined the way ahead and won for *Carte Blanche* its first award. A faded picture in CAP's viewing room shows Faure holding a *Star Tonight!* TV award: 'Bill Faure triumphs with *Carte Blanche*'. The show was described as a trailblazer, a blend of 'sociological awareness, sophistication and audacity'.

Watts, just 40 at the time, was an affable SABC sports presenter and, according to Louis Moller, not CAP's first choice to extend the frontiers of hard-hitting TV journalism. But he was M-Net's choice, and clearly the right one, because he's still around today, an instantly recognisable two-metre-tall figure. He recalls the Alexandra story as a reflection of the times, times in which township reporting on the SABC consisted of police unrest reports and warnings of 'mob' violence.

But, mostly, those early shows were a hotchpotch of ideas, with no particular style, other than a refreshing and brazen one. There were wacky issues and personalities: an interview with Cocky 'Two Bull' Tlhotlhalemaje of Capital Radio and 702 fame; the early James Bond girls, Ursula Andress and Britt Ekland, interviewed live in a make-shift studio that doubled as an edit suite; mating lions in the Kruger National Park; alternative Afrikaans music and theatre. Budgets were small, and staff skeletal. Producer-director Susan Stos worked directly under Bill. She was a new arrival to South Africa from the Canadian Broadcasting Corporation (CBC) and still remembers the terror that went with breaking new ground. She soon got to grips with the strange ways of a strange country, but not before being hauled over the coals for broadcasting a picture of Nelson Mandela – an illegal act at the time – and for having the nerve to edit an interview with Minister of Health Willie van Niekerk, which M-Net then had to rerun apolo-getically in its entirety. And she had to put into practice Bill's often 'mad' ideas, like having a Great Dane as a studio guest. Faure was a showman, not a journalist, and was not overly concerned with cred-ible sources or ethics. 'Smut! We need a bit of smut!' was his regular refrain.

But he chose someone completely unlike him as *Carte Blanche*'s first executive producer. Theologian-turned-TV-producer Pieter Cilliers was producing the magazine show *Potpourri* when Louis and Bill approached him. Bill arrived to collect him for the interview in the ostentatious Rolls-Royce, which had Cilliers' SABC colleagues craning their necks to see the two getting into it. A former dominee, who was later to come out as a gay Christian in his book *'n Kas is vir Klere*, Cilliers saw the *Carte Blanche* job as his opportunity to break free from the state broadcaster's controlling influence. In a *Sunday Times* article in March 1989, he told Barry Ronge that the time had come to 'get off the ambulance full of maimed, wounded and weary creative people' at the SABC. Louis Moller remembers the mercurial Bill and the perfectionist Pieter butting heads on many occasions. But to Pieter, the fact that he was allowed to argue his point, after the rigid controls at the SABC, meant total freedom. He proceeded to lay the foundation for solid investigative journalism and instilled in producers the art of telling personal stories on television, which no one else in South Africa was doing. A working visit to CBS's *60 Minutes* in New York helped him to shape the show. The narrative became king.

With the winds of change blowing from Parliament, Cilliers found himself constantly reminding journalists, so used to self-censorship, that they could in fact report on stories like the mixed marriage of 'Protas and Suzanne Madlala' (1989), 'Blacks Living in White Areas' (1990) and the 'Return of Land to the Mfengus of the Tsitsikamma' (1991).

Gradually, South African stories took centre stage on *Carte Blanche*, until then hugely reliant on *60 Minutes* for content. Derek Watts recalls hosting 'funny little shows', then crossing over to the mighty Mike Wallace for a big-budget story from the US. In those days, *Carte Blanche* was 58 minutes long, with only two minutes of ads, which meant a lot of airtime for a small team to fill. But exposés eventually became part of the weekly *Carte Blanche* diet, and the show began impacting decision-makers and role-players in one of the most fascinating periods of South African history. Cilliers describes his three years as executive producer as the most challenging, liberating, exhausting and rewarding of his life.

But eventually the never-ending deadlines, of waking up on Monday after Sunday's show and having to start the process all over again, got the better of him and Cilliers moved on to produce the more light-hearted *Premiere* for M-Net, but not without having pulled *Carte Blanche* in the direction it needed to go. Ruda Landman credits him with creating solid journalism and for building the presenters into the personalities they became. Linda Vermaas, who produced regular stories for *Carte Blanche*, took over from Cilliers as executive producer in 1992. Newspaper articles from 1993 make mention of her 'livelier approach'. M-Net began providing budget for three local and one overseas insert, which upped ratings considerably. Faure told the *Star Tonight!* (22 April 1993): 'We are very pleased, she is hitting the right formula'.

Stories on Linda's watch included one on hermaphrodites, as well as one on penoplasty – risky surgery to enlarge and lengthen the penis. Derek, who presented the show, recalls being concerned when he and producer Clive Morris noted the sizes of the members being enlarged, because they looked 'normal'! There was Ruda's memorable visit to the threatened silverback gorillas of Rwanda, showing intimate scenes of the animals' daily lives, and about which she's still asked to this day. There was also Derek's 'yoo-hoo' to the Queen across a London street, to tell her he was looking forward to her upcoming visit to South Africa. 'Thank you, thank you very much' was the unexpected response, which astonished royal-watchers and delighted viewers back home.

By the time Faure succumbed to an AIDS-related illness in October 1994, *Carte Blanche* was firmly established in a rapidly changing South Africa. But the country hadn't changed enough for him to feel comfortable about disclosing his status. Louis Moller by this stage was long gone, worn down by the all-consuming nature of the show – the late-Saturday, early-Sunday-morning viewings with lawyers and anxious producers – and had become a dairy farmer near Plettenberg Bay. Bill visited him there in those final months, his intellect and his health fast fading. 'Sad, sad, sad ...' is how Moller sums it up.

Bill's obituary was carried in the *New York Times* on 20 October 1994:

William C. Faure, who gained international recognition for the television mini-series 'Shaka Zulu,' died on Tuesday at the age of 45. His company, Combined Artists, said the cause of death was kidney failure. Mr. Faure directed 'Shaka Zulu,' a 1985 drama made in South Africa about the 19th-century Zulu warrior king. It became one of the most popular mini-series on syndicated television in the United States when it was shown in 1987.

In South Africa, Faure's death made headlines. In *The Star*, Barry Ronge mourned the passing of 'a grand and unforgettable showman ... who quite simply led the field'.

In a tribute on *Carte Blanche* that Sunday, Ruda spoke of his visionary genius, which had enabled him to create and control spectacles of enormous proportions. 'His spirit still guides *Carte Blanche* into shaking complacency ... bringing to the screen a social and ecological conscience. His passing leaves a gaping hole in the South African television industry, for no one will ever know the brilliant productions that he might still have created.'

But the show had to go on. Before he left, Moller had brought on board Jon Sparkes, an executive from Toron Film Studios, which made local movies for the international market. He'd first met Faure in 1985 on the set of *Emily Hobhouse*, which Sparkes had co-produced and Faure had directed. Sparkes was told he was looking for trouble, working with the most undisciplined director in the industry. The documentary came in ahead of schedule and under budget. So he had no qualms about becoming Bill's business partner at CAP when Louis left, although he had doubts that M-Net and *Carte Blanche* would survive. Two and a half decades later, he's still controlling the company finances, still easy on the eye, and still hovering on the periphery of *Carte Blanche*. Faure, he says, would be amazed that his legacy has lived on.

So it was in those years, when the close-knit team gathered at the Houghton house where Faure lived, worked and died – with his ever-present pet python, 'Naughty Boy' – that the seed was sown for South Africa's premier investigative and current affairs show.

With Sparkes as managing producer and the familiar faces of Ruda Landman and Derek Watts, *Carte Blanche* slid gently into the new South

Africa, careful not to lose its grip on its traditional and loyal viewers. The new era took the show into Africa and beyond, and into the heart of some unforgettable stories.

Rick Lomba and the Luanda Zoo

Derek Watts counts it as the worst experience of his long career. Managing producer Jon Sparkes describes it as one of those dreadful moments in the history of a company that has been touched by mercifully few tragedies over the years. Linda Vermaas, the executive producer at the time, now living in Thailand, wrote in an email 18 years after the incident: 'It was an exceptionally sad chapter ... a drop of lead in my heart ... and played a role in my eventual decision to move on from CB.'

From the start, it had been a difficult shoot. Angola in 1994 was a country forgotten by the world, despite massive destruction and the deaths of an untold number of civilians. An attempted ceasefire, the Lusaka Protocol, was to be signed later that year between Jonas Savimbi's UNITA movement and the ruling MPLA, but in March, when *Carte Blanche* arrived, the team found a country ravaged by two decades of conflict. The drive from Luanda airport into the capital showed the effects of intense civil war on a desperately poor population.

But *Carte Blanche* had come to report on animals, not people. The local government had closed the Luanda Zoo because there were simply no funds to run it. But the animals remained, caged and hungry. In an unusual operation, organised by the Johannesburg Zoo, 30 wild animals were to be captured, drugged and relocated to South Africa. It was a massive coordination project, headed by the Johannesburg Zoo's manager of animal collections, Quinton Coetzee, now a popular motivational speaker. Each animal crate was custom-made: you couldn't, for instance, put a black-shouldered kite in a big crate in case it tried to fly and damaged its wings. The six-person team had to bring along, on a cargo plane, everything that might not be available in a country with plenty of mineral resources and weapons, but maybe not drawing pins, generators, angle grinders, bolt cutters and veterinary drugs. The plane, which was infested with rats, was on loan from the Angolan government.

Dealing with officials at the airport was the first hurdle: the dart gun and the animal crates were impounded. South Africa and Angola had been at war until 1990, so guns of any description were treated with utmost suspicion. Days of wrangling to get the paperwork sorted out left little time for the real task at hand: immobilising, capturing and crating the animals.

Interviewed by Derek, Quinton mentioned the five tigers in a small enclosure and the logistical nightmare of trying to get them out. 'If you dart one and it goes down, there's a strong possibility that the others will eat it, so you may have to dart them all at the same time, or build an enclosure in which we can put them one by one.' And in words that would come back to haunt him: 'We are going to have to plan this very carefully ... how are we going to do this in a very limited time and with no losses?'

While negotiations at Customs continued, Derek and cameraman-producer Rick Lomba got to meet the animals and the small band of Samaritans who'd been looking after them.

Rick was an experienced wildlife documentary filmmaker, who'd done several stories in Botswana for *Carte Blanche*, and had made a big impression internationally with his documentary, *The End of Eden*, which showed the effects of cattle ranching on Botswana's wildlife and had led the World Bank to review its aid policy in the region. The subsequent *Gardeners of Eden* and *Quest for Survival* had cemented his reputation. He was a gung-ho character, a veteran of many mishaps, who often strapped his camera on a microlight to follow herds of animals or to capture on film the vastness of areas like the Okavango and the Kalahari. One of his favorite expressions was: 'Any landing you

11

walk away from is a good one.' But he was not to walk away from the Luanda Zoo.

Rick, said Linda Vermaas, although not a core *Carte Blanche* producer, had been the natural choice for the zoo relocation story. There wasn't enough space on the cargo plane for a full crew and Rick was a one-man band – he could shoot and produce, and he knew his subject.

Derek recalls a long walk he and Rick took through the streets of Luanda one night, both of them struck by the contrast between their lavish hotel, which even had lobster on the menu, and the acres and acres of poverty surrounding it; by the barren cages at the zoo filled with starving animals and the brimming supermarkets in parts of the city.

At the zoo they'd met an American expat named Joanna Field, who had made it her life's mission to save the animals. Her husband was well connected in Angola and had helped get the necessary government authorisation for the rescue operation. Every other day, she and a helper named João bought meat for the animals at the local market. There's a shot, filmed by Rick, of João feeding five emaciated tigers, known to eat up to seven kilograms a day. A piece of raw meat gets stuck between the bars at the top of the cage. One of the tigers is there in a flash, defying gravity, the meat devoured.

Once the crates and capturing equipment had been released by Customs, the team had to get moving: they had one day to do what they'd planned to do over three. They began darting animals like the buffalo and ostriches, which were going to a farm outside Luanda because of disease-control regulations in South Africa. There were no spare crates for them, so they were lifted onto the back of a truck. An ostrich and a buffalo died, probably from stress-related causes. Derek stood next to the truck where the dead ostrich was lying, describing it as a 'tragic start to the operation'.

Phase two was the animals destined for South Africa. First were the pythons because there was no danger of them hurting themselves if the drugs wore off on the flight home. Then came the monkeys and lemurs. The bears, lions and tigers were last; if they woke on the journey they could rub their noses raw on their cages, or damage their claws. It all went according to plan. Not surprising, said Coetzee, an ex-military man, because there'd been months of precision planning. But no reconnaissance had been done. Impossible in a war zone, he said.

The oblong-shaped tiger enclosure was divided into two, with an interleading gate through which, at times, the animals could move freely from cage A to cage B. The gate could be closed by pushing a lever on the outside. At the end of the enclosure was another gate, set in a wall in the zoo grounds and opening into an alley that went all the way round to the rear of the cages. The aim was to isolate the tigers by closing the gate between the cages. Once in cage B, the tigers would be darted, and then moved out the back exit, a low door, and along the passage into the zoo grounds. Rick was in and around the alley filming the process: once a tiger was immobilised, three men lifted it onto a sling-like contraption with handles and onto a forklift. It went without saying that the gate between the two cages and the exit gate to the alley couldn't be open at the same time, or the not-yet-drugged tigers would escape. Derek remembers walking back towards the tiger cages with Quinton Coetzee when they realised that one of the big males had moved from cage A to cage B, which meant it could be darted. But the exit into the alley had been left open. And Rick was in the alley.

In an interview with Ruda Landman aired on Sunday, 20 March 1994, Derek said: '... there was just a streak, that tiger went for the gate, everyone just screamed and I heard five shots ring out and someone say "call an ambulance ..." I didn't know it was Rick, but I knew that somebody was in that alley behind those cages and you can't get out; you are trapped there.'

The 190-kilogram cat sank its fangs into Lomba's throat. Moments later, the animal was shot by Quinton Coetzee with an Angolan guard's rifle.

Diana Lucas, who edited the final story, said she could hear Rick talking to the tigers in the last seconds of the tape, telling them they'd soon be on a plane to a better life. But it was too heartbreaking to use, so the last shot in the edited story is a close-up of a huge male tiger, green eyes staring through the bars of the cage behind which, at that stage, it had had no escape.

The devastated team was now in a tricky situation: an entire zoo had been boxed and had to be loaded onto a plane at Luanda airport. They had no choice but to leave Rick's body there, alongside the tiger, and undertake what Derek still describes as the longest flight of his life.

Before they took off, he'd managed to get through to his wife, Belinda, in Johannesburg to tell her the news. He asked her to break it to Rick's wife, Brita.

The petite Mrs Watts has lived and breathed *Carte Blanche* as much as her husband over the past 25 years and this is her most harrowing memory. Belinda didn't know Rick's wife and wasn't sure what to do. So she phoned CAP directors Bill Faure and Jon Sparkes and quickly found a babysitter. She remembers Bill arriving in the Rolls-Royce, smartly dressed in a cravat and suit for some reason and by then using a cane or crutch. They made their way to the home Rick shared with his wife and two daughters. As soon as Brita Lomba saw the three of them on her doorstep, she said: 'Oh, my God, it's Rick.' Then: 'I have all his favourite foods in the fridge, he's coming home tomorrow.' Belinda says they spent hours with her, as friends came round, but there was no way of getting more information out of Luanda. Jon recalls seeing photographs in the living room of Rick's two little girls, Nikki and Kim, who were fast asleep in their beds at the time. He thought: 'They are going to wake up tomorrow and find out that their dad is dead.'

The following day, Belinda, Linda Vermaas and Ruda were at the cargo section of what was then Jan Smuts International Airport. Out on the tarmac, Ruda addressed the camera: 'It's five o'clock in the morning and we're at air freight waiting for the plane to come in. This is not the end that any of us would ever have wished for. Derek is alone on that plane.'

It was a difficult call for Linda. The focus of the story was meant to be the successful airlift of an entire zoo to another country – an amazing feat. Now that focus had been overtaken. Or had it? She wasn't yet sure how to deal with it for that Sunday's show; all she knew was that Derek's arrival, and that of the animals, had to be documented.

In fact, because of heavy fog over Johannesburg, Derek was being rerouted to Gaborone. Together with the zoo staff, he was extremely worried that the animals' tranquilisers would wear off during the five-hour delay. They finally touched down at 10am and Belinda met an emotionally drained and exhausted Derek. In an interview with Ruda, red-eyed and fighting back tears, he pondered her question: 'Was the exercise worth it?'

'Only if the animals make it ... if half of them die, then it's something that should not have happened.'

On the tarmac, the new arrivals were opening their eyes to a brand-new world. Not a single animal was lost on the journey. Rick would've loved the 'success' of the mercy mission, said Johannesburg Zoo director Dr Pat Condy. In the newspapers, he called Lomba's death a 'freak accident', and said that the tiger had slipped through a safety gate.

Brita Lomba sued the city council, as owner of the Johannesburg Zoo, for negligence. In a case that dragged on and was later settled out of court, zoo staff were found responsible for opening the gate between the two cages while the back door of cage B was still open. The council paid Brita's legal costs, but there was no financial settlement, she says, because the costs were separated from the liability.

In a tribute aired on *Carte Blanche*, there's a last picture of Rick, taken by Derek. He's sitting on his camera case, having a smoke break, surrounded by bales of straw and looking hot, tired and cheerful. On the back Derek had written: 'Rick Lomba minutes before he was killed by a tiger in Luanda.'

In a letter written to the *Carte Blanche* team a month later, Brita Lomba said: 'Thank you for the sensitive and understanding way you handled Rick's painful death with regard to me and the little girls. The tribute you produced within such a short time frame was remarkable in its honesty and caring. Even the old cynic would've approved of it, although he always preferred to generate action from behind the camera and to stir up some controversy ... It is still hard to grasp that a man filled with such restless energy is no longer around.'

below the belt 3

When Ruda Landman hung up her microphone in June 2007, after almost 19 years of anchoring *Carte Blanche*, she joked that one of the things the show had given her was a sex education. Bill Faure's recipe for 'a little bit of smut' had not died with him. The show rarely held back when it came to issues of sexuality. Topics included how disabled people had sex, penis piercing and, much later, extended massive orgasms and sex fantasy clubs. Ruda had come a long way since her childhood in the Northern Cape town of Keimoes on the banks of the Orange River and her early career in the South African Defence Force, but there were still things that surprised her. Like the transvestites of Beaufort West.

'*Maak jou reg vir 'n man en dan sal jy 'n man kry in Beaufort-Wes,*' said Masmilla Maans, one of this trucking town's nonconformists, who every evening tucked her tail between her legs, donned a Goldilocks wig, short skirt and high heels before hitting the streets. 'R300 for a good fuck or suck,' was how she bluntly put it. What puzzled Ruda, and made her apologise for being '*dom*', was how on earth Milla had sex with men without them knowing she also had a penis? 'Easy,' said Milla, 'I just sit on him.' Ruda still looked confused and later returned to this line of questioning with another she-male called Priscilla, who laughed, saying there were plenty of 'hazel-strikers' out there. What she meant was that their clients knew exactly what they were getting. The fact that there was a penis lurking beneath the sexy feminine clothing simply added to the fantasies of the heterosexual men who picked them up. And pick them up they did: on the N1 between Cape Town and Johannesburg; in front of the NG Kerk in the middle of town; even a block away from the police station – 'in case of trouble'. Farmers, truck drivers and travellers all stopped to sample the wares of the Queens of the Desert.

Masmilla had a strange attraction; she was sinewy and long-limbed, with full red lips and a sharp sense of humour. She said she asked God to forgive her line of work, and He did. How else would she make ends meet? There were simply no jobs for overt gays in platteland towns like Beaufort West. Masmilla's mum, Sarah Maans, a homely woman in a *doek*, was a little unsure of how much she should reveal on camera about her unusual child, whom she had christened Jack. She didn't approve of Masmilla's sexual proclivities, but accepted them. He began dressing up in girl's clothes as a little boy and had never stopped. She called him 'my baby'; he was the youngest of nine and the only one who was still with her, caring for her. By day, Masmilla played the domesticated daughter, rushing about cleaning, baking bread and hanging up the washing, pegs clipped onto her short skirt. But when the sun went down, she began prepping for a night on the town.

Producer Carol Albertyn Christie, who directed the shoot, was struck by Sarah Maans' non-judgmental acceptance of her unusual child and loved Masmilla's candour, and the way all the she-males played up to the camera, relishing the attention, slightly ludicrous in their ill-fitting wigs, clownish dabs of rouge high on their cheekbones, gap-tooth grins on painted lips.

After several incidents of abuse and stone-throwing in the streets, in which the 'girls' clearly gave as good as they got, they approached social worker Lorraine Deysel to teach them to behave like 'ladies'. She helped them organise a march to demand their right to be accepted in society and drummed into them that swearing in the streets was a no-no. Be polite and command respect. But sometimes they slipped: when potential customers arrived, it was money, not manners, that counted. '*Ek wil die jongetjie hê, die een met die brilletjies,*' said Masmilla, rushing over the road when two truck drivers pulled up.

It was an amusing but also poignant story, set at the start of the Western Cape winter, and the images of Masmilla and the girls trying to flag down truck drivers in the rain and sheltering in shop doorways were atmospheric. As the weather lifted one afternoon, there was a wonderful scene of these Queens of the Desert dancing with gay abandon to 'Lola' by The Kinks, a rainbow stretched over the stark landscape. The song lyrics were about a romance between a young man and a transvestite in a Soho club. Beaufort West might be a far cry from London, but there were similarities:

Girls will be boys and boys will be girls
It's a mixed up, muddled up, shook up world, except for Lola
Lo-lo-lo-lo Lola

Stories of a fairly explicit nature like this one invariably evoke a reaction, and there are always those who question the need to cover this kind of subject at all. But *Carte Blanche*'s mission statement is clear: 'we resist the usual and challenge convention ... we strive to open minds, stimulate debate, nurture understanding and tolerance ... and we do this with the conviction that our audience has the right to see it all.'

Executive producer George Mazarakis, who'd worked at SABC current affairs before a short stint as a lecturer in Journalism at Rhodes University, found the show a breath of fresh air when he took over from Linda Vermaas in 1995. In those days, the Broadcasting Complaints Commission of South Africa (BCCSA) was still finding its feet, and there was far more scope to peek beneath the underbelly of society, to examine the sexual peccadilloes of strait-laced communities. The stories were in no way voyeuristic; they related directly to the subject, the tone empathetic and non-judgmental. And they had a message – as in the curious case of Estefan Els.

Sex Change – June 1996

Esme, as she was then, was 31 years old, with a desperate desire to be a man. So desperate that she was willing to risk all – her friends, her livelihood, her bank balance, her health, her reputation. She was an online video editor, which, in the pre-digital era, was the final stage of videotape production, and she'd crossed paths with *Carte Blanche* producers on occasion. Carol Albertyn Christie, who'd worked at Penguin Films with Esme, described her as 'seriously butch'. Kelly Lilienfeld, the *Carte Blanche* researcher assigned to the story, found her a curious contradiction. Her cropped hair and stocky build may have been masculine, but she dressed in various shades of neon pink, loved sending notes on floral scented paper, and had an unusual collection of crochet doilies. Carol wondered if her radical decision to have a sex change could have been avoided if Esme had embraced her butch-dyke self, strapped on a dildo and got on with it. But it seemed to Carol and Kelly that Esme's conservative background made her feel that she had to be one thing or the other.

Society's understanding of gender identity was still inchoate back then, and so *Carte Blanche* decided to chronicle Esme's transition from female to male. It would be a unique and enlightening story, but not an easy one, because it meant following her for months and months, being there for the hysterectomy, as the hormone injections that suppressed female characteristics and stimulated male ones began to take effect. Kelly recalls egocentric adolescent behaviour the one minute, and a crying heap of hormones the next.

But both she and producer Diana Lucas had to make a conscious effort to remain emotionally uninvolved. Cameraman Mike Yelseth felt involved all the way, however, and Estefan treated him like a buddy, even showing him 'her' porn magazines.

Esme had minimal support from close family, and the *Carte Blanche* team wondered if she wasn't relying too much on her therapist, who was doing a doctorate on gender reassignment. Was Esme an ideal candidate for life-altering surgery, and was she getting the right professional advice? And there was the slightly uncomfortable thought that she might be enjoying having a TV crew following her every move. Kelly remembers on several occasions telling Estefan that the journey could be put on hold at any time. But there was no stopping her, and so the crew was there when her breasts slowly disappeared and she became a 'he'. His facial hair grew, and Mike gave Estefan advice on how to shave before filming the process. They documented the painful growth of skin on Estefan's forearm, injected with saline solution, which would eventually be moulded into a penis by a plastic surgeon. It would be a permanently erect, but fully functioning, phallus.

But the final operation to connect the blood vessels to the groin failed. The blood supply to the penis stopped and there was a danger that gangrene would set in. Kelly remembers visiting the hospital two days after the failed phalloplasty and being nauseated by the putrid smell. George Mazarakis and Billie O'Hara visited too and felt sick and sad for Estefan, who had become part of a tragic statistic: the 15 per cent failure rate of sex change operations. His newly constructed penis had to be removed in an emergency operation, leaving him in no-man's land – that complex middle ground between male and female.

Diana, a highly skilled and creative producer, experienced Estefan as a sometimes too willing case study; he understood television, and, as a conventional bloke in the making, insisted on carrying all the heavy filming gear and opening doors for her. But, as sometimes happens, particularly with stories of a personal nature done over a long period – in this case, almost two years – the subject can become emotionally reliant on the producer. Not an all-consuming obsession, but a difficulty in drawing the line between a working relationship and a need to share all. Diana felt the heartbreak of Estefan's shattered dreams, but for her the main part of the story ended after the unsuccessful operation and she moved into the edit suite for post-production. Kelly remembers a heated argument in edit about the final visuals: should they show Estefan's scarred forearm in place of his manhood – a failure? Or the eventual ending that spoke of hope and the promise of a new life?

For Estefan, the story was incomplete because the desired result hadn't been achieved. Despite taking out a bank overdraft and being short of a further R50 000 to fund a second operation, Estefan remained determined to get the body he wanted – a man's. But he got involved with someone Mike described as 'a nasty piece of work': a blonde 'poppie' and a bad influence. To fund a new attempt at the elusive penis, Estefan stole equipment and committed fraud.

Fast forward to 1997: the *Carte Blanche* cameras found Estefan in a police cell, lying on a narrow bed reading a newspaper with the headline

'Unique funeral planned for Princess Di'. In an interview with Ruda, he broke down, regretting a ruined life and years of jail time ahead. In her book *Off Camera*, Ruda wrote that, despite the lengths to which Estefan had gone in order to become a man, the crew experienced and responded to him as a female. Every time they worked with him, they had to remind themselves that Estefan was a man – in contrast to Masmilla in Beaufort West, who, with her stuffed bra, seemed a woman through and through.

There was a follow-up story in June 2000, by which time Estefan had been released from prison early for good behaviour. He now sported pronounced sideburns and had a deep scar on his back – the legacy of a second attempt to grow a penis. He was living in a borrowed caravan in a garden in Alberton, on Johannesburg's industrial East Rand, and was not nearly as happy as he had been in the female section of Diepkloof prison. There, he had been a novelty and the subject of much attention. Now he had nothing – no job, no money, no sex organs. This time Ruda interviewed him in the caravan not much bigger than a prison cell, a stuffed toy resting on the bed behind him. In a voice that sounded like it still needed to break, he said he had come to terms with his body and felt 'one hundred per cent male'. He wanted to go fishing, to chat to men about their sex lives with women, about shaving. But male society didn't accept him and females were unsure of his intentions, so he lived a lonely isolated life.

Swingers – 1995

Presenters have dipped in and out of *Carte Blanche* over the years. There was Michele Alexander, who produced and presented her own stories and who did the first transvestite prostitution story in 1996, in which she couldn't resist feeling their squishy latex bra fillers. The late Manu Padayachee, the first black continuity presenter on M-Net, was famous for the words 'Please do not adjust the colour on your sets, I look this way'. Manu was the face of some *Carte Blanche* gems like 'Post Office Theft', in which postal workers were filmed taking the contents of parcels certainly not addressed to them. And then there was the stylish Les

Aupiais, who says she's still defined by the sex stories she did.

Les has amusing recollections of an eye-popper she presented on swinging. The Oxford dictionary describes swinging as 'to move to and fro', while Wikipedia says it's 'partner swapping ... non-monogamous behaviour, in which singles or partners in a committed relationship engage in sexual activities with others as a recreational activity'. Les remembers it as a long night of trying not to look shocked.

It wasn't the show's first venture into voyeurism. In 1995, on a *Carte Blanche* set with silver and lurid pink lettering, Ruda said: '*Getroude mense wat nie omgee om hulle maats met ander te deel en self uit te vind watter ander seksuele moontlikhede 'n mens nog kan ontdek nie*.' Prolific producer Jan Lampen and Manu had visited an upmarket swingers' venue called X-pose, run by two glamorous middle-aged women, Michelle and Kathy, dressed in black evening wear and sporting scrunched hairdos.

The club was for members only and there were 8 000 signed up – 'even Afrikaners', Michelle made a point of mentioning, although, said Kathy, 'you can't mix classes, it just doesn't work'. No mention of black patrons, but presumably in 1995 it was still a whites-only thing. The entrance fee of R400 per couple included hot and cold snacks, booze, parking and condoms. When not used for private swinging parties, the house was a fully operational casino and brothel.

Michelle and Kathy locked arms with Manu, who was rigged with a radio microphone, and took him on a tour of the establishment. One of the bedrooms had one-way glass so that patrons at the bar could look in. But there were house rules: if the bedroom door was open, you could join in; if it was closed, stay out. Manu questioned Michelle about being seen as promoting promiscuity; she said it was about being open and honest.

The story began in the home of Frank and Sasha, a swinging couple getting ready for a night out. They didn't mind showing their faces on camera; they loved the lifestyle and it had made them more secure in their relationship, allowing them to act out their fantasies, which had begun as pillow talk. Sasha fantasised about being in bed with a woman and Frank needed to watch others doing the deed. At first they tried picking up partners in an ordinary club, but that didn't work out, so they joined X-pose.

The average ages of swinging couples at X-pose was between 30 and 50, and many said joining had stopped them cheating on their partners. Debora (identity hidden) said she had joined because she was bisexual and hadn't had a chance to explore relationships with 'ladies'. Her husband Graham had always fantasised about 'having sex with two females at once' and with 'two couples in one environment'. Manu asked how they avoided emotional involvement. Emotions took a back seat; they reserved those for their marriage.

Sexual Fantasies – 2005

Ten years on, and there was Les, dressed in a black pinstripe suit, trying to be matter-of-fact as a much younger crowd openly explored its sexuality. Behind her, a couple groped on a bed suspended over an indoor pool. On the dance floor, two scantily dressed women were locked together, groin to bum, while a naked man, with a pronounced G-string tan, pressed against them from the front. There were no ugly people. Bodies were bronzed and beautiful, faces hidden behind garish feathers or Phantom of the Opera masks. Bras were taken off on the dance floor; tongues ran suggestively over taut tummies.

The story was a revealing look at what went on at 'sex fantasy' clubs hidden in out-of-the-way suburbs. To the unsuspecting, it was rather shocking. This time, Ruda's studio link made it clear: this was adults-only stuff. 'You're invited on a vicarious visit to a club north of Johannesburg, where young people live out their sexual fantasies, often very publicly.'

The club was a bit like a run-down hotel; there was a pool, a little restaurant, a big lounge area and plenty of bedrooms. The owner and hostess was former hairdresser Lara, who used to listen to her clients' fantasies while styling their hair in a salon; now she fulfilled them in a saloon. She allowed single women into the club, but not single men. A sign on a door read: 'NO will be the most respected word in the club; no single men unless accompanied by a couple and he must leave when they leave.' And, said Lara, no touching: 'A lady can stand naked next to a man while ordering a drink at the bar with her nipple touching his shoulder, but he's not allowed to touch her.' Another rule was no jeans and no takkies, which was odd, because most people ended up with their kit off anyway.

Cameraman Grant Nelson and Les spent nine enlightening hours at this private swingers' club. The result was a racy, pacy ten-minute insert. At 2am, while doing a piece to camera poolside, Les wondered why her feet were getting wet, looked down, and saw a couple having sex, making sure they were close enough to be captured on camera. Les's immediate concern was for her leather shoes; her next was whether she was expected to join in. She also spent much of the evening trying to ensure that whatever Grant was shooting wasn't X-rated. But she was powerless to prevent oral sex on the dance floor and full sex on the bed suspended over the cuddle puddle, even though, Grant said, they had specifically asked the couple concerned just to 'pose' for a shot. One Adonis was concerned not about his nakedness but that he might be filmed without an erection.

Les interviewed the 'posing' couple, Michael and Michelle, partners for two years. They got their thrills by flaunting their undiluted sexuality. They never had sex with other couples, but enjoyed doing it in public and watching others. At this club, it was less about swinging and more about sharing – and a lot about women satisfying their bisexual needs.

A man named Peter said his ultimate fantasy was to watch his wife Jackie getting it on with other women and succeeding every time.

'The chances of my wife picking up a girl and me picking up a girl ... my wife would pick up some other girl.'
Les: 'You reckon?'
Peter: 'Yes.'
Les: 'The odds are in her favour?'
Peter: 'The odds are in her favour.'

In the obligatory voice-of-reason interview, sex therapist Marlene Wasserman said bisexuality was the suppressed desire of many who feared being labelled as in the closet, or confused. She often counselled women who suppressed their desires to be with both sexes. And according to a nightclub poll at a club in Britain, quoted in the piece, nearly 50 per cent of female revellers had had some sort of sexual experience with a woman. The visuals used were of two women – one of them bare-chested, kissing deeply, hips gyrating and looking the ultimate in bisexual chic.

But for Les, the most bizarre cameo scenes in her long extraordinary evening had nothing to do with sex at all. In the restaurant, at a small table for two, scant metres from the action, an elderly couple sat eating in companionable silence, as old married couples do. They looked neither left nor right. Perhaps they'd come because the steaks were good, Les concluded. And moving quietly from bedroom to bedroom was a housemaid, who spent the entire night changing sheets.

For months afterwards, Les says, she was quizzed about this story. But she was never again asked to do tuck shop duty at her children's school.

Breaking the Censorship Shackles

Derek Watts says his memoirs, when he eventually gets down to them (at the mention of which his wife Belinda rolls her eyes), will be called 'Please Can You Close Your Legs For The Opening Shot?', in reference to a story he did on South Africa's self-appointed king of nudity, Beau Brummell. He was about to interview Beau's naked 16-year-old daughter Cheyenne on growing up in a nudist colony, and cameraman John Parr was forced to ask that question. It was 1992 and Brummell, in a move he said was to celebrate Mandela's release, had opened his whites-only nudist colony, Beau Valley, to black nudists. As if that wasn't enough, he'd decided to go the whole liberated hog and invite gays, too. Now Beau was facing financial ruin. The white shareholders had pulled out because of the 'blacks who walked around with erections and gays who had sex in the swimming pool'.

Derek, John and then-producer Linda Vermaas remember few details of the story and more about being the only fully clothed people in a sea of nudity. And they were struck by Beau's beautiful teenage daughter, who had grown up completely at ease with being naked in front of

25

adults. But she was omitted from the final edit because, said Linda, it didn't seem appropriate. In any event, the story that went on air had little to do with Beau's new-found liberal ideas and resultant financial woes and more about South Africa's confusing censorship laws.

In an interview with a fully clothed Derek, the naked 1960s pop singer and B-movie actor complained about a police raid in which brochures advertising Beau Valley were confiscated, as well as some foreign naturist magazines. The raid posed an interesting question for a South Africa emerging from a repressive and strictly censored era: what exactly defined pornography?

The raid on Beau's house at the nudist colony had been conducted by the South African Narcotics Bureau (SANAB). Captain Piet Senekal recited to Derek a long list of what was considered obscene under the Publications Act of 1974. The Act's definition of obscene ranged from licentiousness and lust to lesbianism. But, said the captain, nudity was not pornographic. So what law had Beau Brummell fallen foul of? Captain Senekal wasn't too sure, but said they'd received 'complaints'.

It was clearly no simple matter, so Derek and Linda headed off to the old Publications Appeal Board, where they were told by chairman Daan Morkel that while sexual titillation wasn't deemed undesirable, 'provoking lust' certainly was. Derek asked if the Beau Valley brochures of naked people sailing, swimming and braaing were lust-provoking. Chairman Daan, the *oranje-blanje-blou* of the old flag behind him, wasn't sure, but he said one wouldn't like to see them in cafés, or in dentist 'shops'. How about at a nudist colony, which is where they were? Daan conceded that if limited to select people, they couldn't be 'undesirable', but said that the Board never found anything to be 'desirable'. Derek looked baffled and concluded that perhaps pornography was like an elephant: hard to define, but no mistaking it when confronted by it.

The entire *Carte Blanche* story featured images the Board would definitely have considered undesirable, even a full-frontal from the movie *Lady Chatterley's Lover*, screened on M-Net a few weeks before – a sign that apartheid was crumbling and a new world was beckoning.

Derek and the Dominatrix

That was Derek's first on-camera encounter with a '*kaalgat*' case study, but it was certainly not his last. He still has nightmares about Demi the Dominatrix, who used to thrash respectable businessmen in her Johannesburg boudoir. Once a sex worker, Demi came to realise that she was spending more time flagellating her clients than actually doing the dirty deed, so she became a dominatrix instead. Clad in a revealing leather get-up, Demi simply had to tie up her clients, beat them till they squealed, drip hot wax onto their naked backs, and occasionally draw blood with a barbed whip. In this way, she said, her body remained her own and she quadrupled her income. 'No sex!' she repeated. They were welcome to 'hand relief', but they had to do it themselves, as part of the humiliation. She, as the goddess, could not touch. She'd stumbled onto a winner: satisfying fetishes without having to spread her legs too wide. Occasionally, she said, she saw couples who wanted to experience pain together – a turn-on for them. So the wife would watch, as a prelude to lovemaking, while Demi beat the living daylights out of her spouse. But mostly her clients were well-heeled businessmen, who would sneak a furtive visit after work. This was 1996 – long before *Fifty Shades of Grey.*

In a scene that would probably not be shown on *Carte Blanche* in the less daring 21st century – bound (so to speak) by the BCCSA's code of conduct – Derek walked into shot, brandishing a riding crop and talking to camera about the rise of S&M joints in the suburbs. He walked to a door, which was opened by a bare-breasted Demi, clad only in crotch-less panties held up by a few leather straps. She took Derek into her torture chamber and proceeded to lash a willing supplicant. She said she was often asked to pretend to be a teacher meting out discipline to grown men seeking relief after a day in the boardroom. Occasionally, she said, she got them to bark like dogs, or to dance with a broomstick. As the camera crew left, a grey-haired, grey-suited man with a briefcase arrived at the garden gate. Derek will never forget the look on his face when he saw them.

Whipping was nothing new; the *Kama Sutra* describes various forms

27

of flagellation, and as far back as the 14th century there are reports of people willingly being bound or whipped before or during, or instead of, sex. But it was certainly a new subject for South African television audiences.

A magazine article published in 1995 asked the question:

> What is it that's still keeping M-Net viewers glued? One could sum it up in three words: controversy, caring and downright cheek. Controversy because anything goes ... no subject is taboo and presenters often have to barge in where angels fear to tread ... and cheek because there are some stories that make everyone grin – like Derek's interviews with prostitutes and men who have had their assets enlarged! Ultimately, *Carte Blanche* works because it unearths dramatic, colourful stories and brings them right into the living room of every M-Net viewer.

Kinks Culture – 2003

The subject was revisited by Ruda in 2003 in another look at the sexual revolution, in which, according to the story, 'erotic experimentation was redefining sex'. Out went peno-vaginal or 'vanilla' sex; in came new forms of sexual expression in which secret desires for objects, aromas and touch become reality. High-powered businessmen by day, sometimes with lacy lingerie beneath their suits, wanted bondage and discipline, domination and submission by night – an elaborate form of foreplay with the mind as the biggest sex organ.

Clinical psychologist Gareth Hunt, interviewed by Ruda, said that the common perception was that these practices were deep, dark and dysfunctional, but if consensual, and if they provided relief and decreased anxiety, they could only be therapeutic, creating a type of psychological equilibrium. The bondage was often an art form – an example being the Japanese art of rope-tying known as *shibari* – and about how the ropes were applied, the pleasure being in the journey, rather than the result.

In most of these stories, the case studies were unconventional, to say the least, and it is hard to imagine that they would sell the sex revolution concept to the missionary types. Cameraman-producer Grant Nelson said they were sourced from classifieds in the newspapers, as well as from a corset-maker who was into bondage. Ruda interviewed 'Miss Canes', who looked like a typical cuddly granny doing her shopping, squeezing paw-paws in the supermarket. But she was actually an aged transgender who practised BDSM. Anatomically a male, she also had breasts. From the supermarket, the shot cut to Miss Canes putting on her bondage gear: suspenders, lacy top over small breasts, big tummy and penis bulging from beneath a short satin skirt. Not a sexy sight by any stretch of the imagination, but this former pastry chef, with a fetish for dishing out bondage and discipline, said she was on call round the clock. 'Sex ... you can wake me at midnight. It's like waking me up for an ice cream.'

She said it wasn't unusual to receive a phone call at one in the morning from people who felt like a jolly good hiding. Pain was an essential part of sex for some. In many ways, South Africa's political history carries the seed of S&M culture: men in uniform inflicting pain and getting pleasure out of degrading others.

Ruda interviewed a dominator called Torch, who had a penchant for medieval torture. He was dressed in an executioner's mask and leopard-skin scants. Domination was his turn-on: 'It's about being able to put people in a position with just the right amount of force, control and to hold them there.' When not chaining up men and helping them play out their submission fantasies, he was an organic farmer, an ordinary guy whose fetish gave him the same rush as jumping out of a plane or bungee jumping off a bridge.

The camera cut to Ruda, in a neat cardigan, standing in front of swaying bondage gear: 'Many otherwise ordinary people have urges and desires that society condemns as abnormal ... their partners would never understand and yet they want to act it out.'

One of these was James, a cross-dresser who visited his dominatrix, Mistress J, every week to play out a psychodrama. Mistress J had huge breasts that spilled from a cutaway bodice as she laid into James's G-string-covered buttocks. Medical role-playing was a big favourite, and Mistress J had a box full of oxygen masks, drips and rectal thermometers. While lots of kinky play went on in her dungeon, Mistress J said it never included 'full-house' or oral sex and definitely no animals. She once gave short shrift to someone with a foot fetish who wanted her to trample on live birds.

Generally, her clients felt ten years younger after a session under the whip. Ruda looked doubtful and couldn't see the attraction of being beaten black and blue, but conceded that perhaps what was important was that society was coming out and that people were no longer afraid about being seen as different.

As she said in that very first broadcast back in 1988: '*Carte Blanche – alles is moontlik ... en dit gaan nie net ons naam wees nie, maar ons leuse vir die program* ... watch this space.'

romance 4

Although not many *Carte Blanche* staffers live in connubial bliss, over the past quarter of a century the show has tried to put as much emphasis on love and romance as it has on libido. Coming up with relationship stories that don't reek of cynicism isn't always easy, but there are those who never give up on love – even the diminutive, straight-talking Dr Ruth, who once said: 'You should not engage in oral sex with someone you are not in love with.'

'Private Dancer' told the story of Allie, the girl-next-door who learnt to lap dance to reignite some passion in her marriage. There were sex surveys to find out what kept couples going after the seven-year itch had set in, and no shortage of new research on love: Esther Perel, author of *Mating in Captivity*, theorised that too much closeness stifled desire; Dr Donatella Marazziti, an Italian biochemist, told *Carte Blanche* that love could be equated with obsessive compulsive disorder (OCD) and was a product of the brain's reward-seeking circuits – nothing to do with the heart. By studying monogamous and non-monogamous species of voles, American behavioural scientist Larry Young proved that enduring love was nothing more than chemistry, which triggered a flurry of speculation on the creation of a 'love pill', containing hormones like oxytocin and pheromones, to bring the honeymoon feeling back into shaky relationships.

Then there was the story of the polygamist in Utah with six wives. This was produced by Eugene Botha, a professor of Theology, who finds unusual *Carte Blanche* topics in his travels around the world as a guest lecturer. The polygamist, Ivan Jenkins, pointed out that this was his God-ordained lifestyle because, according to the Bible, Abraham and Isaac and David and Solomon had been polygamous: 'And my ancestors ... So I thought, "Hey, this is what I ought to be doing. If I want to go where they've gone, I've got to be a polygamist also."' Fortunately for his 47 children, 188 grandchildren and 34 great-grandchildren, his ancestors weren't cannibals.

Although polygamy is illegal in the US, the story pointed out that it was slowly being accepted, because it simply wasn't practical to imprison 40 000 polygamists who were otherwise law-abiding members of the Mormon faith. Ivan, his wives and the younger children didn't live in a compound, but in one big house, and the seven adults had their own rooms. Not everyone's cup of tea, perhaps, but it worked out just fine for Ivan: 'Say, like Monday night I'd go and stay with Carol and the next night with Colleen, and the next night with ... it just depends on circumstances. If somebody was sick we'd just pass that up. If I was sick I'd just stay alone in my room.'

Psychologist Christopher Ryan, interviewed on *Carte Blanche* in 2011 about his book *Sex at Dawn*, said monogamy was unnatural and that humans were genetically programmed to be as promiscuous as their closest genetic relatives. While we might be gifted with more intelligence than gorillas, bonobos and chimpanzees, our base animal natures were the same. Fidelity, said Dr Ryan, was a far-fetched concept.

No *Carte Blanche* story is complete without real-life case studies to illustrate the point. Producer Carol Albertyn Christie found Annie, a polyamorist, who was open to the idea of having multiple intimate relationships with different people, as long as the focus was on honesty and communication. Like monogamy, the jealousy that besets so many modern relationships wasn't a natural human state either, she said: 'You know when we were children and were jealous and our parents said that's unacceptable, and you have to learn to share? Now, as adults, we think jealousy is completely acceptable,' said Annie, with a knowing air.

Adultery and perceived immorality, like the subject of evolution, tend to get Auntie Boksburg rushing to her computer to fire off a missive immediately after broadcast: 'What about AIDS?' or 'Just because something occurs "in nature" doesn't make it right!' 'WE DO NOT COME FROM APES!' screamed another email.

'Can't someone find us a "normal" relationship story?' sighed executive producer George Mazarakis in a research editorial meeting one winter morning. It was decided that 'normal' in the 21st century could be online dating. The proliferation of dating websites and the increasing access to computers have made it completely natural to meet one's match online, circumventing the time-consuming and anxious process that defines traditional dating. Frogs can be eliminated with the click of a mouse and there is no need for hanging around in pubs and clubs waiting to catch someone's eye.

Producer Nicky Troll had tried online dating and seemed perfect for the story, having regaled the office with colourful encounters of her own. She interviewed the perpetual lookers, as well as happy couples like Hayley and Ray, who'd got married after meeting online.

Ray: 'My opening line of my wedding speech was: "It's amazing what you can find on the Internet."'

There was another couple in their mid-sixties, who'd been wary of hitting the dating scene after long marriages, but who'd moved in together six months after meeting online.

It was a warm and fuzzy story that ticked all of George's boxes. But it sparked a follow-up that revealed a much nastier side to the online dating game. Loneliness could, it seemed, lead to extraordinary vulnerability and naivety in normally intelligent people. Some viewers also complained that their hearts and their wallets had fallen victim to con artists on certain dating websites. So Nicky mimicked them – she created a fake profile. Clearly, if she was going to attract those with less than honourable intentions, the trick was to imply that she had a bit of cash.

'Tina, aged 38, newly divorced, good financial settlement and looking for love and nurturing and someone to travel with,' ran the fake profile. Within days she'd made contact with a handsome grey-haired army captain named Roux Prinsloo. He was with the United Nations, based in Pakistan. And he was, he said, 'a one-woman man because he loved wholeheartedly'.

33

But this was the same Roux Prinsloo who'd spun yarns to other *Carte Blanche* viewers.

Tracy: 'He sent me poems every single day ... very charming ... and the picture he sent of himself was just mind-blowing.'

Rachel: 'He couldn't wait to come home and be with me after the darkness of the Pakistani jungle. I was his light and the love he had been waiting for.'

But neither Tracy nor Rachel had spoken to Roux. For that, he said, he'd need money to buy a satellite phone. He provided details of a so-called satellite company and Rachel transferred R4 850 to an FNB account. 'Thanks a lot,' emailed her handsome hero, but he was having problems getting the phone to work. All was not lost, though; he'd been granted leave and soon he and his new sat phone would be heading to South Africa to meet her. He just needed R5 000 for a helicopter to pick him up from the military base to take him to the airport. Amazingly, both Tracy and Rachel came up with the cash. In the interviews, presenter Devi Sankaree Govender couldn't believe her ears: 'What were you thinking?'

Well, said Rachel, she'd thought that if he left Pakistan the next day, he would be in South Africa in two days. Then she'd get her money back. And she'd get him as well – that was the first prize.

Devi: 'Did it not cross your mind that maybe something was going on here?'

Rachel: 'Not at all, because the emails were so real. It was all so real.'

But there was nothing real about Romeo Roux Prinsloo. Not even the photograph. And he certainly wasn't in Pakistan. Nicky traced his address from the bank account into which the women had paid the money. She and Devi set off, hoping to confront the online heartbreaker. They ended up in a village called Oskraal in the North West: the address had been false.

Devi: 'From the jungles in Pakistan to this rural setting in Oskraal it seems that internet dating can take you places.'

They'd reached a dead end. The police were unhelpful. Former Hawks spokesperson McIntosh Polela said the difficulty was that whoever was behind the scam was part of a global syndicate and the SAPS had no jurisdiction to chase cyber-based crimes. But Nicky knew that the scammers were in South Africa because she had an informant at the bank, who'd told her the account was active. The scammers had made R32 000 in 17 days.

She'd found another case study, named Monique, a divorcee who'd had an online relationship with a 'submarine engineer' named Josef Werner. He'd sent her flowers, spoken to her on the phone and told her about a big contract he had signed with Shell SA. Monique became worried when he disappeared from cyberspace for a few days, but he reappeared to tell her that there'd been an explosion aboard his submarine. He'd lost big money and needed her help. She smelled a rat and recorded the conversation.

Josef: 'I need £2 400. I have £300 with me.'

Monique: 'How do I know you are going to pay me back, Josef?'

Josef: 'My pretty, my pretty, I will pay you back once I get back; paying back won't be a problem.'

Nicky phoned Shell SA, who'd never heard of Josef Werner, or his so-called contract. With the help of a private investigator, she managed to triangulate Josef's cellphone and discovered that it was active in Kempton Park. Devi gave him a call.

Devi: 'Are you really in the UK?'

(West African accent): 'Yes, why do you ask?'

Devi: 'Because I know you're in Kempton Park and that you are lying. Your real name is not Josef. What is your real name?'

(West African accent): 'You know ... you know, you know how stupid you are?'

Devi: 'How stupid am I?'

(West African accent): 'You're very, very stupid by calling me and telling me shit ... please don't call this number again!'

After broadcast, *Carte Blanche* was contacted by more women who'd fallen for similar online ruses. They couldn't resist men in uniform, they said, so they overlooked the poor spelling in the emails and, once they'd made phone contact, thought the exotic accents to be European. One of them, Suzette, had recognised the voice talking to Monique: 'He was calling her "my pretty", he was calling her the sort of endearments he used for me and I felt intense anger.'

Josef had made Suzette feel alive, youthful and attractive, and she had willingly parted with R250 000. When her life savings ran out and he suggested she sell her car, she finally became suspicious. To show that he was good for the money, he'd sent her the same Shell contract and a cheque made out to him. Now she felt scorned and wanted revenge.

Someone else whose love turned to rage after watching *Carte Blanche* was Elize, who'd been online with 'Josef' for three months and had been head over heels. Except ... his name was Andrew Cole. 'I don't think I ever fell for anyone like I did for this one. Ooh, me meeting a petroleum engineer, wow! And he wants to come home to me?'

Too embarrassed to show her face on camera, Elize – a successful and attractive businesswoman – told of her excitement as the time drew near for their first meeting. 'Andrew' had sent her his flight arrival times. She had filled the house with flowers and chocolate hearts and told all her friends. Then she'd waited at the airport ... and waited and waited, scanning the faces in the arrivals hall for one that matched the photo. But he never arrived.

All in all, Elize had given him R500 000 – most of her savings.

The 419 Romancers had cashed in close to a million just from the women who'd contacted *Carte Blanche*. Suzette wanted to lay fraud charges and managed to obtain bank statements for the accounts she'd paid money into. From these, she noticed that cash withdrawals had been made from ATMs in Kempton Park. But she wasn't sure what to do next and handed over the information to Nicky, who did a company search which showed that the bank account belonged to a company called Ebernat Motors. The only director was a Ghanaian national named Ebenezer Nartey. And most of the money from Ebernat Motors went into an account held by a property investment company called FALDNK, which Suzette had also paid money into. The account holder was another Ghanaian named David Febri.

Nicky discovered that David and Ebenezer were Facebook friends. Several addresses were attached to the company details, so she drove to every one of them, most of them dead ends, but finally matched a housing complex to a Facebook picture of David and Ebenezer posing outside in front of luxury cars. No one was home, but a check of the letterbox showed an envelope addressed to David Febri.

Nicky then phoned two numbers attached to the company records. The person who picked up the second call identified himself as David Febri and asked if Nicky was phoning about 'the car'. She didn't know what he was talking about, but said yes and established that he'd put an ad in the paper wanting to buy a car. He agreed to meet her on the rooftop of a shopping centre the following day to have a look at her car.

Devi was busy catching crooks elsewhere, so Nicky hooked up with presenter Chantal Rutter Dros for the follow-up. Also on board was cameraman Dudley Saunders, a veteran of many a skirmish and certainly not afraid of fraudsters. But just to be safe, they picked up two 'bodyguards' as backup. It was just as well, because David Febri arrived with two well-built friends. Perhaps he was planning to do more than just 'look' at Nicky's vehicle. While Dudley and Chantal stayed out of sight, Nicky led them to her 'for sale' car. When she gave a prearranged signal, Dudley and Chantal emerged, camera rolling. Chantal was pleased that David was shorter than she because it gave her the courage to challenge him. She felt desperately sorry for the women who'd been misled, and contempt for the heartbreaker, who naturally denied all. No, he'd never heard of Ebenezer Nartey. Chantal showed him the Facebook picture to jog his memory.

David: 'I think ... No, it's not Ebenezer Nartey.'

Chantal: 'Who is it?'

David: 'This guy is from Congolese [sic].'

He was as slippery as they come, and became aggressive when challenged, but Chantal stood her ground, prompted by Nicky, who was shouting the odds in the background. But David shouted louder:

David (hand on camera): 'Okay, that's enough! It's enough before I break your camera. I've spoken to you! I'm done with you!'

(David's friend): 'Just get out from our faces! Don't show us any cameras here – we are not actors! You can't show me on the camera!'

David: 'You are not the judge to judge me! Thousand of proof or evidence; it's none of my business, let's go!'

With a screech of tyres, David and his comrades sped off. Very soon, the Facebook pictures disappeared from cyberspace.

Nicky and Chantal never found Ebenezer, but it was not for lack of trying. They went back to the house, where a neighbour told them that David and Ebenezer were 'wealthy men' who worked as a team, running syndicates, chatting online and duping people. Everyone knew that, he said, but the police weren't interested. They said the women had been willing participants who'd been duped.

Elize: 'For me the biggest thing is the deceit part. You know, the money ... it can come back.'

Suzette: 'For me, it wasn't so much about the money, for me it was about having lost what I thought I had found.'

David and Ebenezer are probably still in cyberspace pretending to be gallant heroes looking for true love, but hopefully finding the hearts of *Carte Blanche* viewers, at least, much harder to break.

war stories 5

When George Mazarakis took over as executive producer in 1995, a position he has occupied ever since – making him *Carte Blanche*'s longest-serving head – he felt it was important to have the show's presenters telling stories in other countries, at a time when access to international broadcasting was much more limited than it is today. In those days of bigger budgets, wherever the news was – or even wasn't – *Carte Blanche* would go. There were trips to NASA headquarters, to Bosnia, to Egypt (to meet up with Graham Hancock and Robert Bauval), to report live from conflict-ridden Jerusalem and Palestine, and even to the Persian Gulf to board a nuclear-powered aircraft carrier.

USS *George Washington* – 1998

In 1998 Iraqi leader Saddam Hussein was giving UN weapons inspectors the run-around, and US President Bill Clinton, although embroiled in the Monica Lewinsky sex scandal, was threatening air strikes. Saudi Arabia, Bahrain and the United Arab Emirates (UAE) were hesitant about allowing the US military to use their bases to attack targets in Iraq. *Carte Blanche* needed to get to the Persian Gulf. But how do you base a story on undefined, tension-filled rumblings?

It was decided that the aircraft carrier USS *George Washington*, among the biggest warships ever built, deployed in the Gulf to monitor and control Iraqi airspace, would be the perfect vehicle. Researcher Anna-Maria

Lombard began a fax-intensive mission (because email was still in its infancy), and within a few months producer Diana Lucas, Derek Watts and cameraman Mike Yelseth were on their way to Bahrain to do a story they still talk about today.

From Bahrain, they'd been assured that they'd be able to get themselves onto the mighty vessel. This would be one of the few ways to tell the story of the military manoeuvres going down in the region, so they weren't the only journalists trying – it was a news circus. Diana and Derek felt like poor country cousins compared to the other networks and news agencies, with their satellite dishes and the best equipment money could buy. Diana wrote 'Carte Blanche Newsroom' on a piece of paper, stuck it on the door of her room at the Bahrain Holiday Inn, and then relentlessly pestered the US Department of Defense's Mid-East Press Office, which, with the region on a knife-edge, was having second thoughts about allowing distractions on board its floating airbase. Diana, mindful of how much had been spent getting them there, phoned the office every day until they had no doubt who she was: a South African, representing a programme that was broadcast to the whole of Africa, and she was very sure President Mandela would want to see the USS *George Washington* on local TV.

There's nothing worse than waiting for a story that might not happen when you're expected to come back with a cracker, so they halfheartedly filmed a piece on Bahrain as a playground for the rich, the Sun City of the Persian Gulf. But finally one of Diana's hourly calls to the Press Office yielded results: they were to be ready the next day to board a helicopter bound for the supercarrier. They would be allowed 24 hours on board. Mike took a nap on the chopper and when he woke up, 40 minutes later, they were approaching a ship standing 20 storeys above the water: four and a half acres of sovereign territory floating in international waters. His opening shot, from one end of the ship to the other, lasted almost 20 seconds – the ship was as big as four football fields.

Immediately evident was the ship's radar tower, and, because of it, Mike covered his camera with a lead-lined bag to protect the film stock. But there was still interference, and an explanation was given in Derek's opening voice-over: '... as we stepped on board, the constant radar signals that would detect the first signs of enemy action were so intense it affected the sensitive electronics of our camera and tape ...'

Derek appeared on camera looking hot and windswept, fighter jets behind him, and holding a microphone covered in a fluffy sock to mini- mise noise. The flight deck was incredibly loud, with planes landing and taking off at a furious pace. Because there wasn't enough room on the flight deck for all 75 aircraft, Derek explained – as Mike panned and tilted down to include them – the vessel had four giant elevators, which constantly moved planes that weren't in use to the hangar bay, the 'garage', two decks below. The high-speed hydraulic elevators were powerful enough to lift two F-14 Tomcat fighter jets at a time.

The flight deck also wasn't long enough for the planes to make ordi- nary landings or take-offs, so for take-offs they hooked onto one of four massive catapults, each consisting of two steam-driven pistons that got the aircraft up to high speeds in no time. In his onboard digs one deck down, a fresh-faced pilot named Mike Amos was getting ready to fly the US Navy's premier attack jet, the F-18 Hornet, capable of bombing ground targets with killer accuracy. One of the carrier's glamour boys, Amos told Derek that the catapult shot, which shoved him back in his seat with a force four times greater than gravity, was 'a great feeling'.
Derek: 'Are you the envy of the crew?'
Mike: 'Sometimes ... but who wants to get shot at?'

But he did at least get to escape every day, something everyone wanted to do after months at sea. Cameraman Mike filmed pilot Mike hopping into his Hornet, shaking Derek's hand, and then taking off: 0 to 160 miles per hour in less than two seconds. He had with him everything he needed to survive in case he had to eject – radio, knives, water, signalling devices like flares and smoke, and a couple of pieces of candy.

Because of the constant noise, visual signs and gestures were the main forms of communication on the flight deck. Everyone was colour-coded: for example, the Red Shirts – the fire-fighters – loaded the missiles and attached the aircraft to the catapults. It was precision stuff, and the dif- ference between life and death, said Derek, could be the thumbs-up sign giving the all-clear to release the catapult. At night, the green-shirted maintenance men emerged to prepare for the following day's mission. The *George Washington* was a floating city that never rested.

This was a real boy's story, but there were also 36 women on board. Lieutenant Courtney Smith was filmed getting ready for take-off in her ES-3A Shadow dual-engine jet. She spoke American military jargon, but from the sound of it she did surveillance: 'We have various sensors that can pick up emissions and let the rest of our battle group know what's radiating.'

Derek looked impressed and wondered if her husband was, too. She said she'd met him in the military so he was pretty clued-up, but conceded that it couldn't be easy for him to wave goodbye as his wife sailed over the horizon in a confined space with more than 5 000 blokes.

Back at Vulture's Row, an observation area on the carrier's tower, Derek and Diana watched 30 planes that had been surveying Iraqi territory coming in to land in rapid succession. Landing on a runway as short as 320 metres was as demanding and dangerous as a catapult-assisted take-off. Four steel ropes, called arrester cables, were laid across the runway for the plane to hook onto. If it hooked number one or two, the pilot was too close to the stern; number four meant the plane only just made it. A 'Top Gun' landing was when the plane hooked cable number three.

Not content with just interviewing pilots taking off from the flight deck, Diana, who has great persuasive powers, managed to organise an interview in the control tower with the 'foreman of the factory', Lieutenant Commander Gary Brookheider. Here, those on duty dressed in bright yellow crewneck sweatshirts. Gary coordinated the movements on the flight deck – not by computer, but with a series of cut-out model planes on a Monopoly-type board. He said it was functional, had evolved over 50 years, and that in the event of a loss of power during an air strike they were still able to do the necessary. Each model was cut to the exact scale and dimensions of the aircraft on the main deck and mimicked their movements.

Below deck was a sweet-faced chap named Jason, just 23, who had the daunting task of turning dials to set the correct tonnage as each plane landed and caught the arrester cable on the deck with its tail hook. Although it looked complicated, he said it wasn't: a basic hydraulic system that not only stopped the plane, but cushioned the blow. If the weight was wrongly set, or if the pilot came in at the wrong speed, the arrester cable could snap and ... well, he didn't want to think of what would happen then. 'It could kill a whole bunch of people on the flight deck.' So, concluded Derek, while Jason took instructions with his headphones on, amid all this high-powered technology, the safety of the whole operation depended on twiddling the right knobs.

Apart from the two thousand-odd marines on board, there were another three thousand crew members below decks, who often didn't see sunlight for months on end, because the open areas were considered too dangerous for anyone other than essential personnel. There were canteens galore, a gym, callbox phones, a post office, cinema and a games arcade. With crew members coming and going all night according to their shifts, sleep was an interrupted affair in tight quarters. Diana was placed in the care of a GI Jane and managed to find a bunk to grab some shuteye in the early hours.

This cruise was the first on which crew members were allowed to light up. Mike took a shot of some smokers on a weather deck, huddled around a bin overflowing with cigarette butts. Derek called it a 'victory for smokers' rights'. Ten years later, a costly fire on board the USS *George Washington* would be blamed on smoking in an unauthorised place. The fire caused US$70 million damage to a ship that cost $5 billion to construct.

Derek and Diana would travel the world extensively on a *Carte Blanche* ticket, but the story of the USS *George Washington* remains near the top of their list of all-time favourites. These days, it isn't uncommon to see the inner workings of aircraft carriers on the History Channel, but that wasn't the case back in 1998. The segment was given 25 minutes on air, longer than what is required for the traditional Sunday 'formula'. The piece was first broadcast on 8 March 1998, the day on which the United Nations warned the US against bombing Iraq because of Saddam Hussein's non-compliance with UN weapons inspections. The crisis dragged on and, nine months later, Operation Desert Fox saw major air strikes on Iraqi targets.

Sally Trench in Bosnia – 1995

Ruda: *'Kan daar vrede in Bosnia wees? Dis die vraag wat die hele wereld vra nou dat daar 'n sestig dae wapen stilstand is in die oorlog wat byna vier jaar lank al woed ...'*
Derek: 'It's a fragile truce and a bloody war that has raged so close to the seemingly sophisticated heart of Europe. Yet despite the abundance of TV news footage, it's a war that has remained rather remote for many people.'

One of the ways of making far-off wars less remote is to find a strong central character with whom viewers can identify and around which the greater story can be told. George Mazarakis, newly arrived as executive producer, had heard a radio interview with a remarkable-sounding woman who was doing remarkable work with children of war in the former Yugoslavia.

Looking weather-beaten in a straw hat, and with an upper-class British accent, Sally Trench had been around the block. Expelled from five schools for resisting authority, in 1967 she'd gone to live among London's homeless. She'd written a book about her experiences, *Bury Me in My Boots*, which had gone on to sell more than a million copies. She had used the money to establish a charity called Project Spark, and now helped juvenile delinquents. Suffering was her business.

Sally had seen on television the plight of children in Bosnia and had decided to do something about it. For three years, she'd led truck convoys carrying food, medicine and supplies across Europe to Bosnia. She'd hired volunteer drivers and taken them with her, working her way around the refugee camps, rescuing children hiding out in remote villages.

Sometimes, she said, she was so scared that she was 'almost shitting in her pants', but couldn't turn her back on the children of Bosnia. The only thing she could be sure of, once she'd negotiated her way across the border from the relative safety of Croatia, was that she would find no happiness. She'd once located a group of children hiding out in a mountain cave, where they'd fled after Serb nationalists had attacked their village. Sally arranged for helicopters to pick them up, but the site was too hilly to land, so rope ladders were dropped for the kids to grab onto. But while some were trying to climb up the ladders, they were shot by soldiers alerted by the noise of the choppers. Twenty-five of the original group of 68 children made it to safety and Sally took them back to England with her.

But since then, British immigration authorities had clamped down on refugees. Unable to remove any more children, she instead did what she could on the ground. Those she helped were kids who spent their mornings picking flowers for their parents' graves, their afternoons foraging for rats to eat, their nights sleeping in abandoned buildings. Sally created schools and youth centres for them. When the sniper fire got too bad to be outside, she had trenches dug and they got on with their lessons in subterranean classrooms. School time was more therapy than anything else, because most of the little pupils were so traumatised they couldn't concentrate for more than a few minutes at a time.

Her faith kept her there, despite witnessing horror upon horror: drunken Serb soldiers systematically raping 14-year-old girls; Muslim women being herded into deep-freeze containers to die; children being put into concrete mixers. In London she'd employed a driver named Mo. If she'd checked his British passport, she would've seen that his full name was Mohammed. Soon after she'd crossed into Bosnia with Mo, he was captured and tortured to death. She blamed herself. But she took no sides, enjoyed no protection.

The *Carte Blanche* story was assigned to producer Jan Lampen, whose assistant, Kate Barry, was then a TV rookie; she is now one of *Carte Blanche*'s top investigative producers. It was Kate's job to locate Sally, which she did through her Oxford-based charity, and arrange to meet her in Croatia – Bosnia being far too dangerous. Kate flew ahead with cameraman Paul Morkel to film Sally doing her thing and to make the necessary arrangements so that when presenter Derek and producer Jan arrived it would be smooth sailing.

Kate and Paul negotiated their way around a country in the dying stages of a devastating civil war. They took advantage of the fragile truce and crossed into Bosnia, eventually arriving in Mostar, once a magnificent city tucked between hills and divided by the Neretva River. The most famous thing about Mostar had been its 16th-century 'Old

Bridge', a UNESCO World Heritage Site, which connected the Muslim eastern and Croat western halves of the city. It had stood for 429 years until 9 November 1993, when it was bombarded by tank fire until it collapsed. Kate found a little gallery on the river bank called Don't Forget, filled with paintings of the ruined Old Bridge, once one of the most recognisable landmarks in the Balkans. Now it was a poignant reminder of suffering and loss.

Mostar was bustling; businesses had reopened and Kate and Paul filmed the amazing ability of people to carry on. No one could've been unscathed. Although the world's focus had been on Sarajevo, the capital, Mostar had been one of the worst-hit cities in all of Bosnia. The camera shots they took were tinged with sadness. A girl of five or six stood by a car wreck, picking up thick pieces of shattered windscreen and slowly dropping them into a container. Boys ran around with make-shift guns – war was the only reality they knew. Unless the peace lasted, five-year-olds would become soldiers by the time they were ten.

Somewhere in this tragic city, Kate had to find Sally Trench. It had started raining, and she and Paul sheltered in the ruins of a shop: two South Africans, standing silently with strangers who'd been through years of unspeakable horror. Written on the walls in red paint were the words 'People of the world, help us'. After a while, the sun came out and suddenly, out of nowhere, appeared a truck with a GB sticker. God had smiled on them and delivered Sally Trench.

They followed the truck to some ruined buildings, and there she was, barely able to open her door because of all the children who'd gathered around. She was 50 then, small and wiry, with thick grey hair and the look of someone who favoured strong drink above food. But her voice was booming and she didn't mince her words in expressing her displeasure at seeing Kate, Paul and especially the camera. She had told them she would only meet in Croatia, and she'd meant it. Did they have any idea of how dangerous Bosnia was?

They made an arrangement to meet up in the Croatian city of Split, about 100 km away, and then stole a few shots of her with the children, before she vanished with a terse flick of her hand and nod of her head.

Kate and Paul headed for Split, where they were to overnight and meet up with Derek and Jan, who were due to fly in. Along the way, they stopped to film burnt-out homes and crowded cemeteries. A carload of drunken and heavily armed soldiers pulled up and tried to take the camera, accusing them of filming propaganda. They managed to pacify them by telling them they were from 'Mandela's country' and agreed to accompany them to the nearest police station to 'talk'. In the ensuing car journey they managed to shake them off and fled, with the horrible reminder that whoever wielded the gun was king.

This was confirmed by Sally when Derek interviewed her in the countryside outside Split. Both of them were wearing slightly ludicrous straw hats – hers war-torn, his brand-new. She said: 'The man on the ground here wants to fight; the politicians in Geneva don't … anarchy at its worst … if I can bring a little bit of hope in total darkness behind those front lines then it is absolutely worthwhile. And I do it because I am a servant of God.'

Sally was one of those rare people who have to act in the face of suffering. She was also deeply eccentric. Every now and then she would throw her head back and burst out with an almost inappropriate guffaw. Once, she said, her convoy had taken a direct hit; a driver was killed and she was flung to the ground. When she came round, blood was pouring from her mouth. She'd assumed the worst: internal injuries. She'd lain there for hours before it dawned on her that she wasn't dying after all, but had merely lost all her front teeth, so she began picking them up out of the dirt. She was later taken to what remained of the shelled Mostar Hospital and, while waiting for treatment, watched doctors amputate a child's leg without anaesthetic. 'Suddenly I'd never felt so well in my life: I got up and walked out.' Another roar of laughter.

The day after the interview, Kate and Paul travelled with Derek and Jan to Mostar, where Derek did links in Sniper's Alley, in front of ruined buildings pockmarked by gunfire. They almost got arrested for pointing the camera at something they shouldn't have; not knowing the history, they weren't quite sure what. They were marched off to the police station, where a translator established that they were actually there to film Sally Trench. 'Oh, that maniac', was the response. 'Let them go.'

But they weren't done with Sally. They caught up with her in Oxford, where she'd just arrived home in her Ford truck after a successful mission: no one had died. It was here, in the peaceful English countryside, that Sally gathered supplies and recruits for the next trip. But right now she was having the first of many whiskies. Her antidote to weeks of tension was to get completely plastered and then sleep for 48 hours.

'She's certainly no wilting wallflower,' Derek told Ruda back in the studio.

As George had predicted, the story of Sally Trench found in viewers a common humanity, making her selfless attitude hard to ignore. South African schoolchildren held fundraisers to support her efforts. In 1996 *Carte Blanche* did a follow-up when Sally came to say thank you.

Derek approached her unannounced at a school in Benoni. She took one look at him, uttered an expletive, gave the cameraman the finger, then conceded: 'I would never have thought of coming to South Africa until you followed me to Bosnia last year, and from that film on *Carte Blanche* I had so many thousands of letters and people so generously sending me money. And then I realised that there are a whole lot of people here who want to help.'

Her work hadn't ended there, she said. She was busy with a project to train the brightest young minds in Bosnia at institutions all over the world, so they could return to rebuild their shattered country.

In 2004 the Old Bridge across Mostar's Neretva River was reconstructed, once again linking the town's Croats and Muslims.

Sally Trench and Project Spark now have a South African Project, which helps children in informal settlements. In an online newsletter she described South Africa as 'magnetic ... nothing ever happens rationally ... or even consciously ... yet there is always a significant silent cry for help that persists, unrelentingly.'

And it is those silent cries that spur her on.

Extraordinary Rendition – 2005

On 31 October 2005, Khalid Mehmood Rashid and his housemate, Mohammed Jeebhai, were abducted in Estcourt, KwaZulu-Natal, by a group of armed men under cover of darkness. Why should we care, asked *Carte Blanche*? Because, said presenter John Webb, standing in Church Square in Pretoria: 'Today it's Khalid Rashid ... tomorrow it could be you or me.'

It was a story that *Carte Blanche* refused to let go. What first piqued the interest of producer Susan Puren was a short column in the *Sunday Independent* in late 2005. A Pakistani national, legally living in Estcourt, a town not known for much other than pork processing, had vanished into thin air.

Susan had a nose for news and a good network of contacts. There were far too many unanswered 'who, what, when, where and why' questions in the newspaper article. Researcher Nikki Lindsay was dispatched to the Pakistani Embassy in Pretoria, where she sat around for hours before being told they knew nothing about Khalid Rashid. That really got Susan going.

She suspected it had to be connected to the United States's unconventional 'war on terror', which began after the 9/11 attacks and came to include a secret global internment network that depended on the co-operation of foreign intelligence services. Anyone suspected of having links to al-Qaeda – even though in a country legally – could be abducted in well-planned operations, sent overseas to be interrogated, often tortured, and then disappear without a trace.

In 2003 in Italy, for example, the CIA had abducted the Imam of Milan, Abu Omar, as he walked to mosque for noon prayers. He was smuggled to Cairo, even though he held an Italian asylum passport. After four years of detention, an Egyptian court ruled that his imprisonment had been illegal. In November 2009, 22 CIA agents and two Italian secret agents became the first people to be convicted for this abduction. The trial cast a spotlight on the controversial American practice of extraordinary rendition – the extrajudicial transfer of a person from one country to another.

South Africa's slightly schizophrenic foreign policy leaned towards terrorism being dealt with by the United Nations and recommended that caution be exercised when supporting the actions of the United States and its allies. But in 2004 *Carte Blanche* had done an interview with

Ronnie Kasrils, then Minister of Intelligence, that indicated the opposite: 'We will cooperate with other services throughout the world because international terrorism is one of the biggest problems that the globe is being confronted with at present.' Could the Thabo Mbeki government be involved in international abductions, too? Had there been 'cooperation' in Estcourt?

Eyewitnesses told Susan and John that up to 20 armed men had entered the house Khalid was sharing with Mohammed Jeebhai, an Indian Muslim cleric, bundled them both into unmarked cars, tied and hooded, and then vanished into the night. Their landlord, alerted by the commotion, was confronted by two men with rifles, who told him to stay inside if he knew what was good for him. He said he'd heard British accents, suggesting that British Intelligence had worked with South African officials in abducting the two men. Nikki got hold of the British Embassy, but they knew nothing either.

When family and friends of the pair had tried to track them down, police had told them to contact Home Affairs in Pretoria. But Home Affairs was unhelpful, and played dumb when Susan and Nikki made inquiries. *Home Affairs official*: 'You'll have to speak to our head of communications ...'

Head of Communications: 'They said I shouldn't speak on these issues ...'

On 1 November 2005, Rashid and Jeebhai were secretly locked up at the Cullinan police station, outside Pretoria. Jeebhai, who was blindfolded when he was bundled into a car, had no idea where he had been taken. Three days later he was finally given something to eat – a packet of fruit. The packaging, he told *Carte Blanche*, had a label indicating that it had been bought at the Cullinan Spar. While Mohammed was never questioned, he'd heard Khalid Rashid, in the cell next door, being taken in and out at least twice a day. After five days, Mohammed was dumped at the Lindela repatriation centre on the West Rand and was at last able to phone his family and friends. They were to organise an urgent interdict to prevent Home Affairs from deporting him. But there was no sign of Khalid.

Mohammed's friends contacted lawyer Zahir Omar, an energetic, flamboyant character who said the secret to his boundless energy was a cold shower every morning of his life, even in the frosty Highveld winters. He was a devout Muslim who refused to shake Susan's hand when they first met, because it wasn't allowed by his faith. But he realised that, in the hunt for Khalid Rashid, he needed the media as much as they needed him. He would eventually become one of Susan's most valued contacts. Omar took the matter to the High Court, accusing Home Affairs of violating the Immigration Act. Home Affairs was instructed to disclose Khalid Rashid's whereabouts, an instruction they initially ignored.

In the absence of any official explanation, Susan and John Webb did some snooping around in Cullinan. Susan told police that her gardener had gone missing and that she needed to check their incident book. There, amazingly, she found the names of Khalid Rashid and Mohammed Jeebhai. They'd been booked in at 3:30 in the morning as 'illegal immigrants' and Home Affairs officials had signed Rashid in and out of the cells no fewer than nine times in the days that followed. Yet everyone, from the police all the way up to National Intelligence, was pretending to know nothing about Khalid Rashid. They just kept passing the buck. For example, the response of the South African Police Service (SAPS) was: 'After carefully going through this enquiry, we realised that really it should be Home Affairs that should be responding on this.' Nope, said Home Affairs, it was actually a matter for the National Intelligence Agency (NIA). The NIA said: 'Well, it sounds largely like a police matter, so they would be the people to talk to.' The head of SAPS crime intelligence simply put down the phone in John's ear. The story was becoming intriguing. South African officials were clearly trying to hide their involvement, but why?

It was probably because Rashid had been sent to an American prison camp and not 'deported due to a visa problem', as Home Affairs later told the High Court. But, if he was part of al-Qaeda or the Taliban and not merely an innocent person residing in South Africa, why hadn't due process been followed?

It seemed that the South African government, aided by the British, was taking its cue from the US and allowing illegal kidnappings. A huge breakthrough in uncovering the chain of events came when a plane spotter at Lanseria airport gave Susan a picture of a Gulfstream II jet that had been parked on the runway. The only reason he'd become suspicious was because he had been told to stop taking pictures of the plane. Susan traced it to Waterkloof Air Force Base and, because she had the plane's number from the viewer's photograph, was able to get a flight plan. The jet was owned by a charter company from Kyrgyzstan and had been leased by the government of Pakistan. Another source told her that 'some Pakistani men' had received emergency visas. Standard procedure for deportations is on a commercial flight from a point of entry.

Susan and *Carte Blanche* stayed with the story, refusing to be fobbed off by government's silence on the whereabouts of Khalid Rashid. It merely heightened the mystery – why all the secrecy? Human rights advocates like Jody Kollapen and Rudolph Jansen said the incident had all the trademarks of abductions by oppressive governments, governments that didn't have functioning courts.

But in court, a battle was raging. Home Affairs produced a letter from the Pakistani government stating that Rashid had arrived home after being deported as an illegal immigrant – except he hadn't been illegal. Nobody had even bothered to check his passport, which was still lying at his house in Estcourt, and his family in Rawalpindi told *Carte Blanche* on the phone that they hadn't heard from him in months.

Bizarrely, but drawing obvious parallels, Zahir Omar enlisted the help of former apartheid death squad commander Dirk Coetzee. 'That's exactly the way we acted. You know, abduct the guy, afford him no rights and eventually he disappeared,' Coetzee said outside the High Court.

Then something extraordinary happened, which came to be known as 'The Samoosa File Incident'. A box containing samoosas and drinks was delivered to a late-night court sitting. A Home Affairs file containing key documents was picked up with the box by the man who'd delivered the snacks, a part-time law student named Yaseen. The so-called Samoosa File revealed that Home Affairs had been economical with the truth. But the judge said its contents couldn't be made public. Enraged that the file had been 'stolen', Home Affairs bigwigs enlisted the help of plainclothes police heavies to threaten Yaseen outside court. Yaseen found himself catapulted into the spotlight. He was warned not to speak to *Carte Blanche*.

But Susan managed to get hold of his affidavit, which revealed what he had gleaned from the Samoosa File, that Home Affairs had been protecting the Minister of Intelligence, who'd been requested by Britain to assist in the capture of Rashid, who was wanted in connection with the London bombings of July 2005. But, as Zahir Omar pointed out, Rashid had been living in South Africa at the time. And in the unlikely event that he'd slipped out of the country to take part in the London bombings, why wasn't he in England facing trial? Where was he? The British Foreign Office would only say that it was a matter for the South African authorities.

Susan flew to Pakistan, but was unable to find Rashid. She interviewed his weeping mother, who said she'd neither seen nor heard from him since his disappearance.

In 2007, Amnesty International located Khalid Rashid in an Islamabad jail. He'd been detained incommunicado for 17 months. No charges were ever laid against him. He refused to speak about what had happened.

In 2009, South Africa's Supreme Court of Appeal held that the arrest, detention and deportation of Khalid Rashid had been unlawful, effectively proving that *Carte Blanche*'s investigation was accurate in every respect.

'A hollow victory,' said Zahir Omar. 'But I would like to thank the journalists of *Carte Blanche* whose efforts were pivotal in saving the life of Khalid Rashid and exposing the Mbeki administration's involvement in Bush's war on terror.'

Radovan – 2010

While Khalid Rashid found himself *persona non grata* in South Africa, it seemed that the dregs of Central Europe were A-OK. The collapse of communism and the brutal disintegration of the Balkans were said to have contributed to an unheralded 'success' story: the globalisation of crime. And if you had plenty of money, it seemed, South Africa was a safe haven.

In 2005, Czech fugitive and alleged underworld kingpin Radovan

Krejcir fled his home country in dramatic style, while police were searching his villa in Prague. He first lay low in the Seychelles, then got bored and wrote a book revealing that he'd once funded the election campaign of the Czech Social Democratic Party in return for 'special favours'. It was a bad move, because in 2007 an extradition treaty was signed between the Seychelles and the Czech Republic and Krejcir was forced to run again. With a false passport he flew to South Africa, where, being on the Interpol red list, he was arrested at the airport. What should've been a routine extradition application – after all, Krejcir was wanted for conspiracy to murder, forgery, tax evasion, extortion and abduction – turned out a little differently. A Kempton Park magistrate accepted his explanation that there was a conspiracy against him in the Czech Republic and Krejcir walked away to a new life, very impressed with the South African justice system.

He began using his cash to surround himself with influential people in the local underworld, but only shot to prominence after the murder of strip-club owner Lolly Jackson in 2010. Krejcir was well acquainted with Lolly's alleged murderer, George Louka. He'd met him in the Kempton Park police cells and, after his release, had introduced Louka to Cypriot banker Alekos Panayi, a dab hand at laundering foreign currency. Louka allegedly fronted for Krejcir, opening a bank account for him in Cyprus, so that Panayi could help him get his millions out of Europe. Lolly Jackson was another of Panayi's clients. Soon they were all one big happy mob family. But things got nasty, as they do when mega-money is involved, and Jackson accused Panayi of stealing from him. He forced Panayi to sign an IOU for R1 million, gave him a few smacks, and then sued him.

Panayi wanted revenge. He enlisted the help of an ex-cop named Ollie Olivier, who was investigating Jackson on behalf of various clients and who had a bulging file of affidavits. *Carte Blanche* producer Joy Summers obtained Panayi's affidavit, in which he came clean about the laundering syndicate. She presented the story at an editorial meeting on Monday, 3 May 2010, planning to take a few weeks to unravel the details of how it worked. But that night Lolly Jackson was shot dead.

Joy had to move fast to get the story out for that Sunday. Ollie told her that George Louka had been the trigger man and that the police were hot on his trail. She and cameraman Dudley Saunders hung around the east of Joburg for several hours that night, waiting for the arrest. They went home disappointed. Louka had skipped the country.

The next day, presenter Devi Sankaree Govender was assigned to work with Joy on the story. She'd interviewed Lolly years before about a planned red-light district in Durban. He'd given her a Teazers' lifetime access card, which impressed her husband until he found out it was non-transferable. Devi was shocked that Jackson had been killed, as were his staff, who said things like: 'A great man has left us ... he was loved by many.'

Others, like Andrew Phillips, who ran a competing strip joint, were less complimentary: 'Anybody who did business with Lolly got stitched. He couldn't help himself. It was like it was encoded in his genes.' Ollie agreed: 'He would exploit every person that [came] his way, whether that was a bank manager, whether it was a cleaner, a chef in the kitchen, a dancer, or even his admin staff.'

Devi: 'Was there anything good about Lolly Jackson?'

Ollie: 'He drove nice cars.'

The story, clearly not a tribute, gave insight into the fast world in which Lolly Jackson moved, and the name Radovan Krejcir kept cropping up. The allegations were that George Louka had been Krejcir's front man.

Joy decided to find out more for a follow-up story. The Johannesburg underworld was a fascinating place, and she learnt more about it from Juan Meyer, a former business partner of Krejcir, who was convinced that he too was about to be taken out. Meyer was a beefcake, but surrounded himself with a posse of bodyguards, sure that he was next on Krejcir's 'hit list'.

He implicated Krejcir in currency smuggling, as well as in the murder of Uwe Gemballa, a German supercar conversion specialist who'd vanished soon after arriving in South Africa for discussions with Krejcir's right-hand man, Jerome Safi, about opening a franchise. By no means squeaky-clean himself, and later arrested for VAT fraud, Meyer also fingered several high-ranking policemen as being on Krejcir's payroll.

Joy wasn't sure where to start: there was no shortage of allegations, but few people were willing to go on camera. With no stomach to investigate Johannesburg's underbelly on her own, and with a looming deadline, she enlisted the help of colleague Bernadette Maguire.

It seemed that the only way *Carte Blanche* could make this story different to the reams of copy already written was to speak to the man himself. Bernadette, who has a way with shady characters, was assigned to find Radovan Krejcir and secure an interview.

They had access to affidavits written by investigator Paul O'Sullivan, who was trying to bring down what he called 'the evil transnational crime syndicate of Radovan Krejcir'. The Czech was, said O'Sullivan, 'a criminal psychopath buying his way into all aspects of society' and should be removed from 'the public domain before any more persons vanish'.

One of the affidavits was from Johannesburg urologist Marian Tupy, who said that Krejcir had threatened him and forced him to falsify his medical file to say that Krejcir was dying of cancer so that he could get a presidential pardon in the Czech Republic and cash in on an insurance claim. Dr Tupy also stated that Krejcir had bragged to him about murdering Uwe Gemballa, and that, if he wasn't so busy with lawyers, 'more people would disappear'.

Bernadette interviewed a clearly terrified Dr Tupy, but they left him out of the final story, fearing that his life would be in danger if he were shown to have spoken out against Krejcir.

O'Sullivan's role in the story made it even more convoluted. Was he simply a philanthropist, spending millions of his own in an effort to rid South Africa of corruption, or was he – as was often alleged – on the payroll of a foreign intelligence agency?

Despite all the serious allegations against Krejcir, he certainly wasn't in hiding. Most days, he held court behind specially fitted bulletproof glass at the Harbour Café in Bedfordview. Champagne flowed as Radovan entertained an assortment of characters and made his deals. His Porsche, Lamborghini or Ferrari occupied a prime parking spot near the entrance. It was at the Harbour Café that an apparently spaced-out George Louka had pulled up in Lolly Jackson's Jeep and announced to Radovan and his henchmen that he'd just killed the strip-club magnate. Then he'd bought two packets of cigarettes and disappeared, later surfacing in Cyprus.

Bernadette was nervous, but reckoned that asking Radovan for an interview wouldn't exactly put her life in danger. She walked in with presenter Bongani Bingwa and cameraman Andre Gous, who left his camera in the car so they would not be too conspicuous, and found a table. They must've made an odd trio: Bernadette is slightly hippie-ish, with a mane of waist-length black hair, Andre looks not unlike a pre-1994 security policeman, and Bongani is very much the face of *Carte Blanche*. They spotted Radovan Krejcir immediately, holding court in an area surrounded by fish tanks, eating sushi and drinking cocktails. He vaguely resembled Ratko Mladic, the notorious Serb military commander, with a full face and cropped hair.

Bernadette approached him and was greeted with his trademark laugh. He'd thought they were undercover cops. No, he hadn't heard of *Carte Blanche* and no, he certainly wasn't going to do an interview ... the media were never fair to him.

It was at this point, recalls Bongani, who'd hung back, that Bernadette began using her feminine wiles, deciding that flirtatious persuasion would be the way to go. She remembers it differently ... she merely gave Radovan her word, in the friendliest way she could, that he would be given an opportunity to respond to every allegation that *Carte Blanche* had against him.

Radovan said he would consider it and that she should make contact with his second in command, Jerome Safi – the same Jerome Safi who'd allegedly been Uwe Gemballa's last contact before disappearing off the face of the earth.

Bernadette didn't know anything about Safi yet, and wasted no time in getting hold of him. He told them to be at the Harbour Café the following afternoon at half past five; he would see what he could do.

Joy was delighted; in the meantime, she was trying to link what Juan Meyer had said in his interview to the affidavits she had. And she'd managed to trace a Czech journalist who'd been investigating Krejcir for years and did a video link-up with him.

(Investigative journalist, TV Nova): 'Radovan is a very ambitious businessman in the Czech Republic, and belongs to a group ... that became very rich after the Velvet Revolution in the 1990s. He is a very

controversial person ... his story is like one from a Hollywood movie ... he even had a shark tank in his house and he could watch the shark inside ... when [Radovan] escaped, the Czech Chief of Police had to resign because it was his fault ...'

On their way to the Harbour Café the following evening, Bernadette received a phone call from Jerome Safı. 'What do yous like to drink?' the Lebanese go-between asked. It was going to be a long evening. When they walked in, Radovan and the Kir Royales were waiting for them. He began regaling them with stories of how unfair the world had been to him. Bongani sipped slowly in case they were granted an interview, but the hours ticked by and the booze kept flowing. Radovan, it seemed, could drink anyone under the table. Also at the Harbour Café that night was Ivan Savov, Krejcir's business manager. It would later emerge in court that Uwe Gemballa had been murdered at a house rented by Savov.

Joy arrived later and remembers feeling distinctly uncomfortable drinking Champagne with one of Eastern Europe's most wanted men. She was glad it was Bernadette, and not she, who had to convince him to talk, and made an early exit.

Eventually, after several hours of Champagne cocktails and Jägerbombs, punctuated by Radovan laughingly phoning George Louka in Cyprus and Marian Tupy, 'his friend the doctor', he agreed to do the interview the following evening. Bernadette was elated, Bongani was slightly unsteady on his feet, and Joy, when they phoned her, was antsy. It was already Thursday ... the story was for that Sunday, and she reckoned they'd blown it – they should've done it while they had him. Now he would simply disappear.

After a tense night and a nervous morning, Bernadette, Bongani and Andre arrived at the Harbour Café for the interview – but there was no sign of Radovan. More frantic phone calls to Jerome Safı, whose number Bernadette now had on speed dial. Jerome arrived, took them outside to three black BMWs with tinted windows and ordered them to switch off their cellphones and lock them in one of the cars, so they couldn't be traced. Then he got into a car with Bernadette, while Bongani and cameraman Andre followed on a convoluted journey at high speed through the streets of Bedfordview, as if they were shaking off a tail. It was, said

Jerome, because Radovan was 'in hiding'. He didn't explain what made the Harbour Café a safe place to hide from assassins – perhaps the bulletproof glass. They finally arrived, via a circuitous route, at Radovan's R20-million mansion on a cliff, with a view to die for and a glass elevator. There were splash pools, tasteful furnishings and, of course, fish tanks.

Bernadette felt slightly edgy without her phone. No one had any idea where she was. Krejcir's idea of a welcome was: 'First we drink, then we do interview, then I keeeel you!' And he fell about laughing. Bongani laughed too, but couldn't relax – this guy seemed untouchable. While Andre was setting up the camera and lights, Radovan told Bongani that the only way to tell if a man had good taste was to check out his watch and his shoes. South Africans, he said, confused taste with fancy suits, shirts, cologne and 'bling'. After Lolly had been killed, he'd gone to his house, just up the road, to see the body and only had to look as far as his feet to know it was him. 'Lolly had no fucking taste in shoes,' he said. Part of him was Radovan the alleged godfather of organised crime, and another part was a character who enjoyed old-world values and sophistication, Bongani decided.

He and Bernadette were in a hurry to do the interview and get the hell out, but were aware that Radovan would try to outsmart them, so they opted for the slowly-slowly approach. They would first warm him up, and then ask questions like: 'Uwe Gemballa ... what happened to him? One of the allegations is that you ...' – Bongani made a sawing gesture at his throat, with accompanying sound effects – '... you took care of him.'

Radovan reacted instantly: 'I taking care of him? Why are you asking me? How I know what happened to him? I never see Uwe Gemballa.'

According to Juan Meyer, Gemballa and Radovan had had an agreement to stash cash in imported cars, as a way for Radovan to get hold of some of his European fortune. But a Porsche had arrived without the cash and things had soured. When Radovan had had words with Gemballa, he'd allegedly responded: 'You're a wanted man in Europe, don't threaten me.'

But Radovan just laughed and repeated to Bongani that he'd never set eyes on Gemballa. As for Juan Meyer: 'He is not normal, it is very simple. This person, he needs the psychological hospital ... it is just the bullshit ... it is just the nonsense.'

Bongani: 'Did Lolly Jackson owe you money?'

Radovan: 'Look, I gave him some loan from overseas ... direct to the Teazers ... I won't say how much ... but it is true there is outstanding amount ... He was my friend, he was my buddy.'

And so it went on for 45 minutes while Radovan stuck to his story: he was a victim. After the interview, while the Cypriot house staff served drinks, Radovan pointed at some oil drums in the corner of his garden, which he jokingly said were filled with acid. If the *Carte Blanche* story wasn't to his liking ...

Back in the edit suite on the other side of Johannesburg, Joy was frantically phoning around, trying to locate Bernadette and Bongani. She hadn't heard from them for hours, and why would their phones be switched off?

They were still resisting Radovan's efforts to ply them with liquor on his magnificent veranda and eyeing the acid-filled drums. But finally Jerome took them back to the Harbour Café. Mission accomplished. Now Bernadette and Joy had 48 hours to put the story together.

It wasn't the last they heard of Radovan. He phoned Bernadette several times over the weekend to check if the story 'was still going out'. To her, it seemed like a subtle threat, and when he requested to see the story on the Sunday morning before broadcast, she switched off her phone.

The story was part of *Carte Blanche*'s first high-definition (HD) broadcast, on 5 September 2010. On HD screens in living rooms across South Africa, Bongani looked sharp and intense: 'This is the Harbour Café in Bedfordview ... it is here, behind bulletproof glass, that fugitive Czech billionaire Radovan Krejcir ... wheels and deals and makes plans to move his money around the world ... but some who've had dealings with him fear for their lives ...'

It was 17 minutes of entertaining television, and concluded: 'Radovan Krejcir is a wanted man in the Czech Republic ... just why on earth is he living a life of luxury here in South Africa?'

Radovan phoned Bernadette the following day to say he'd been 'shocked' at what all the people who'd been interviewed had said about him. And he'd been particularly interested in the news footage of his arrest in Prague. She was relieved to be finished with Krejcir, but for the next few weeks checked her rear-view mirror while driving.

Months later, Bongani found himself in Bedfordview to meet a friend for a meal at the Harbour Café. Within minutes, members of Krejcir's entourage sidled over to find out if he was 'OK'. When it came to paying, the waiter said there was no charge. There was no sign of Radovan, but his reach extended far.

Six months later, Joy received a phone call from Juan Meyer, Krejcir's arch-nemesis. He said he had reliable information that a contract had been put out on his life – as well as on Paul O'Sullivan and Cyril Beeka, a former MK operative who ruled Cape Town's underworld.

Four days later, Cyril Beeka was dead – killed in a drive-by shooting. He'd had business dealings with Radovan that had gone sour, said Meyer. At Beeka's birthday party the previous year, he and Radovan had apparently had a punch-up and Radovan had needed stitches. Was this a case of when blood is spilled in the underworld, 'blood must be picked up'?

It was alleged that Radovan had flown in three Serbian assassins to do the deed. Bernadette asked him to comment, but he declined: why, whenever anyone he knew got killed, was it Radovan's fault, he asked?

In a bizarre development a few days after Beeka's killing, police, accompanied by Paul O'Sullivan, raided Radovan's home and claimed to have found a 'hit list'. Radovan was arrested – at last. Was there evidence that would stick?

Paul O'Sullivan, who'd worked tirelessly to put Krejcir away, treated himself to a Guinness in Radovan's corner at the Harbour Café. He phoned a friend in the Czech Republic, saying: 'When the people of Prague realise I am sitting at Krejcir's table in the Harbour Café, they will rejoice.'

But the best the state could come up with against Radovan were fraud charges. Ten days later, he walked out of court on bail, ordered a Czech beer at the Harbour Café and said: 'Saluté, Paul O'Sullivan.'

In 2012, the NPA dropped all charges against Radovan.

tall stories 6

In his book *Into Thin Air*, widely acknowledged as the definitive account of the deadliest season in the history of climbing Mount Everest, mountaineer Jon Krakauer says: '*Everest* has always been a magnet for kooks, publicity seekers, hopeless romantics and others with a shaky hold on reality.'

Sean Wisedale, the first South African to climb the Seven Summits – the highest mountains on all seven continents – says he is all of those things. He got his first glimpse of Everest (called 'Holy Mother' in Tibetan), in 1996, when he accompanied Derek Watts and producer Diana Lucas to Kathmandu, Nepal, as cameraman to interview Cathy O'Dowd after she'd become the first South African to summit the world's highest peak. It had been a controversial team effort that had resulted in much mudslinging, quite a bit of it on *Carte Blanche*.

O'Dowd, then a novice, is now the first woman to have summited Everest from both south and north. In 1996 she was accompanied to the top by two Sherpa guides and by Ian Woodall, the team leader. Woodall's British compatriot, Bruce Herrod, the team photographer who had trailed hours behind them, never made it down. A year later, his body was found near the base of the Hillary Step.

The South African team had originally consisted of seven climbers, but the allegedly dictatorial and generally unlikeable Woodall had managed to alienate them all. The experienced Andy de Klerk, Andy Hackland and Ed February had all pulled out, as had the team doctor, Charlotte Noble. Some of them had left before the expedition even reached South Base

Camp. Krakauer quotes Andy de Klerk: 'Woodall turned out to be a total control freak ... And you couldn't trust him. We never knew when he was talking bullshit or telling the truth. We didn't want to put our lives in the hands of a guy like that. So we left.'

In addition there'd been a big spat with the sponsor, the *Sunday Times*. Woodall had banished reporter Ken Vernon from Base Camp and told editor Ken Owen, who'd arrived to sort things out, that he was going to 'rip his fucking head off'. In 1997, both Woodall and Vernon published very divergent accounts of the South African Everest expedition and had a heated live debate on *Carte Blanche*. It ran for a full 40 minutes, with Derek trying unsuccessfully to bring it to an earlier conclusion.

Woodall was blamed for not having forced Herrod to turn back when he, O'Dowd and the Sherpas had encountered him going up while they were on their way down. It was after noon, regarded by many experts as too late in the day to ascend a killer mountain. Woodall was even accused of not giving his close friend, Herrod, enough oxygen. What kind of person was this?

The Everest expedition was a big story and one that *Carte Blanche* needed in a hurry. Derek's account of how the decision was made to go to Everest is amusingly recounted in the foreword to Sean's book, *Freeze Frame*: 'There is no doubt that the life of Sean Stephen Wisedale changed radically at a *Carte Blanche* editorial meeting on 4 June 1996 ... it was announced that we had an exclusive interview with Cathy O'Dowd ... as soon as she returned home. Half-jokingly I blurted out, "That's too late. Every newspaper in the country will have interviews with her! We must get over to Kathmandu this week ... now."'

That afternoon Derek, Diana and Sean boarded a flight to Nepal. The only advice from executive producer George Mazarakis before they left was that Diana, whom Derek describes as 'a bit of a whirlwind', should tone it down in case she triggered an avalanche. She brought her shrill voice down to a whisper: 'Don't worry, George, I can be very, very quiet.'

They arrived in Nepal without having had time to arrange media accreditation. Sean had, said Derek, 'a huge pile of gleaming aluminium cases of equipment'. He and Diana decided that, at the first hint of trouble, they would pretend they didn't know Sean, enter the country as

63

visitors and hire a cameraman in Kathmandu. It had been the deadliest season ever on Everest. Some of the world's top climbers had died, and there had been widespread negative publicity about the number of inexperienced climbers being allowed on the mountain. So perhaps the authorities at Kathmandu International Airport were feeling lenient, because the *Carte Blanche* team got their visas.

Carte Blanche had already done two stories on the controversy, using a model of Everest, which, needless to say, had captured none of the drama going down at South Base Camp and beyond. The first story had dealt with the return home of climbers Andy Hackland and Ed February. They'd called the expedition a 'farce' and said that if the remaining South Africans got to the top, it would be thanks to the top Sherpas hired by Woodall to 'push them up'.

The second story, on 19 May 1996, had been more positive and told of the hopes and fears of the families of Cathy O'Dowd and Deshun Deysel, the last South Africans left from the original team. There were shots of their parents listening to live radio reports from 702's Patrick Conroy at South Base Camp, who explained that the bad weather and a bottleneck on Everest that had contributed to the deaths of ten climbers had made it impossible for the South Africans to stay on at the final camp before the summit. So they'd descended all the way down to rest until conditions improved. Sports scientist Tim Noakes explained to presenter Manu Padayachee that there simply wasn't enough oxygen at Camp IV, on the South Col, to remain there: 'All the human being is at 8 000 metres is a massive lung ... you are not really conscious.'

On 25 May 1996, Ian Woodall and Cathy O'Dowd confounded the experts when they planted the South African flag on Everest. They returned to Camp IV, in the death zone (above 8 000 metres), to wait for Bruce Herrod, who radioed them at 5pm to say he'd got to the top: 'I'm just chuffed to fuck that I've finally made it ... It's been a long time coming, mate, and I will be real careful on the way down ... I'm not going to screw up now ... thanks for all your support ... over.'

They never heard from him again and departed Camp IV the following morning. They were the last team left on Everest.

By the time the *Carte Blanche* team got to Nepal, Bruce Herrod was presumed dead and Cathy and Ian had arrived back in Kathmandu. They were dressed in light Nepalese cotton clothing and looked relaxed as they dodged motorcycles in the narrow streets. Cathy, said Diana, was 'amazing television', as some people are. It has nothing to do with looks and everything to do with being forthright, confident and sincere.

Newspaper reports in South Africa had lashed Woodall for failing to order Herrod down, so Derek felt he needed to grill Cathy and Ian in the interviews. Kathmandu is a busy city, so they found a quiet spot at a Buddhist retreat with mountains in the background. They were interviewed separately because, apart from the fact that it always makes for easier editing, Diana felt Ian's strong personality might be inclined to take over. She needn't have worried: Cathy was more than able to hold her own on camera and completely disarmed Derek.

She said she was tired of all the 'armchair mountaineers' back home. 'Bruce was so terribly pleased when he passed Ian and me and learnt that we'd made it. There was no stopping him. It was a real triumph for Bruce and people should remember that.'

It had been a perfect day, surprisingly warm with no storms coming in. Bruce would've been quite capable of descending in the dark: he had on a down suit and was fully equipped to sit it out in those weather conditions. He'd had a cylinder of oxygen and they'd stashed two more for him on the route down. Listening to him talk on the radio, he hadn't been tired or frightened. She smiled broadly: 'He was a strong man who was unbelievably chuffed about what he'd achieved.'

Derek: 'When did it hit you that Bruce wasn't coming back?'

Cathy (smile fades): 'When I woke up the next morning and there'd been no radio calls, I knew.'

Ian had sat at Camp IV for hours waiting for his friend. He could see most of the route to the summit from the South Col and there had been no movement on the ridge.

Derek challenged him: 'As expedition leader, shouldn't you have tried to get Bruce to turn back when your paths crossed?'

That, said Woodall, would've been like telling the late Ayrton Senna not to drive on the day of his fatal crash. Herrod was a better and stronger climber than he was. He wasn't 'a bank manager who'd paid lots of money to be pushed up' – a reference to the commercialisation of Everest, where underqualified mountaineers pay thousands of dollars to adventure companies to nanny them to the top of a mountain that had once been the ultimate challenge in human strength and endurance.

Quietly filming all of this was Sean Wisedale, who had never climbed a mountain in his life. Sixteen years and many peaks later, he calls Ian Woodall a 'compulsive bull-duster ... if you aren't on the summit of Everest by 13:00, you must turn around.'

But the 'Wiseman', as Derek calls Sean, held his tongue at the time, listening and learning. The following day, Diana, who, says Derek, is 'relentless when it comes to getting her own way on a shoot', somehow persuaded an experienced Nepalese Air Force pilot to take them to South Base Camp to film Cathy 'in situ'. In those days, such a flight was considered dangerous; they would be pushing the Squirrel helicopter to its limits. Because it could only take four people, Diana, to her dismay, had to stay behind. In 2005, a high-altitude helicopter landed on the summit of Everest for the first time, and nowadays there are daily flights to and from the mountain during the spring climbing season. But in 1996 choppers had difficulty getting enough lift in the thin air.

In what was certainly a television scoop, Cathy, the woman of the moment, took the mic and, while Sean filmed out of the window, gave them running commentary: 'We are about to cross the first major test for us, the Lamjura Pass ... this was the first time we got our legs into gear ... that there is the gateway to the Western Cwm ... There's Camp IV, where we sat for four days in a raging storm ... and directly below us the Khumbu Icefall, a formidable moving frozen rapid ...'

They landed briefly at South Base Camp. They were the only living souls on Everest – no tents, no trash, just rugged, jagged beauty.

'An extraordinary feeling,' yelled Derek, above the roar of the rotor, which the pilot couldn't turn off in case it didn't start again. 'Base Camp Everest ... deserted after climbing teams from around the world have returned home.' Cathy, standing next to him in her thin cotton shirt, looked overcome. Derek couldn't resist giving her a big kiss, which he said got him into trouble back home.

It was, he says in the foreword to *Freeze Frame*, a moment that left

Cathy in tears ... Sean Wisedale put down his Sony Betacam camera for a moment, looked towards the summit and said: 'I am going to come back here and climb this hill.' Moments later, they clambered back into the chopper for the long flight back down the Khumbu Valley, entranced by the vision of Everest and slightly dazed from the lack of oxygen.

The following year, Sean and his camera helped to cement *Carte Blanche*'s reputation as the most-travelled current affairs show in South Africa. He followed adventurer Mike Horn – who was travelling down the Amazon River unassisted on a hydrospeed board – went on sailing adventures and learnt to understand weather patterns, knowledge that would later stand him in good stead on the world's highest peaks. He would attach himself to expeditions as the cameraman and bring dramatic stories back to *Carte Blanche*. George Mazarakis remembers many tortured viewings with the fiery-haired Sean, who had the perfect temperament for mountain climbing, but certainly not for putting up with criticism of his storytelling abilities. Sean recalls Big Boss George as being harder to budge than any mountain.

Aconcagua, the Stone Sentinel – 2002

In 2002, Sean went to Aconcagua, in Argentina, and brought back to *Carte Blanche* a beautifully filmed story called 'The Stone Sentinel'. Aconcagua is the highest point in the Andes, the world's longest mountain range. It's one of the peaks needed to complete the Seven Summits – the ultimate challenge for Jon Krakauer's 'kooks, publicity seekers, hopeless romantics and others with a shaky hold on reality'.

The leader of this particular expedition was Sean Disney, one of the world's most experienced mountain guides. He coordinated the preparations, which involved hauling food, tents and climbing equipment over long distances. In the final stages, heavily laden donkeys traversed the arid Andean foothills to Base Camp.

Sean Wisedale interviewed Disney intermittently on the journey. Because there was no presenter, the interviews were direct to camera, which gave a gritty, diary feel: 'For two days we're moving half a ton of equipment from South Africa to Base Camp and that's where we start our assault on the mountain. It's a huge logistical mission.'

The two Seans were among 11 South Africans who'd set off to conquer Aconcagua. Among them was Sue Wadley, a Johannesburg physiotherapist new to the rigours of high-altitude climbing.

When they arrived at Base Camp, at 4 200 metres, the first thing Sean filmed was a rescue, which put things into perspective. A lone climber had been brought back on a stretcher. He had water on the lung, and was lucky to have been found. But Sean managed to inject some humour into the story, filming signs on the ablutions at Base Camp: 'Toilet ticket – $20; Shower – $10; Three showers – $25.'

As they set off for Mount Nido, a crucial step towards acclimatising, conditions worsened. Sleet came down in sheets, and two members of the team dropped out. One of them was cricketer Lawrence Seeff. Sean captured a close-up of him wheezing to camera: 'I've got no words ...' Then followed a long shot of him walking away until he became just a speck.

The remaining nine climbers took three exhausting weeks to get to the high camp, from where they would attempt the summit, which would take 14 hours. They set off in darkness, but within an hour weather conditions worsened, to the point that Disney ordered them back to camp. Sue Wadley was livid. She'd come there to get to the top.

Then a blizzard set in, pushing temperatures down to –20 °C. Sean Wisedale filmed the exhausted climbers making their way to camp, barely visible in the snowstorm. In an interview with Disney, huddled in his tent, the expedition leader explained: 'What we were experiencing was becoming a little too hard ... we were getting storms in the afternoon ... it was getting very cold ... and for the season, it shouldn't be like that.'

Despite her earlier disappointment, Sue Wadley had only praise for Disney: 'That's what makes a guide a guide. He judged the weather correctly, and, even though I was fuming, six hours later his predictions were right.'

Half the team was suffering from altitude sickness, so Disney took them back to Base Camp and called off the expedition. It had been the worst season on Aconcagua in 25 years.

But the wiry Wisedale, despite being weighed down by camera equipment, wasn't ready to give up. Bargaining on calm after a storm, he remained behind with Sue. Twenty-four hours later, their break came. Back in South Africa, when interviewed by Ruda, he explained their decision: 'It was good weather; we had no idea when it would get bad again and the idea was to get back up there as quickly as we could ...'

The rest of the shoot belonged to Sue. She was the only expedition member left for Sean to film. Soft, knee-deep snow made the going painfully slow, but finally they were rewarded with what looked like an amazing sight, even on television: a view of Mount Aconcagua that few have witnessed. From the upper slopes, its vast shadow ran for hundreds of kilometres over the Andes. They were almost at the top.

Sean described their emotions on reaching the summit: 'You know that this is what every step was for, and all the pain and discomfort that you went through, that you achieved that goal, and that's absolutely amazing; it was worth it.'

Summit – 2004

'I had to get back, hey ... I meant it, Derek. You remember that helicopter flight. When you looked out those windows and I looked up at the Himalayas and the helicopter is flying at the highest it can fly and those mountains are two and half kilometres higher than you, then you know there's something special there.'

Since the 1996 trip with Derek and Diana, Sean Wisedale had found ways and means to get back to Everest. He'd hooked up with Alex Harris and Sean Disney, South Africa's big boys of mountaineering, in an unsuccessful attempt on Everest's north face. Jetstream winds had prevented them from climbing higher than 7 300 metres. He'd followed them to Mount Vinson in Antarctica, carrying his hefty Sony Betacam camera to the top and producing an award-winning documentary. After Aconcagua, he'd climbed Alaska's Mount Denali (also known as Mount McKinley), the highest peak in North America.

Then, in 2003, he got another chance to return to Everest, again as filmmaker. It was supposed to be Alex Harris and Sean Disney's seventh summit, the first time any South African had achieved the feat. But after two attempts, the team was beaten back, just 400 metres from the top, because of unforgiving weather. Defeated, they made their way back to Base Camp.

The *Carte Blanche* script of that particular incident reads: 'It had been a team decision to throw in the ice pick and head home, but one member was about to mutiny.' The word 'mutiny' still irritates Sean. His team-mates had left, he was still at Base Camp waiting to fly out, when suddenly a weather window opened up and the American team that was still there decided to go for it. Sean, feeling fit and hydrated, made a spur-of-the-moment decision to join them. He got to the summit half an hour before them, planted the flag of the sponsor, Discovery, on the highest point on earth and headed back.

'How much of that event was destiny and how much was my own choice I have no answer for. What I do know is that Mother Nature waits for no one and that exactly seven years after I had said to Derek at Base Camp, "one day I will come back and climb that hill," I did.' He had climbed his fourth (and the toughest) of the Seven Summits.

By the time *Carte Blanche* hooked up with him again, only Kilimanjaro was beckoning. The filmmaker had become the story. Derek, who'd climbed Kili some ten years back, was in. So was Diana. Derek donned what felt like a rather thin anorak, but was told to put on lots of layers underneath it and he'd be fine. There were shots of him striding along a mountain path in his shorts, displaying what Sean called 'an innate sense of style and fashion ... designer shorts and space-age trainers, without socks ... a spectacular mountaineering first.'

Derek, puffing slightly, commented: 'Kili is the highest free-standing mountain in the world and it's a challenge that takes climbers from tropical rainforests to permanent ice caps in just five days.' But by the time they'd reached the highest camp, they'd been through a blizzard, and Derek was soaked. He managed to crawl into his tent, and described the next eight hours as the worst of his life. He didn't have the strength to remove his wet clothing and was convinced that if he fell asleep he would never wake up. He was sharing a tent with the team doctor, a fastidious man who seemed completely uninterested in his plight. There was no doubt in Derek's mind that he was developing hypothermia, and what still traumatises him to this day was that no one gave a hoot. He lay there in his sodden gear, unable even to lift his arms to eat a biscuit, let alone get changed. It was only after Philip the cameraman, Sean's brother, suffered a seizure and had to be evacuated that Derek got the chance to move down the mountain, where he recovered sufficiently to change his sodden clothes.

In the meantime, Sean Wisedale was making history. With the rest of the party, he left for the summit of Kilimanjaro in the early hours. A line of shadowy figures with headtorches reached the 5 895-metre Uhuru Peak at half past seven on the morning of 19 February 2004.

But there was no presenter or cameraman on hand to record the moment. So Diana became the somewhat shaky camera operator, shouting from the roof of Africa: 'SEAN, BOY ... YOU HAVE SHOWN US ... THE FIRST SOUTH AFRICAN FOR SEVEN SUMMITS!'

Sean, in a much quieter voice, muffled by the wind, said it was a privilege to be there. His Seven Summits journey had helped him find his talent. Everyone had their own mountains to climb, he said; everyone should find their talent.

Many kilometres down the mountain, Philip had recovered and Derek was at last tucking into the biscuits he'd been longing to eat while drenched and immobilised at High Camp.

In *Freeze Frame*, published in 2005, Derek wrote: 'Cameramen come from a tough school and in this regard Sean was at the top of his class ... a team player supreme ... but when it's down to the make or break moment, he has a focus, drive and sheer physical strength that is staggering, almost supernatural.'

rugby fever 7

Search for 'rugby' on the *Carte Blanche* website and a host of stories will pop up. These were usually instigated by Derek Watts and were indicative of the profile of the typical *Carte Blanche* viewer. In 1998, Derek decided that coverage of what happened behind the scenes at the fiftieth test between the Springboks and the All Blacks – part of the Tri-Nations – would be essential viewing. Executive producer George Mazarakis remembers Derek nagging him endlessly until he eventually gave in. The conditions were that Derek took only a cameraman and produced the segment himself – no problem for a former sports reporter. Derek got hold of New Zealand Tourism and they agreed to help set up a story. He and cameraman Mike Yelseth arrived on South Island upbeat and ready for a cracker. They anticipated having limited access to the All Blacks, but no doubt being allowed to attend a training session or two, and to interview some of the greats – Taine Randell, Jonah Lomu, Carlos Spencer, Andrew Mehrtens, the list was endless.

But Tourism New Zealand's idea of behind-the-scenes time with the All Blacks was a cocktail party at Parliament House, and interviews with recently retired captain Sean Fitzpatrick and Prime Minister Jenny Shipley. When Derek inquired about filming a training session, he was told no, that was it – no more access. So all they had on tape was ten minutes of socialising and an interview with a politician and a former player. A Kiwi journalist confirmed that the All Blacks didn't do interviews 48 hours before a match. Beating South Africa, he said, had a special taste – the boys needed to focus.

So Derek hastily changed his focus – and switched camps. Coach Nick Mallett, captain Gary Teichmann and the Boks were relaxed: they allowed *Carte Blanche* to film breakfast at the team hotel on match day and invited them into their change room at the ground. There were interviews with locks Mark Andrews and Krynauw Otto. (For once, Derek wasn't looking down!) Andrews said he always had time for the fans, without whom the players were nothing, and he loved seeing folk from home when on tour.

But there was a small problem: Derek, under the auspices of New Zealand Tourism, was meant to be showcasing this lovely country and its most famous export, but even an attempt to film the not-so-lovely All Blacks getting into their team bus at the hotel was met with hostility. Where to stand without 'breaching protocol' got technical.

Doorman: 'Playse get off the hotel prawperty.'

Derek: 'Where does it end?'

Doorman: 'Acrawss the rowed.'

Derek: 'What! You own the street?'

Doorman: 'Ye-e-e-s.'

Match day saw Derek at a sold-out Athletic Park, being silly and asking for a boerie roll and biltong, then taking his seat among the fans and cheering the Boks to a 3–13 victory, the first on New Zealand soil in 17 years. He grabbed a quick interview with Joost van der Westhuizen near the dressing room after the match. Joost cocked his ear towards the stands and said: 'It sounds like death out there.' Rugby is a religion in New Zealand, and losing is not taken lightly. But Derek and Mike had a sudden rush of blood to the head and decided to try to access the All Blacks' dressing room. After a lengthy altercation with an official, they were unceremoniously booted out.

That was the end of the broadcast story, but two weeks later the All Blacks arrived for the return match and must've watched *Carte Blanche*. Derek was at a New Zealand Tourism function the day after the broadcast, as were Jonah Lomu and Sean Fitzpatrick, who had a few choice words when a photographer asked Derek to pose with them for a picture.

And there were more choice words for Derek in a letter to the *Natal Mercury* on 21 August 1998, headed 'Watt An Example of Bad Manners'.

A viewer complained about Derek trying to force himself into the All Blacks' dressing room in New Zealand, saying his rudeness had set a bad example.

The Springboks set a fine example and won the Tri-Nations that year.

Joost – November 1998

This insert also reflects a happy chapter in Springbok rugby's fortunes. The Boks, led by Gary Teichmann and Nick Mallett, were at the top of their game – on the road to a record 17 consecutive Test wins. While George Mazarakis was (and still is) unsure of the difference between a ruck and a maul, he's pretty good at assessing the mood of the moment. The 27-year-old Joost van der Westhuizen had just captained the Blue Bulls to a Currie Cup victory over Western Province, and could do no wrong. It was the eve of the Boks' European tour, during which Joost was to play his fiftieth test match, and Edward Griffiths had just written his biography. Ruda Landman, looking a bit star-struck, spoke to Joost and his pretty blonde wife, Marlene. The golden couple, it seemed. Producer Victoria Cullinan was assigned to the story; it was one of those rush jobs, decided on Monday morning after the Currie Cup final, and Joost had limited time before he flew out. So they were interviewed separately – Joost after a training session, Marlene in her big empty mansion outside Pretoria.

With Joost, the tone was celebratory. At times, Ruda's questions seemed gushing: 'How did you feel when you were first chosen for Northern Transvaal? How does it feel to be a sex symbol?' Joost laughed it off. Marlene did not. In an extraordinarily frank interview, she revealed her true feelings about being a Bok wife.

She said she was counting the cost of having a famous husband, whom she knew would become a legend. She hated the way women blatantly threw themselves at him when the couple were on a rare night out together, how female fans sent pictures of themselves and described their wildest fantasies, how rugby management deliberately excluded wives from local functions. In 1997, her husband had spent eight months away from home on tour

In a pretty sundress and pearl necklace, she admitted that she couldn't live with the loneliness, something her 'pa' had warned her about when she'd decided to marry her childhood sweetheart in 1995, soon after the Rugby World Cup.

In his interview, Joost described Marlene as "*n baie groot kultuur mens*' who, unlike him, read books and wrote poetry. When he was abroad, she sent him faxes, jokes and Bible texts to cheer him up. But what was clear was that he didn't need that much cheering up – he was a whole lot happier than Marlene. Once a year, he said, they'd take a trip to Botswana or Mozambique, and when he did have time off at home they locked the gate, disconnected the phone and caught up.

But it was clearly not enough for Marlene, who, it seemed, was sorry she'd ever married him. And it created a dilemma for Victoria because she wasn't sure if the story should be celebrating a star player, or commiserating with his wife, who felt like a widow. Ruda said they were so concerned with the final cut that they actually phoned Marlene to find out if she was happy with her statement: '... *en nou, as ek terug kyk, dink ek ek sou 'n ander pad geloop het.*' But she said she had no problem with that going out on *Carte Blanche* because it was the truth, and Joost, she said, was well aware of it. Her childhood dream was to be happily married, not lonely.

On the Tuesday after the programme aired, November 10 1998, TV writer Janet Smith wrote in *The Star*: 'Perhaps Marlene van der Westhuizen didn't anticipate losing her television virginity quite this way. As the wife of a top Springbok rugby player, one would almost expect her to show a dreary coyness on personal questions ... instead Marlene did something quite unexpected ... she told the truth. Without putting too sentimental a point on it, it was rather a moving and shocking television moment.' Then, towards the end of the column: 'It's likely that this most interesting rugby marriage will survive ... we hope so, because Marlene certainly deserves it.'

Hindsight is an exact science. We know now that Joost began an affair with high-jumper Charmaine Gale while married to Marlene, which continued after he'd wed singer Amor Vittone.

Towards the end of the interview, Marlene predicted that Joost was going to become "*n groot legende*' and that they would never be able to enjoy their privacy again. The price of fame, she said, was high.

Joost was to find out just how high.

Kamp Staaldraad – November 2003

Humiliation, abuse, demoralisation and excessive physical pain are often associated with military training, and still play on the minds of South Africans old enough to remember the conscription that was compulsory for white men from 1967 to 1993.

So why would a country enjoying its first blush of freedom want to subject its elite rugby players to a military-style boot camp, when they could have been training in air-conditioned gyms and heated pools, assessed by sports scientists, or watched by adoring fans on a lush green field?

But no, there were the national heroes buck naked, grovelling on the ground and looking cold and miserable. A nattily dressed Gideon Sam, the Springbok team manager interviewed in the aftermath of the furore, reckoned that Kamp Staaldraad was 'mild compared to black initiation', which was merciful, considering the deaths and injuries associated with some bush initiation schools. Rugby, he said, was about toughness and discipline, and he recommended this type of training to other teams to 'build spirit', even though professional rugby had developed into a thinking game with flair and innovation: chess with brawn.

The *Carte Blanche* story of Sunday 23 November followed a week of headlines and telling photographs that went around the world, describing the Bok regime as 'old school' and a reminder of a brutal past: 'Boks Trained at Gunpoint'; 'Naked Players Forced into Freezing Lake'; 'Exclusive Photos of the Ordeal the Boks Were Put Through on Eve of Rugby World Cup'.

Analysts criticised this approach, the brainchild of coach Rudolph Straeuli and his security man, Adriaan Heijns, as harking back to the pre-democratic era, which had stressed '*kragdadigheid*' (efficiency). It quite simply gave the wrong impression to a nation trying to explore diversity and cultural dynamics. How would a quick-fix approach like this, which ignored process, contribute to a winning side? It didn't help that the pictures came hot on the heels of the Boks' disastrous Rugby World Cup campaign in Australia, which saw them defeated 29–9 by the All Blacks in the quarter-finals. So, clearly, being forced to stay awake all night, huddled naked in a muddy puddle with a torch shining in their eyes and listening to a taped recording of the haka on an isolated farm near Thabazimbi had not had the desired effect. Kamp Staaldraad was to be Straeuli's undoing.

In an attempt at damage control, the unedited Kamp Staaldraad tape was slipped to *Carte Blanche* to correct the perception that the players had been forced to participate against their will and at gunpoint. But it certainly showed their nakedness. After the broadcast, Kamp commandant and security consultant Heijns was threatened with legal action by indignant players. It was bad enough that photographs had been leaked to the press; now team management had willingly handed over the tape for the Boks to be seen in all their glory on national television.

But it was a scoop for M-Net. Tim Modise, who presented *Carte Blanche* in studio on the night, said: 'We bring you exclusive footage of what went on during the much-criticised rugby boot camp. Was it appropriate training for the World Cup tournament, was it immoral, did it smack of the old South Africa? Ruda investigates ...'

The story was produced by Sophia Phirippides, who was pushy and tenacious but not rugby-savvy. Researcher Seamus Reynolds gave her a crash course in the ins and outs of the game, so that she didn't come across as clueless when she and Ruda interviewed the players and team management in Johannesburg. Because of the short turnaround time, with little over 48 hours for post-production, the interview with the Durban-based Straeuli was done by freelancer Terence Pillay, who knew as little about sport as Sophia. He arrived in Straeuli's office dressed in an arty gold Gideon shirt and proceeded to inject camp into Staaldraad: 'So Rudolph, let me get this picture clear – it's our national team, the Springboks, naked in freezing cold water, pumping rugby balls, and being filmed doing it ... Our national team, naked! What were you thinking?'

The question never made the final cut, but had Sophia and Seamus rolling around in the edit suite. Straeuli probably wondered why he'd ever agreed to do the interview. Looking decidedly hot and bothered, he said it was all about team-building, and to toughen up the boys, mentally and physically. The exercise in which they had to fill rugby balls with water had to do with unbalancing them to test coordination skills. And the nakedness, said captain Corné Krige, interviewed by Ruda, was to stop their sandy shorts chafing when they got into the dam. No, said Adriaan Heijns, looking in need of a bit of PT himself, the nakedness 'sort of levelled the playing field'. There are bizarre shots of the Springboks in their birthday suits, getting in and out of a dam carrying makeshift rafts and doing an exercise with their bottoms in the air.

Whether Heijns himself would've liked to have been seen naked on television wasn't asked of him. But he reckoned that being in the nude took away pretences. Just how wasn't explained. The furore that broke out after the Sunday headlines had caused a bit of a shutdown within SA Rugby, so access to players was stage-managed, with only 'safe' interviews allowed: Krige, Joost van der Westhuizen and Ricardo Laubscher. They tried their best to get across the message that the benefits of the boot camp far outweighed the discomfort. There was no comment from the burly Gcobani Bobo, who had expressed his disapproval of Staaldraad in press reports. Producer Sophia can't remember if there were preconditions as to who could be interviewed; Seamus remembers trying to get hold of Bobo, without luck. But the script is cleverly written and the shot selection speaks volumes.

The story opens with a luxury Bok bus on some sort of victory parade in the good old winning days, then cuts to players pushing a cattle truck on a farm road, hopping on one leg in the veld, crawling through pipes that served as foxholes and jumping out of a helicopter into a dam. Food and sleep deprivation were among the tough-guy tactics used, and footage shows players having eggs broken on their heads, yolk running down their faces.

Ruda commented: 'This looks so childish and unnecessary. Why?' Adriaan Heijns explained that the players had been given instructions on how to cook an egg in the bush, and those who didn't get it right got punished because small things were important in rugby and in sport generally.

Joost described the egg-cooking exercise as 'creative fun'. Sports psychologist Andre Roux questioned the need for enforcing discipline at the cost of individual creativity. He said the tactics used were more applicable to those wanting to go out and kill, not for peak performance from an elite sports team.

Former Bok communications manager Mark Keohane was accused of leaking the Staaldraad photographs to the newspapers, even though he'd already resigned from SA Rugby. The source of the leak was later identified as the team's video analyst, Dale McDermott, who'd felt uncomfortable about the goings-on at the boot camp. His decision to release the footage cost him everything. He committed suicide in 2005.

Sophia Phirippides and her partner Jonathan Pienaar, who did the video editing, won a CNN African Journalist Award in the Sports category for the Staaldraad story, beating seasoned sports journalists. Kamp Staaldraad did nothing for Rudolph Straeuli's career, and a few months later he was sacked. In 2006, Adriaan Heijns decided to cash in – and the notorious DVD went on sale for R300. But a group of players, including Corné Krige, obtained an interdict to stop Heijns from distributing it, saying it infringed their privacy and that the copyright belonged to SA Rugby.

Adriaan Heijns now lives in New Zealand. But both he and Mark Keohane were to feature on *Carte Blanche* again the following year.

Mark Keohane Tells All – July 2004

Joost van der Westhuizen once described the appointment of Mark Keohane to the post of Springbok communications manager as 'the darkest day in the history of SA rugby'. To which Keohane countered on *Carte Blanche*: 'Personally, I consider naked Boks holed up in a pit singing our national anthem for four hours while they listened to the haka as the darkest day in our rugby history.'

Keohane, a sports writer with a reputation as a muckraker, among other things, joined the Boks in 2000 and effectively became rugby's spin doctor. He resigned in protest in 2003 because, he said, of the way rugby management dealt with racism. He wrote a best-selling book entitled *Springbok Rugby Uncovered*, which became the subject of a *Carte Blanche* story, because rugby not only sells books, it also attracts viewers. Chapters in the book include: 'Laager Mentality' and 'Descent into Darkness', subtitled 'Rudolf Straeuli's self-destruction'.

The final straw for Keohane was the way team management handled the Geo Cronje–Quinton Davids affair. He said a clearly racial incident, in which Cronje had refused to share a room with Davids, had been swept under the carpet. In the story, he was quoted as having said: 'These people are anti-black, and half the time they don't even know it.' As communications manager, Keohane was ideally placed to spill the beans; he knew exactly what went on between the players and the coach, the exchanges, the nuances. He told Ruda of an incident in which Gcobani Bobo had been congratulated by Straeuli on making the team, but the coach had felt it necessary to include the words 'on merit'. According to Keohane, he then said to the centre: 'Don't go mess it up for your people like the last three black guys did.' Keo accused Joost van der Westhuizen of a similar patronising approach towards Bobo. When congratulated on his eightieth Test match, the veteran scrumhalf is said to have told Bobo, a product of Dale College and Rondebosch Boys' High: 'Go and do it for your people like I did it for my people.' If Bobo had hoped his people were all South Africans, Joost had put him right in a way that didn't exactly echo the famous words of Francois Pienaar after the 1995 Rugby World Cup final.

In the interview with Ruda Landman, Keohane referred at length to the relationship between Straeuli and Adriaan Heijns, with the latter, he said, feeding the coach's paranoia by checking his hotel rooms for bugs and warning him of bomb threats, which Keohane doubted ever existed. He said Heijns' influence on the team had been felt long before the Staaldraad debacle and that Straeuli was treated like the president of a very powerful country. He wanted to know everyone's moves, had players spied on, and changed arrangements at a whim because of imagined dangers.

This time, rugby's top guns were less keen to make themselves available to *Carte Blanche* for interviews, so producer Kate Barry included unused clips from the 2003 Staaldraad interviews in which Corné Krige accused Keohane of undermining the confidence of the Boks. Rudolph Straeuli intimated that Keohane was maliciously divisive. Heijns was interviewed, and said that although he'd sometimes walked the former coach to his room, he had never tucked him into bed, and that all information regarding bomb threats had been obtained from a contact in the police.

'There's more politics in sport than in Parliament,' was Tim Modise's wry comment in studio after that story.

Joost – 2009

Early one Sunday morning in mid-February 2009, Derek Watts received a phone call asking if Joost van der Westhuizen, now long retired from rugby, could come into the *Carte Blanche* studio that night to counter claims by *Rapport* and celebrity gossip magazine *Heat* that there was a video portraying him as a philandering drug-taker. But, reasoned George Mazarakis, how on earth could Joost come onto the show proclaiming his innocence without *Carte Blanche* having seen the footage? What if it *was* him, and not someone who 'looked like him' (as he claimed)?

A few days after the Sunday headlines had screamed '*Joost in Seksvideo*', the tape was shown to journalists at the office of a Sandton law firm. Someone looking remarkably like Joost was seen snorting methcat, a psychoactive stimulant, with Marilize van Emmenis, an exotic dancer. *Carte Blanche* producer Susan Puren went along with a fashion designer friend who had, on occasion, dressed the famous Van der Westhuizens. He had no doubt it was Joost, nor did Susan, who said his skew little finger was a dead giveaway.

But it was to be nine months before *Carte Blanche* touched the story: it felt too much like tabloid sleaze, sex and sin. Joost and Amor, our own Posh and Becks, who embraced family values and lived the high life that came with lucrative sponsorships and appearance money, had been knocked off their pedestals.

In November 2009 presenter Devi Sankaree Govender interviewed Joost following the publication of his book *The Man in the Mirror*, marketed by the publisher as 'the truth and nothing but the truth and guaranteed to blow your socks off'. By the time the book was published, Joost had reached rock bottom; he'd had to confess to his loyal wife, who'd made a point of publicly 'standing by her man' and was an emotional wreck. He said it felt as if he hadn't slept for months, which is why he'd suffered a much publicised fit.

'Why the lies?' asked Devi. 'To protect myself. I was scared,' said the man who had faced some of the most fearsome players in world rugby and who had enjoyed Kamp Staaldraad. But the pressure off the field was worse than anything he'd ever had to face on the loose-head side of the scrum. He spoke of the terror that his mobile phone had come to represent; every time it rang it was trouble. First, the blackmailer wanting money; then, after the release of the video, the media wanted comment. 'On Saturday afternoons it was *Rapport* ... Sundays it was the Afrikaans press ... on Wednesdays, *Huisgenoot* ... Tuesdays, *Heat* magazine ...'

Producer Susan, the veteran of many *Carte Blanche* scoops over the years, found this one difficult to unravel in ten minutes, the standard length of a *Carte Blanche* insert. It may have been a story about a book, but the intrigue and deceit made it complicated. She had cellphone records from a source, indicating that 'security consultant' Mike Bolhuis had spied on *Heat* editor Melinda Shaw on behalf of Joost to find out who'd given the magazine the incriminating tape. Melinda, looking not unlike former *News of the World* editor Rebekah Brooks, was incensed at this 'invasion of privacy' and was planning to sue Bolhuis. She did have the grace to add that it was ironic that she was complaining about her privacy being invaded, given that the invasion of privacy was *Heat*'s stock in trade.

The tape, it turned out, had been handed over by Marilize van Emmenis's former boyfriend, Anthony de Beer, who'd wanted to 'make a few bucks'. He'd first tried to make them out of Joost, who had set up a meeting with De Beer at a golf estate in Centurion, allegedly to exchange R500 000 in cash for the tape. Instead De Beer got an empty suitcase and a thick ear from Joost's heavies.

But the point of the *Carte Blanche* interview, and of the book, was for Joost to say sorry to those he had disappointed. His eyes filled with tears when he answered Devi's last question.

Devi: 'So, where to from here now, Joost? What happens?'

Joost: 'Where to from here is to work on my relationship with my wife, my family, especially my kids – two angels – to fix my life.'

But things were to get a whole lot worse.

Joost: From Hero to Zero and Back – 2012

The problem with a show that's been going for 25 years is that, eventually, it feels like it's all been done before. Every so often, the *Carte Blanche* team gets together for a brainstorm to come up with new ideas, which often tend to sound very much like old ideas. At one such mini-conference in 2012, Derek decided that the show had lost the 'common touch' and that doing a reality-type, character-driven insert on a person with whom viewers could identify would provide a much-needed lift. And what better subject than Joost, now fighting motor neurone disease (MND), a catastrophic degenerative condition.

Derek had recently been to a function where Joost had given an address. His speech was slurred, and nothing in his movements recalled the deft scrumhalf of old. But the humour was still there: 'I ushed to have to b-b-be drunk to t-t-talk like thush', he joked.

In 2011, Joost had been diagnosed with amyotrophic lateral sclerosis, an aggressive subtype of MND that attacks the central nervous system, causing progressive disability and death. At first, he said, he withdrew, but then he decided he would fight the disease – a full-time job.

A story like this can't be knocked out in a few days: the producer needs the total cooperation of the subject – to be in his face and space. Joost, so used to life in the limelight, was on board, which was half the battle won for insert producer Odette Schwegler. It was to be a 'reality' shoot, which is impossible unless the case study is totally committed.

Some of the shooting days overlapped with another story Derek was busy with, so Odette – along with cameramen Bruce Cuningham and Thomas Pretorius – started without him. Bruce's first *Carte Blanche* story had been in 1992, about a war between Joburg's punks and skinheads. Twenty years and 150 stories later, he described the Joost story as one of the best. Odette knew exactly what she wanted; she briefed the team and then gave them the freedom to get on with it. They had to be there for Joost's appointments with his neurosurgeon and biokineticist, for when he met up with his Bok buddies for a Rugby Legends' golf day, and for his work with J9, the foundation he had set up to help fellow MND sufferers.

For budgetary reasons, *Carte Blanche* shoots, unless investigative, are usually confined to two days and a single camera. Planning is of the essence; interviews and set-up shots of case studies are done in one location, and then it's on to the next. The CAP offices are a favourite for rush interviews; the subject is made to do a quick whip around the fountain outside, looking purposeful. But this story was to be longer than the usual ten minutes, so there was time to make it as real as possible – no set-ups, no pretences.

Odette and the crew had arrived at Joost's upmarket Sandton address at seven in the morning. The lift opened directly into his bachelor pad. This was not done to impress, but in case he might one day be confined to a wheelchair; he'd already had several tumbles on the stairs. But now he'd just woken up and looked a bit sleepy. With two cameras focused on him and sound operator Connley van der Westhuizen (no relation) scrambling for position, he good-naturedly took them through his morning routine: 'This pills [sic] is my breakfast every morning.'

The story began with a montage of shots of Joburg morning traffic and the Sandton skyline. The opening lines ran: 'Clumsy fingers, slurred speech and a weak grip – the seemingly benign symptoms of a fatal disease.'

Joost took a big swig of syrup from a bottle – 'for my voice'. He said he was meant to measure it with a syringe, but it was too finicky for his fingers. 'So I just gooi.' He was completely at ease with the camera and joked about the challenges of his life. Once he'd had to put a rugby ball into the middle of a scrum; now he had trouble scooping up powdered medication without spilling it: 'This is the funny part – getting the powder in the cup.'

The visuals were everything. The script was artfully kept to a minimum; the words simply nudged the story along: 'This once-super athlete has learnt to accept his limitations ... and has invited us into his life.'

When Derek joined Odette and the crew for the interview, he asked Joost how long he had. Joost replied: 'Two to five years ... I am doing research every week. That is how we got to the drugs I'm using now.'

Derek: 'And it's this Mongolian goat weed ... what is it?'

The experimental treatment was obtained from the serum of Tasmanian goats and was expensive: Joost had to inject it twice a day, at £200 a pop. That's about R170 000 a month. It had shown promising results in multiple sclerosis patients – lessening the symptoms, and in some cases reversing them. Now in phase two of clinical trials, the hope was that the experimental serum would slow down the devastating effects of MND.

Joost was one of only eight MND sufferers in the world on the treatment, and thought it was working. When he was diagnosed, he was told he'd be in a wheelchair in twelve months. It had been double that time already and he was still on his feet and going to the gym – the next stop for our cameras. Joost took the frozen vials along because his hands were now too unsteady to inject himself.

Bruce filmed from the passenger seat while Joost drove. He glanced at his phone, muttered to himself about not seeing his children, complaining that his ex-wife never answered his calls and messages. It might've been calculated to exact sympathy from viewers, but it didn't come across that way. At the gym, the team filmed his rigorous training schedule, worked out by a biokineticist, to hold on to what muscle strength he had left. With MND, he said, you got something called 'foot drop', in which it became a struggle to pick up one's toes. So his exercises focused on small movements to build strength in the wrists, feet and hands. What struck Odette was seeing this once-dexterous athlete struggling to do a simple thing like spinning a ball in his hands. The effort was visible in his face, his jaw clenched in determination. What kept him going? His two young children, Jordan and Kylie.

It was a much humbler Joost than the one Ruda had interviewed back in his prime with the long-suffering Marlene. He said he'd learned from his mistakes and now surrounded himself with positive people. MND had shown him the reality of life. And he had no shortage of friends, some with lots of money, prepared to help him out.

Joost, Bruce and soundman Connley set off in a helicopter early one morning for the Swartkops golf course near Pretoria, while Derek, Odette and Thomas raced to meet them on the greens. The event was a fundraiser for Joost's foundation and his own medical bills. Among the big hitters lending support were James Small, Pieter Hendricks and Jannie de Beer.

At breakfast that morning, Joost had bent down to slurp his coffee, no longer able to pick up the cup. For Odette, this was the most telling shot of all. He laughingly pulled out his chair to get to the cup and said something about not rushing him.

The shoot coincided with his quarterly visit to his neurosurgeon, and the first since starting the experimental treatment. According to Dr Pieter Kritzinger, Joost's body hadn't deteriorated further in three months and in some areas there was even a slight improvement. Hope. Crouched behind Bruce to keep out of the shot – as producers do – Odette shed a quiet tear.

It was a touching story, guaranteed to tug at the heartstrings, but not intended to trash his ex-wife. Odette agonised over whether to include hints of the public acrimony between the two about access to their children: 'If it was a normal divorce, I'd understand, but this is different. This is terminal and I need to spend time with them.' She decided a bit of it had to be in the piece because it seemed so central to his life. But that's what viewers picked up on. Someone even tried to start a Facebook page in support of Joost seeing more of his children. In 24 hours it had attracted over a thousand followers, some of whom commented:

Nancy: What did last night's interview do for me? It made me realise that we are all HUMAN! I hope Joost's kids have access to this recording one day when they are old enough to understand. He has acknowledged his wrong doing and has accepted his illness and he is turning it into something positive.

Hazel: Gee don't we all make mistakes, we all have our own bark in our eye, let's not look for splinters in Joost's.

Johann: *Joost jy kan 'n baie trotse man wees wat alles wil regmaak wat jy verkeerd gedoen het. Geen mens het die reg om te oordeel nie.*

Chantall: Joost had my son of 10yrs and myself in tears, ur such an inspiration and true warrior ... We all make mistakes, nobody's perfect, hence pencils are having erasers!

Christa: *Joost het gisteraand duisende ... let wel ... DUISENDE mense se hart geraak deur sy inspirasie en positiwiteit ...*

Alida: *Dankie dat julle Joost 'n regmatige plekkie op CB gegee het – en – vir diegene wat 'n vinger wys na Joost – gaan lees jul Bybel en bely ook jul sondes.*

Less pleased with the show was Joost's ex-wife Amor, who accused him of using the media to exact sympathy. While she worked her 'gat' off, she told other publications, he drove around in a million-rand car and took little interest in their children's everyday lives, just wanting to be there for the fun and not for the discipline. She went to bed at night wondering what she'd read in the papers about herself the next day and was considering a court order to stop him slandering her.

But in September 2012 Joost tweeted: 'Thanks for ur support. Me and Amor had a long chat and are good friends now, the kids are so happy!'

cars

Of all the topics that viewers comment on to *Carte Blanche*, cars are the top. South Africans love their wheels. The used-car business isn't known for being squeaky-clean, and, each day, web submissions pour in about the illegal exchange of car parts, car dealerships being in cahoots with car finance companies, and even brand-new vehicles bursting into flames. The list is endless, as are the phone calls the day after a car story has been broadcast. Calls are often along the following lines:

Caller: You had a story on last night about Planet Wheels; exactly the same thing happened to me, and a colleague of mine here at work! They sold my car in two months, but didn't pay me the money; next thing I see my car driving around town.

Carte Blanche *journalist*: Yip, it happened to loads of people; that's why we did the story.

Caller: And when I confronted them about the registration documents, they said they sold it with a release note from the bank. Do you want to come and interview me?

Carte Blanche *journalist*: Uh, thanks, but no, we've already done the story.

Caller: But I am in a far worse situation than that one guy you interviewed! He was only owed R40 000. I am owed R75 000!

Carte Blanche *journalist*: I understand, but we have to do other topics too. Maybe we will revisit this again in a few months' time.

Caller: But I thought you guys were here to help us?

   Helping is one thing; producing entertaining television that gets bums on seats is another. And there are more than enough rogue motor dealerships and mechanics to do a different saga every week. Derek's favourite car story was called just that: 'Rogue Motors'. It featured a mild-mannered man named Ray, who was delighted to see *Carte Blanche* at his Pinetown garage: 'Derek, my mate, how are you!' His explanation for selling a leaky kit car with no brakes, a worn battery and faulty steering was: 'No car is perfect, Derek!' There was no shouting, no threats, no hidden cameras, and it all seemed rather polite back in 1992.

Turning Back the Clocks – 1995

Three years later, in 1995, things got a bit nastier. Producer Clive Morris followed up on complaints that used-car dealers were tampering with the mileage of cars before selling them. The story opened with presenter Manu Padayachee having a haircut at a barber shop and wondering if anyone knew that the same could happen to a car. A dealership had contacted *Carte Blanche* after a client had taken her newly bought second-hand car there for a checkup. They'd serviced the car for the previous owner, too, and had a record of the mileage, which they'd noticed was now considerably lower. Clive recorded a phone call in which the dealership confronted 'Affordable Motors', from where the client had bought the car. They were told 'not to fuck with them', and that, for the matter to stand up legally, 'Affordable Motors' had to be caught in the act. So *Carte Blanche* decided to do just that. Clive found someone who wanted to sell his Ford Courier bakkie, which had 260 000 km on the clock but was still in good condition. He asked the AA to check and mark the odometer, after which the owner sold it to 'Affordable Motors' for R23 000.

Four days later, the Courier appeared on the shop floor and Clive sent in a friend, fitted with a hidden camera, to pose as a buyer. The bakkie was on sale for R45 000 and, with only 120 000 km on the clock, had become a whole lot younger. When Manu asked the shopowner, Dave, a *Magnum PI* lookalike with teardrop sunglasses and droopy moustache, how this could've happened, he said it was because they'd bought a replacement speedometer for the bakkie, a second-hand one.

Uh ... right ... but why had the mileage changed?

Dave got irritated: 'I do not change a car's speedo unless there's a problem ... I can sell it with that kind of mileage.'

But for a whole lot less, Dave.

Manu revealed that they'd asked the AA to inspect the car prior to the sale. The AA man was waiting nearby and whipped off the speedometer to reveal that it was exactly the same one, marked with paint and his employer number.

So how did that happen, Dave?

Dave nonchalantly lit a cigarette and blamed the modern workman.

'Do you know who repairs these things these days? Do you?'

Furthermore, he said, every customer that walked in the door was a potential thief, always lying about their car's history.

After the story was aired, a letter was hand-delivered to the *Carte Blanche* offices, addressed to 'the chief nut and wrench mechanic' and threatening to get even. Nothing came of the threats. Six years later, when viewers complained that used-car dealers were at it again, executive producer George Mazarakis decided it was time for another investigation.

Turning Back the Clocks – 2001

The story began with a flashback to 'don't give a damn Dave', followed by Ruda saying: 'That was six years ago, but turning back the clocks is not a thing of the past.'

A viewer named Madelaine had contacted *Carte Blanche* after buying a Toyota Twin Cam from a dealer in Boksburg. It registered as having done 148 000 km, but two days after she bought it things started to go wrong. Smelling a rat, she contacted the previous owners and found that they'd sold the car with 237 000 km on the clock. Nearly 90 000 km had mysteriously disappeared.

Madelaine suspected this was being done to all the cars by this particular dealer, so producer Hayley Levin sent a potential buyer, armed with a camera hidden in a bag, to the same dealership. The salesman,

Dion, showed the buyer a Ford bakkie he described as a 'workhorse', which was going for R38 000 and was marked as having done 147 000 km. But on checking with Wesbank, where the car had been bought on auction, Hayley found out that the mileage had been reduced by 130 000 km. She traced the original owner, a woman called Marinda, who agreed to accompany Ruda and Hayley when they visited the dealership to find out just how the car had shed so many kilometres.

Dion swore that the cars were sold exactly as they got them from the auction floor. The look on Ruda's face was one of scepticism: 'Wesbank gave us a certification of the kilometre readings when they sold them to you. In this instance, this bakkie was 277 000. Please show me what it is now ...'

Dion: '147 000.'

Ruda: '147 000? So what happened there?'

Dion: 'I don't know ... I'll find out for you ...'

Ruda: 'Wesbank sold it to you direct?'

Dion: 'Yes. I suppose so ...'

Ruda: 'You don't have to suppose – we know. In this instance you bought the car with a very specific reading, certified kilometre reading ...'

Dion: '... but one can't be certain ...'

Ruda assured him one could be certain and beckoned to Marinda, who walked into shot and confirmed that she was the previous owner of the bakkie and that it had had 277 000 km on the clock.

Dion began backtracking, saying he'd just returned from a trip to Australia and that all of this had nothing to do with him. He called a colleague, Andy, who could only repeat: 'I dunno, hey ... I dunno ... really, I dunno.'

They had been caught out and were about to lose a whole lot of business. But not without a fight. A few days later, *Carte Blanche* received a letter from the dealership's lawyers, saying that they were covered because the purchase agreement stated that they could not take responsibility for incorrect mileage – something the Consumer Protection Act would take issue with today.

That was only part of the story: Hayley also traced a couple named Charlotte and Fred, who turned back clocks for a living. They worked from home and, like all specialists, on a referral basis: R250 per hour. Fred was something of a stud and Charlotte an East Rand dolly-bird. They both loved their 'job' and had no problem answering a myriad questions from Hayley's undercover agent, David Jones (not his real name).

Fred: 'I did a BM for BMW. It was a car that had 15 000 km on it.'

David: '15 000?'

Fred: 'I put it down to 244 km and they sold it as a brand-new car.'

David: 'Serious?'

Fred: 'Ja ... a big fucking dealer.'

Charlotte: 'I do all of them – any BMW, any Golf, any Audi, any Merc, the digitals.'

Hayley wanted to see how the pair turned back a digital odometer, so she borrowed a BMW and got David to take it to the 'doctor'. Fred simply pulled out the microchip and Charlotte plugged it into her computer, punched in a code and within minutes – and for R550 – the BMW was 48 000 km younger.

Confrontations can be tricky during a shoot, and are usually a last resort after requests for an interview have been declined. No one really feels comfortable with *Carte Blanche* knocking on the door, so the instinct is often to run away and hide, or to become aggressive and defensive. Fortunately, TV shoots are crowded affairs, involving producer, presenter and camera and sound operators. Fred and Charlotte were hardly going to agree to an interview with *Carte Blanche*, so Hayley decided that David, whom Fred and Charlotte now trusted, would ask them to do a 'house call' on six cars in Germiston. The couple duly arrived with their bag of tricks, and the concealed cameraman filmed them from indoors, behind a curtain. Ruda waited until Fred and Charlotte were both seated in one of the cars, hard at work. She then walked over, stood by the driver's door and uttered the words no one wants to hear: '*Ek is Ruda Landman van* Carte Blanche. *Kan julle my se wat julle besig is om te doen?*'

Fred took a while to react. Then he mopped his forehead with a red lappie and found someone to blame. The money he made from doing this – R635 000 in 18 months – was peanuts compared to what those selling the reworked cars earned.

Fred: 'I'll do the job, but do I sell the car? I don't make a profit from the car. It's the guy who sells the car. That's the guy who makes the end profit.'

Charlotte: 'They make much more than the service fee that we charge. So we're not the guilty ones, but the person who is selling it is.'

They hastily packed up their belongings and made for their (no doubt low-mileage) car. But not before asking for payment for the work they'd done.

The first call to the *Carte Blanche* office the next day about the pair wasn't from the police, but from SARS. They thought Charlotte and Fred might owe them some money.

Roadworthy – 1999

This was a *Carte Blanche* car classic that blew the lid off a racket causing carnage on South African roads. The aim was to prove that, for a fee, anything on (or off) wheels could get a licence.

Producer Clive Morris and researcher Hayley Levin sourced an old red Fiat, which they bought for R50 from a scrapyard. They were directed to an 'Oom Smittie' in Roodepoort who, for R650, would register the mangled car at the Midrand municipality. David the private investigator did the undercover filming. Oom Smittie took only four hours to deliver the papers, even though he had never seen the car. The next day, documents in hand, Derek and the crew set off for the Midrand municipal offices, with the red wreck loaded on the back of a truck. The documents had been signed by someone named Karen from the licensing department. Derek tried to jog her memory: 'Do you remember the vehicle?'

The entire office stopped what they were doing to stare. Of course Karen didn't remember the vehicle, but she spent a frantic 15 minutes hunting for the nonexistent roadworthy certificate. By this time the chief licensing officer, Willie, had joined in the search. Eventually Derek called a halt to the panic and led them to the smashed Fiat outside. Karen gaped, gathered herself, and then hastily blamed a trainee: 'I was "learning" a lady yesterday and she did a wrong job.' Willie summoned the trainee, Angie. She looked a whole lot sharper than Karen, knew exactly what was going down, and pointed out that if she'd done the job she would've signed the papers.

Angie was off the hook, Karen in the pooh. Clearly, she had a lucrative arrangement going with Oom Smittie. And her husband, it was later revealed, worked at a testing station that creatively issued roadworthy certificates for vehicles declined elsewhere.

The following Sunday there was an update: Johannesburg Metro Police Director Gerrie Gerneke had watched the story and noticed, peering over Karen's shoulder, behind the counter at the Midrand Licensing Department, a man named Louis whom he'd suspended from another licensing centre for registering vehicles without proper documentation. Louis had managed to get himself employed in Midrand, and was earning two salaries.

Newspaper headlines the following week trumpeted the story: 'Wheels come off for two staffers ... the Midrand Metro Council has suspended two employees ... Sunday night's *Carte Blanche* revealed that a vehicle which was clearly not roadworthy was given clearance and was duly registered ...'

The last shot of the story was of the newly licensed wreck, perched precariously on the truck, being driven away into the sunset.

Anatomy of a Hijacker – 2002

There are all sorts of theories about carjackers: that they work according to orders; that they follow potential victims from shopping malls; that the professionals won't kill drivers in the car because middlemen and buyers don't want blood on the upholstery; that they stake out cars and homes for weeks before pouncing; that they pay the police a protection fee.

This story revealed just how criminals succeeded in a process that involved so much more than seizing a car by putting a gun to the driver's head. They were just a link in the chain, part of a process that also needed loads of paperwork and willing accomplices. Producer Hayley Levin recalls it being a hard sell to George Mazarakis because of the danger that a story like this could end up as a training manual for wannabe crooks.

She found four rehabilitated hijackers, who had done their time and were working for a crime-prevention organisation called Khulisa. Two of them, Mondli and Ben, were camera-shy and merely sat there. The other two, Bongani and Simon, said that they'd lost count of how many cars they'd hijacked in their day. They'd been angry, aggressive and often high on drugs, and would think nothing of shooting if the driver didn't cooperate. But generally they had tried not to attract too much attention to themselves by killing people. The story opened with the four of them sitting on Yeoville Hill, once a favourite spot for interviews because it looks down onto the city centre. Although hauling camera equipment up here can attract attention from the wrong types in the wrong area, Hayley and Derek felt pretty safe in the presence of four hardened, albeit reformed, car thieves.

There is no point stealing a car without the necessary paperwork in place; otherwise you can't sell it on, explained Bongani. So the first stop was the scrapyard. By law, when a car is scrapped it is deregistered, taken off the system. But scrap dealers know there is a market for legitimate paperwork and car numbers and that the ID tags found on the bodywork of a scrap vehicle are part of a hijacker's toolkit.

So Hayley sent undercover David to a scrapyard in Vereeniging. Matthew, a pony-tailed fellow working behind the desk, offered David a red Uno for R3 000. His female colleague chipped in: 'It's code 2, dealer's stock, not scrapped or anything.' The piece of scrap came complete with numbers and a legitimate registration certificate. And Matthew was unconcerned about the role he might be playing in the criminal chain: 'I don't ask questions and I don't hear no lies either. That's the way it goes. I sell legitimate stuff. Once it's out of my yard it's out of my hands.'

Next step, said Bongani, talking to camera from the front seat of a moving vehicle, was to hijack a car of the same make and colour. He said they would drive around the suburbs, as they were doing now, on the lookout for a car that almost matched their ID tags: 'And then we'd

95

follow him and see where he stayed, and when he comes back, maybe after work. The good time of getting the person, or hijacking the car, would be in the early hours of the morning.'

The tags from the scrap car were then replicated, or transferred to the newly acquired vehicle, and the old engine number sanded off. But even with new numbers on the stolen car, it was still not street-legal. Next stop for David was to organise a roadworthy certificate, a change of colour if necessary, and new licence details. This could be done at a nondescript licensing bureau in Mayfair, Johannesburg West, run by an exotic-looking woman named Tabor, with an Eastern European accent and a baby gurgling in its pram. She didn't even need to see the car. Three days and a thousand bucks later, the paperwork was ready: a new licence disc, a roadworthy from a testing station, and the red Uno was now white. They were even kind enough to forge the signatures on all the documents.

The dirty work done, Hayley booked Derek for a day to go and do the confrontations – never pleasant, but always necessary. Matthew from the scrapyard in Vereeniging looked perplexed when the crew walked in.

'Matthew, howzit! Derek Watts, how are you, man? One of our investigators bought an Uno Fire front for R3 000. There's the receipt.'

While Matthew was squinting at the receipt, the owner of the business, alerted by the commotion, appeared out of nowhere and laid into Derek, accusing him of trespassing. Derek explained that they'd been sold a piece of scrap with code 2 papers. The owner refused to answer any questions, and, with Matthew in tow, beat a hasty retreat, leaving Derek yelling: 'WE BOUGHT A PIECE OF SCRAP WITH CODE 2 PAPERS!'

Next stop was Mayfair, where Tabor was far friendlier, giggling coyly and looking at Derek as if he was a talent scout and she'd won a lap-dancing competition. But her body language changed when he showed her the roadworthy certificate and asked her how she'd got it.

Tabor: 'Why must I explain to you?'

Derek: 'Because we've got the forms and we've paid for it ... But the point is, Tabor, do you know the implications of what you're doing? Do you know that you are part of the cycle of hijackings in this country?'

Tabor looked completely nonplussed, asked a worker to mind her

baby, and rushed over the road to call her husband, Abe, who immediately said it was all her fault. Had he been in the shop, this would
NEVER have happened. Tabor poked her head from behind a dividing
wall in the office, opened her mouth, then thought better of it as Abe
carried on: 'This is wrong, totally wrong. I don't know what else to say;
there's nothing more I can say.'

The crew left the speechless Abe and headed to the Lenasia testing
station to find out how they'd issued a roadworthy to Tabor without
seeing the car. The piece of scrap, the papers showed, had passed the test
with only a faulty headlight. Claude, a handsome grey-haired man with
gold chain and watch, gave Derek a glass of Coke and tried to shift the
blame onto his examiners.

Claude: 'I don't test the vehicles, I don't check them.'

Derek: 'But Claude, as the owner of this business, you have to take responsibility for what has happened. You can't just blame the examiner.'

The story ended with Bongani the carjacker-come-good saying that
this brutal crime would continue while the system remained corrupt
and while there were willing accomplices at every turn. After the interview, Hayley drove the guys home. They were amused when they
were stopped by cops on the way, clearly worried about the 'madam's'
safety. For years, when they'd driven about looking for cars to steal,
they laughed, no policeman had ever stopped them.

Hijack Route – 2004

In 2004, producers Nicky Troll and Julie Laurenz – commonly known
as 'the Cows', after their company, Nguni Productions – investigated
cross-border car theft. Their plan was to follow a stolen car from Durban
to Mozambique. A local dealership loaned them a Pajero, which they
parked in West Street, near the Durban beachfront, a vehicle-theft hot-
spot. Transborder theft syndicates were looking for 4x4s, and the team
were assured that within hours it would probably be stolen.

A contact named Russell Edmunds, an ex-cop who ran a stolen vehicle recovery company, helped them to rig the car with four different

tracking systems. The idea was that once the Pajero had been stolen, the thieves would immediately remove one of the tracking devices, not realising there were three more.

Nicky and Julie filmed the parked car from a nearby building. Within 45 minutes a 'spotter' had arrived; he made a call to his thieving buddies, who, in broad daylight, broke into the car in seconds. But they couldn't get it going; there seemed to be problems with the steering lock, so they abandoned it. There were no more takers for that particular vehicle, so the next day the Nguni Cows exchanged it for another, a RAV4 fitted with the same four recovery systems, and returned to their vantage point. The thieves appeared out of nowhere and placed themselves near the car – one working at the lock with an Allen key, the other standing next to him talking on his cellphone facing the busy road, and three others loitering on the pavement. Again, they couldn't get it started, so they brazenly opened the bonnet and pretended to be working on the car until a sixth man arrived, whom Julie and Nicky recognised from the day before. He climbed in and got it going within seconds. All this was caught on camera, but the Cows couldn't use any of the background sound, because all they could hear was their own expressions of disbelief: 'Shit! They took it, can you believe it! All those people walking past …!'

Nicky phoned Russell, who got the tracking company into action, and they set off in hot pursuit, expecting a long drive to the KwaZulu-Natal/ Mozambique border. But the tracker signal showed the RAV4 stopping in a Durban suburb for nearly an hour. It emerged with Mozambican number plates and two 'jockeys' – not the same men who'd stolen it. To Nicky's dismay, instead of taking the expected route along the coast to Kosi Bay, where they'd alerted the police's jacked-up border vehicle theft unit, the jockeys headed inland. Near Pietermaritzburg, the tracking devices were picked up by the tracking company's rather-too-vigilant local unit, which wasn't in on the sting operation. They alerted the police, who arrested the pair. By the time Nicky and Russell arrived, they'd established that they were Mozambican and on their way to Maputo via Mpumalanga. Not anymore. The pair were handcuffed and put into a van, which Nicky rather shakily filmed next to the busy highway. The driver said in Portuguese that he'd been paid R2 000 to take the car to the Komatipoort border crossing, where he was to hand it over to someone else to take across into Mozambique, and then on to Malawi and beyond – wherever the demand was. It was a slick operation that explained how as many as 90 000 cars a year could be hijacked in South Africa and never recovered.

With the modus operandi proven, the Nguni Cows began working on the second part of the story: the work of the border police, who operated in the thick bush of no-man's land, the 20-metre-wide, 30-km-long strip that separates KwaZulu-Natal from Mozambique. In those days, recalls Nicky, the cops were much 'nicer' about allowing the media to film their operations. She and Julie and presenter Devi Sankaree Govender got permission to spend time with the elite Border Unit – the only SAPS formation that specialised in the illegal trafficking of vehicles. What Devi recalls most clearly about this story is that the Cows made her do 11 links to camera, most of them in the dead of night and that only one was used in the final edit. And that she never got a chance to bath or shower.

The trio tagged along with the Border Unit's Inspector BJ Mkhwamubi, who good-naturedly took them on an all-night patrol to find stolen cars. Any tail-lights up ahead were treated with heightened suspicion and ac-celeration. Filming from the front seat, Nicky prayed for them to catch up with the thieves for the story's sake, but feared she'd cop the first bullets should they open fire. As it turned out, two stolen double-cabs made it across to Mozambique that night, but BJ couldn't catch them. Once he saw the tracks, he immediately got hold of a Mozambican police officer on the other side. He didn't want *Carte Blanche* tagging along, so BJ dumped the team and continued the chase. Devi and the Cows made their weary way back to their lodge, which had run out of water.

The next afternoon, while heading home, the car laden with pots and curios after some roadside shopping, they received a call from Russell, who said he'd helped police recreate the *Carte Blanche* sting in West Street, and that they'd arrested the car thieves, who were sitting in the back of a van if they wanted to film them. The bemused police team stood and watched while the girls unpacked their curios to find their camera gear, and at last Devi, with smudged make-up and dirty hair, got her moment on camera: 'The five men who have been arrested by the police following their sting are sitting behind me in this van. We are not allowed to speak to them, but we can tell you that one man we have identified as being involved in our two stings.'

But the police had pounced too soon, before the thieves could start the car. Back at headquarters, they realised that they could only charge them with breaking into a car, not stealing one. So they wanted *Carte Blanche's* original tapes to strengthen their case. This was a dangerous thing to do pre-broadcast, because it could mean not seeing the footage again for months, or perhaps never. It made no sense to jeopardise a good story and weeks of hard work by relinquishing the tapes. Nicky took them to her mother's house, told her to 'hide them and don't tell me where you've put them', and was later accused by a Durban public prosecutor of obstructing justice.

Perhaps this is one of the reasons the police are not as 'nice' as they used to be ... And perhaps it is also because of a story the Cows did called 'Stolen Dockets', which won for Nicky and Julie a CNN African Journalist of the Year award in 2005. It showed just how easy it was to access criminal dockets at Durban's biggest police stations.

Stolen Dockets – 2001

The sale of classified information, criminal dockets and the contents of dockets, like the names of witnesses, isn't unique to South Africa. It's just that our justice system appears to lack effective strategies to deal with corrupt activities. From 2000, more and more cases involving the 'sale of justice' were being reported to *Carte Blanche* journalists, but these were difficult stories to tell, and even harder to prove. Then, in late 2001, came a breakthrough: a mild-mannered attorney named Walter Niedinger phoned up. He'd seen the exam scam story on *Carte Blanche*, in which an education official had been filmed offering to up matric results for a fee (see page 153). Niedinger decided that the only way to get senior police officers to sit up and take notice of the corruption he'd experienced was exposure in the media. Over the next few months, he helped expose a racket involving 12 detectives based at the Randfontein police station.

Following the arrest of a client, Niedinger had been approached by a cop named Soccas, who had told him that, for between R1 500 and R2 000, he could get rid of evidence against his client, change witness statements or have a 'chat' with the prosecutor. Niedinger was outraged, but played along, and at considerable personal risk he set up several meetings with Soccas at the local Wimpy, some of which he filmed.

Producer Victoria Cullinan organised two spy cameras for him (because one invariably bombs out) – one in a bag, the other in a pair of rather bizarre-looking glasses with unusually thick frames to hide the wire. There have been dramatic strides in miniaturising surveillance equipment since those days, but the glasses fooled the Randfontein police.

Victoria got to know the West Rand mining town well, waiting in her car outside the Wimpy, while Walter met with Soccas and his cohorts. Sometimes they pitched, sometimes not. But when they did, it seemed there was nothing they couldn't 'fix'; even serious offences like murder, child rape and molestation could vanish into the ether. *Carte Blanche* couldn't break the law by paying the cops, but Walter was prepared to risk it, reasoning that it was for the greater good. One policeman even brought his son along to collect a bribe, an indication of how blasé he'd become. It was a damning story, one that infuriated then Gauteng Police Commissioner Perumal Naidoo, who said he felt 'tricked' when confronted with the *Carte Blanche* camera evidence, but it resulted in the arrests of three policemen. Walter and his family had to get 24-hour armed protection for three months, his children guarded by two policemen at their crèche.

Victoria won the prestigious WWB Legal Journalist of the Year award for 'a vivid exposé of corruption and disappearing dockets in our courts'.

But the stolen docket saga didn't end there.

Two years later, the Nguni Cows were to prove how easy it was simply to walk into a police station and take dockets without even having to pay anyone. It came at a time when only six out of every 100 police cases resulted in a conviction, and with 75 per cent of them never even making it to court. Nguni got their lead from an organisation in Phoenix, Durban, called 'The Voice' – the Victim Outreach and Information Centre. Its founder, Alvin Brijlal, and his team provided a sympathetic ear to people who had experienced negligence and corruption at the hands of the KZN police. And the most frequent complaint was the constant disappearance of dockets, which resulted in criminals walking away scot-free. Brijlal claimed that, on average, a staggering 25 cases involving disappearing dockets appeared on his desk every month. Julie remembers going to meet him while researching the story and thinking that he was another one of the hundreds who phone *Carte Blanche* with big allegations, without being able to prove them. But Alvin turned out, in Julie's words, to be 'a champ'. She gave him a spy camera in a shoulder bag, and he and a friend walked into the Phoenix police station and helped themselves. No one questioned them, or even turned a hair. Not wanting to commit an offence by actually stealing the dockets, they removed a pile and took them to the toilet, where they could've filched evidence, or changed statements if they'd wanted to. But they took them all back and left the building, passing several policemen on the way, no questions asked. Just to make sure it wasn't a once-off, they got Alvin's mate to do it again – this time to find a specific murder docket. No problem – all that was needed, it seemed, was attitude.

The Cows decided to try one more major station. A police source from Durban Central had complained to them that dockets disappeared regularly from there. He gave them the lie of the land. Nicky, who was just 22 at the time and a rookie eager to cut her teeth in investigative journalism, decided to do it herself. She casually made her way behind the main charge desk and into the control room, where, she'd been told by the source, the dockets were processed. Despite her youth, she must've looked like a plainclothes cop because no one inquired about her presence. She asked someone on duty for the Berea police station dockets, found a chair and paged through them all, most of them involving petty offences. The source had told her that the serious crimes were kept in the safe, so she asked for those too, and got them. According to her police source, hundreds of thousands of rand could be made selling murder dockets. The only time she was interrupted – and her heart sank, thinking she'd been rumbled – was when a policeman asked for help with his computer.

Julie remembers sitting outside in her car 'crapping herself' in case Nicky got caught. But she emerged with exactly what they wanted on camera.

Interviewed by Devi, police spokesman Vish Naidoo seemed shocked: 'Heads must roll. This must be an eye-opener to every one of us to ensure that something similar to this never happens again.'

'Heads must roll, Devi, heads must roll' became an Nguni catch phrase, because, of course, they never did. In 2009, following reports that there'd been a 56 per cent increase in missing dockets, the team repeated the exercise at police stations in Johannesburg and Port Elizabeth. The story, this time presented by Derek, began with Vish's 'heads must roll' comment, and was followed by a heartbreaking interview with a woman who'd been gang-raped in Tembisa, near Midrand. She described how her attackers had pushed her as they left the courtroom after the case had been struck off the roll because statements were missing from the docket. 'We are not like a paper, we are human beings ... paper can get lost, that means I'm lost. I'm not lost, I'm still here.' Her case was eventually reinstated, and only because of the efforts of the NGO People Against Women Abuse (POWA), but it took close on two years to collect all the statements again.

But something had been achieved, because return visits to Phoenix and Durban Central showed dockets under lock and key and CCTV cameras. The obvious solution, an e-docket system, in which documents are scanned into a national digital database, has yet to be rolled out.

the Tuli elephants

In his book *The Elephant Whisperer*, Lawrence Anthony writes: '... there are no walls between humans and elephants except those that we put up ourselves, and until we allow not only elephants, but all living creatures their place in the sun, we can never be whole ourselves.'

A *Carte Blanche* story on the now-famous Tuli Elephants inspired this legendary conservationist to adopt problem elephants and begin reha-bilitating them on his private game reserve, Thula Thula, in Zululand. But, as he said, it wasn't a case of him adopting the elephants, but being patient enough to wait for them to adopt him. And they did.

In 2003, when Anthony returned from a mission to save zoo animals in war-torn Iraq, the wild herd he'd adopted arrived at his gate to meet him, even though he'd been gone for months.

A few days after Anthony's death in 2012, two herds of elephant arrived at his compound on the 1 500-hectare reserve to say goodbye. They hadn't visited the house in 18 months and it must've taken them 12 hours to make the journey.

They'd come to mourn, as elephants do.

Like humans, elephants are recognised as having life-long loyalties, an instinctive sense of family, extraordinarily developed bonding with their calves and a strong sense of death. This interconnection between beings is one of the concepts at the heart of the movement for animal rights, and no *Carte Blanche* story opened the debate better than the 'Tuli Elephants', broadcast on 4 July 1999.

Somewhere in the region of 64 000 people contacted *Carte Blanche* after the broadcast, a volume of feedback never before experienced and not since. An article in the *Pretoria News* on 8 July read: '... *Carte Blanche* once again dominated newspaper headlines and radio talk shows around the country this week after the broadcast on cruelty to young elephants ... M-Net and Combined Artists' offices were inundated with calls, faxes and emails. By Tuesday afternoon, M-Net had to create extra space on its server for viewers to enter the "Rant and Rage" page ...'

Thousands of protesters gathered outside the premises of African Game Services (AGS), the wildlife trading company near Brits that was 'training' baby elephants captured in the wild in Botswana. Tattooed bikers in leather, smart Sandton ladies and their dogs, schoolchildren and grandmothers – all were calling for the arrest of owner Riccardo Ghiazza and carrying posters like 'Hang the Bastards, Free the Elephants' and 'What kind of man allows abuse of defenceless babies?'

In a display of passion uncommon among white South Africans, who just didn't join mass protests, people pushed through the gates at AGS.

A report in *The Citizen* on 12 July 1999 read: 'Angry protesters broke down a gate, shoved security guards out of their way and stormed the premises ... to reach the 14 Tuli elephants being held there ...'

Cartoonist Zapiro summed up the mood:

Zapiro cartoon in the *Sunday Times*, 11 July 1999

The story that caused all this commotion had pulled no punches. The opening shot was of an elephant calf being hit repeatedly on the trunk and over the head with what looked like a short broomstick. The man wielding the blows seemed to be venting the frustration of years. The animal's leg was chained to a post, and when it tried to turn its head to avoid the blows it was beaten on the body. Viewing didn't get any easier as the 16-minute insert progressed. It showed elephants hobbled and chained so that it was impossible for them to lie down. A terrified and confused-looking calf with ropes around its neck was being dragged around by an adult elephant with a man on its back; a row of elephants stood, front legs hobbled, back legs stretched out and chained to posts in poses that cried of submission. They were denied drinking water and were constantly goaded in what could only be an effort intended to break their spirits. There were close-ups of baby elephants with lesions above their eyes, which were clearly caused by a sharp object.

Looking back on the story more than ten years later, producer Hein Ungerer, who today lectures and mentors film students in Cape Town, finds the insert slow and slightly indulgent. But it was a defining moment in his life and changed his perception of animal issues. It wasn't just a story about cruelty to elephants; it was about fairness and social justice. He produced several award-winning animal rights stories in his time at *Carte Blanche*, and was a three-time winner of the Brigitte Bardot International Award, presented to non-American media as part of the Humane Society of the United States's annual Genesis Awards.

The tale of the Tulis had begun in July 1998, when 30 wild calves, aged between two and seven, were snatched from their mothers in Botswana's Tuli Game Reserve, a block of land that juts out into Zimbabwe and South Africa. The baby elephants were sold, in a commercial deal, to animal trader and exporter Riccardo Ghiazza, and were transported by road to his wildlife trading company in the North West province. AGS supplied wild-caught animals to zoos and safari parks around the globe.

The first story that appeared on *Carte Blanche* focused on the outcry that followed the baby elephants' arrival at AGS. It was known that Ghiazza employed Indonesian mahouts, which made local and overseas animal activists deeply suspicious of how they were to be 'trained'. The mahouts' most common tools were chains and ankuses – sticks with sharp metal hooks to stab elephants in the head, or sensitive areas like the mouth or inner ear. So, particularly given the age of the elephants, it wasn't long before accusations of cruelty surfaced. In September 1998, the National Council of SPCAs (NSPCA) obtained a search warrant to assess their condition. Inspector Rick Allen went onto the farm and filmed the training methods. But Ghiazza tried to obtain the tape, even applying to the High Court. Allen was interviewed saying: 'To go to these lengths, one can imagine what is on the videotape.'

But imagine was all the public could do, because Ghiazza obtained an interdict against the NSPCA, and it was ruled that the footage could only be released to international elephant experts, who would make recommendations to the court. Among these experts were Kenyan conservationists Daphne Sheldrick and Joyce Poole.

And so began a bitter court feud. Although the case dealt only with whether or not there had been cruelty inflicted on the animals, the elephants had come to symbolise a much bigger argument between conservation groups on the one hand, and animal rights activists on the other. And at the heart of it was the origin of the elephants. The Tuli Block was owned by a consortium of wealthy South African businessmen, who claimed that the elephants there were slowly starving because of overpopulation; selling them off would also prevent degradation of the environment.

In her book *Animal Rights in South Africa*, activist Michele Pickover described the capture of the elephants as told to her by a wildlife photographer who happened to be there at the time. After a baby elephant had been darted with a tranquilliser fired from a helicopter, the ground crew tried to move in, but were prevented by the mother, who stood over her unconscious baby. So the cow had to be tranquillised too. When she came round, her baby was gone. Her distressed screaming and bellowing could be heard for miles.

And so the baby Tuli elephants, ripped from their mothers, ended up at Ghiazza's torture camp, where he employed the kind of training, based on fear of humans, that the NSPCA wanted to prevent taking root in South Africa. But Ghiazza was well connected ... he had even supplied two elephants to Michael Jackson's private zoo. He had bought the baby Tulis for R12 000 each and could sell them for more than ten times that amount. There were no laws that stood in his way. South Africa was, and is, a country that encourages trade in live animals.

Derek Hanekom, then Minister of Agriculture and Land Affairs, joined the fray. He reinforced the view of animals as a 'commodity' by saying that the training of elephants could give them a better quality of life as they would be 'familiar with human contact' and that training could be a 'viable alternative to culling'.

Carte Blanche first asked Ghiazza for an interview in August 1998, a request he flatly refused. But the furore refused to die down; international and local media hung around the heavily guarded AGS premises, filming the baby elephants from the road, and signs of the brutal mahout-style training were evident even from afar.

In November, Ghiazza realised he needed to do some PR. He cleaned up his act, got rid of the mahouts and allowed the media in. The elephants seemed in much better condition than the earlier images of them, with legs in chains and covered in lesions, had suggested. The odd elephant still had tied feet, but Ghiazza said these were the aggressive ones. In an interview with Manu Padayachee, he said that the training had been 'soft' and that he was not a man who would tolerate cruelty to animals. Furthermore, no one had actually witnessed this cruelty – it was all based on 'assumption'.

But there *were* a few people who had seen the NSPCA footage: producer Hein Ungerer, for one, and Daphne Sheldrick, for another. She had first featured on *Carte Blanche* in 1994, in an insert on raising and reintegrating orphaned elephants into the wild in the Nairobi National Park. She had visited the Tulis at AGS and had testified in court that the footage she'd seen had shown the elephants being hit 137 times in 20 minutes and that each of them had up to 20 abscesses on their bodies.

In June 1999, Sheldrick received another tape in the post, this time depicting the brutal bludgeoning of a cornered baby elephant at AGS. She decided that enough was enough, and, with Hein, hatched a plan. In terms of the court order, it was illegal for the NSPCA to distribute the footage, but the same rules didn't apply in Kenya. And so Hein and

Derek Watts set off for Nairobi to blow the lid off the saga of the Tuli elephants.

The final edited story showed Derek viewing the tapes with Daphne in an edit suite at the Nairobi offices of Camerapix, the company started by world-renowned photojournalist, the late Mohamed Amin.

Derek: 'The footage you are about to see was taken by the SPCA within the last month or two. It could've been much worse without their presence.'

That was hard to imagine, and the comment might have been made to placate the NSPCA, which was under pressure in South Africa for filming the abuse but not being able to stop it. The infamous tape was played, followed by an interview with Daphne who described, scene by scene, what the elephants were going through.

There were horrible images of a baby elephant, its back legs hobbled, trumpeting dismally with its mouth open as it was beaten repeatedly; another was shown kneeling in the so-called killing mode, its ears up; an elephant urinated in terror as it was forced into a corner by a man jabbing it with an ankus.

The only training these elephants were getting, said Daphne, was how to hate humans, how to kill humans. Elephants' ears and skin, which might look tough, were in fact so sensitive that they could feel a feather; and when they put up their tails, as they were doing in the images, it signified pain and terror. The animals had no idea what was expected of them because the beatings were intended to break their spirits; they would eventually turn angry and vicious. 'This has been proved time and time again in circuses and zoos ... one day they will think: "It's shit or bust and I am going to kill this swine."' Hein had got hold of some footage from a circus in Hawaii, where, some years previously, a fully grown African elephant had killed a trainer, pressing down on him with its head and trunk, while the horrified audience screamed in terror and disbelief. The animal had rampaged through the circus grounds, killing two more people, until police repeatedly fired at it. The animal bled to death on a suburban road. The then director of the Endangered Wildlife Trust, John Ledger, took issue with this, post-broadcast, saying: 'the video was cleverly edited to include overseas file material showing other incidents of brutality to elephants ... people poured out their anger at the abuse of Babar the elephant ...'

The *Carte Blanche* story clearly took a moral position: what was happening to these intelligent beasts was wrong and could in no way be defended. There was no attempt to speak to African Game Services, or to the NSPCA, or to alternative wildlife groupings pre-broadcast because, once it was known that *Carte Blanche* had the footage, there would undoubtedly be interdicts launched to stop broadcast. The weekly promo for the show was curious and cryptic: no pictures; just Ruda on screen, hinting of abuse and horror, and that was it.

Once Hein had finished editing the story with Jonathan Pienaar, there was a pre-viewing for final approval. For many *Carte Blanche* producers these viewings are nerve-wracking affairs, involving critiques by the executive producer, the managing editor and, if there are legal implications, lawyers. Executive producer George Mazarakis is widely regarded as a man difficult to please: it's a professional environment and he has exacting standards. The responses to the pre-viewing may necessitate changes to the story structure, or even additional filming, which, with limited time, equals stress and trauma for producers, who may also have already spent their allocated filming allowance. Hein still recalls with satisfaction the stunned silence after this particular viewing: there were no changes.

But there was a cacophony of protest from viewers following the broadcast. The beatings and cruelty were too graphic to ignore. Apart from outraged viewers, who directed their anger at Ghiazza, suddenly there were about-turns from those within the wildlife industry who had initially deemed the removal of the Tulis from Botswana 'ecologically necessary'.

Rhino and Elephant Foundation director Andrew McKenzie, who had been supportive of Ghiazza, resigned after a TV debate on *50/50*, saying he had 'tarnished the name of the Foundation in pursuit of a battle against international animal rights movements'. He later wrote that the Tuli issue had brought about the most pivotal period in the history of conservation in South Africa.

And in an amazing turnaround, the World Wildlife Fund (WWF) South

Africa, part of the sustainable utilisation lobby, released a public statement decrying the cruelty shown on *Carte Blanche*. It asked the public to support a fund to remove the remaining 14 elephants to an alternative facility, to 'preclude any possibility of a further recurrence'.

Human rights groups like People Opposing Women Abuse (POWA) and the Black Sash took issue with what they thought was South Africans' over-reaction to animal abuse and under-reaction to the abuse of women and children, even running a newspaper campaign with the slogan 'The Tuli Elephants don't know how lucky they are'. Pickover deals with this in her book, saying society should recognise the 'interconnectedness of all things'. According to animal rights philosophy, women and child abuse, poverty and racism were 'all part of the same problem: the need for a caring and just society'.

To quote Lawrence Anthony: 'Our inability to think beyond our own species, or to be able to co-habit with other life forms in what is patently a massive collaborative quest for survival, is surely a malady that pervades the human soul.'

Environmentalists acknowledged that the Tuli Elephant saga had achieved what they had been unable to do for years – to make ordinary South Africans re-evaluate their relationships with nature. The weaknesses of the Animal Protection Act became obvious, but there was no significant change to the law.

The men responsible for the beatings were arrested. Riccardo Ghiazza and employee Wayne Stockigt, the man shown beating the elephants in the opening shots of the story, were found guilty of contravening the Animal Protection Act and fined a mere R35 000.

It was a bittersweet victory for the NSPCA. They'd won the case but ultimately could only free nine of the 14 elephants. These were released into the Marakele National Park in the Waterberg, where they were gradually integrated into a wild herd. Lawrence Anthony made an unsuccessful attempt to acquire some of the others for Thula Thula. But, by devious means, Ghiazza decided their fate, dispatching them to European zoos, a hunting farm and an elephant sanctuary. *Carte Blanche* did several report-backs: some of the Tulis ended up at Sandhurst Safaris, a hunting establishment, and at a 'sanctuary' near Hartbeespoort Dam, owned by Craig Saunders, who had been charged along with Ghiazza but was later acquitted. A 2008 visit revealed that some of the Tulis were being used to give rides and to perform for tourists, although Saunders denied that these were the abused elephants. According to the NSPCA, they were all abused.

In July 2007, Riccardo Ghiazza, still trading in animals, was killed when he crashed his black Mercedes SLK on the R512 near Hartbeespoort Dam. Derek was amazed when, some years later, Ghiazza's wife confronted him in a restaurant, saying *Carte Blanche* had contributed to his death.

old bones and young blood 10

The days of our years are three score years and ten; and if by reason of
strength they be four score years, yet is their strength labour and sorrow.

– Psalm 90

Someone who wholeheartedly disputes this biblical quotation is Cambridge-based scientist Dr Aubrey de Grey, who believes humans are capable of not only living much longer, but also much younger lives. He's a biomedical gerontologist – an expert in the field of longevity – and was interviewed by Eugene Botha, *Carte Blanche*'s travelling producer/professor, for a story entitled 'Can We Live Forever?' His opening sentence was startling: 'I think that the first people who could live to as much as a thousand are already alive today.'

De Grey, in his late forties, resembled an Old Testament prophet, with a beard that looked like it'd been growing for a couple of hundred years at least. And it sounded as if he was planning to live that long. Diseases of the elderly had to be combated at a cellular and molecular level, he said, and if the seven types of damage he'd identified could be repaired, it would be bye-bye to arthritis, cataracts, decrepitude and senility. A scientific journal had put up a challenge to anyone who could dispute

De Grey's radical claim that regenerative medicine could be applied to ageing. No one was able to, and De Grey had established the Methuselah Foundation, awarding big cash prizes to scientists who could prolong the life of mice, for starters. The 'Mouse Prize' was first won by a researcher who had succeeded in extending a mouse's life to five years – apparently the equivalent of 250 human years.

The problem, said De Grey, was that old age was regarded as immutable and unavoidable, rather than just another medical problem that could, in principle – and very probably in practice – be addressed by medicine in the foreseeable future. Most of us, he said, were trapped in a 'pro-ageing trance' and needed to snap out of it and stop prolonging decrepitude. The whole of civilisation was about changing nature to achieve a higher quality of life, he said. Ageing should be reversed or postponed.

While the thought of living to 250, let alone a thousand, might not appeal to everyone, avoiding the decrepitude of old age would surely have many takers and could mean fewer alarming headlines like these: 'Abuse of elderly patients rises by a third a year'; 'Financial abuse of elderly becomes more common'; 'Elder Abuse the new societal crime'; 'Retirement home worker convicted of torture'.

The UN General Assembly declared 1999 the International Year of Older Persons, calling for solidarity, respect and exchanges between generations. In January 2000, *Carte Blanche* broadcast a story that made news for weeks, provoked public hearings and ministerial committees and influenced legislation.

It began in 1998 with an email from a viewer, irate because he'd written to *Carte Blanche* before about the abuse of his mother at the hands of her caregivers. Now his mother was dead, he wrote, and might not have been had the alleged abuse been exposed. Such expectations are common: *Carte Blanche* often has to fill the role of social worker, police officer or arbitrator. Once, after a succession of 'if you don't help me I am going to kill myself' phone calls, programme liaison Billie O'Hara – the show's 'listen-hear lady' – went on a counselling course with Lifeline, where she learnt to recognise emotional blackmail.

Executive producer George Mazarakis had received this distressing email, which clearly wasn't emotional blackmail, so he did what he does best: set a near-impossible challenge. It was too late for this viewer's mother, but surely someone in the office would be able to prove conclusively that elder abuse was becoming a real problem?

It was a tall order, but one that Odette Schwegler took on. She was new to the role of senior *Carte Blanche* researcher, but was keen to make an impression. Having replaced Anna-Maria Lombard – a resourceful and innovative journalist who'd moved on, as so many do in this high-stress environment – Odette had big shoes to fill. She began a fishing expedition, deciding to call up old-age homes across South Africa until she got a bite. She knew how slim were the chances of anyone responding positively to a journalist asking to film abuse of the elderly at their institution and of then allowing the film to be screened on the most influential current affairs show in the country.

Joy Summers, managing editor at the time, remembers the story being on the whiteboard in her office for almost two years. She had serious doubts that it would ever come off, but says it was testimony to Odette's indefatigable spirit that it eventually became one of *Carte Blanche*'s most important stories.

Via a network of contacts, including an organisation called 'Focus on Elder Abuse', Odette found a caring administrator at a home on the KwaZulu-Natal South Coast called Sunset Lodge. Gabriel Hartzenberg had long suspected the abuse of infirm residents at the institution. Some of them had complained to him, saying: 'I want you to get me out of here, they're hitting me.' But their senile conditions made them unreliable witnesses, and many were too terrified of further abuse to 'tell on' their caregivers. It had to be proven beyond reasonable doubt. And the only way to do that was through surveillance.

Gabriel suggested that *Carte Blanche* install cameras in the bedrooms and in the showers at Sunset Lodge. Although it would be an invasion of privacy, he suspected that the abuse was occurring in these areas. In those days, installing a hidden camera was more difficult than it is today. The cameras were, as Joy described them, 'great clunking VHS's with tapes that needed to be changed'. Odette ended up going undercover as a temporary carer for a few weeks, to ensure that the tape-changing process went smoothly. Later, Gabriel would send her the tapes every week.

One day, after spooling through hours of footage, there it was: a carer punching and slapping an elderly man in the face. Odette tried to suppress that feeling of delight that journalists get when hard work pays off and a plan comes together – even when the subject matter is unpleasant. The tapes kept coming; in 70 hours of clandestine footage there was enough evidence to show that something was very wrong at Sunset Lodge. The nurses weren't acting in self-defence, dealing with impossibly difficult people, or just having a bad day. They were being mean and cruel to defenceless and infirm people who couldn't protect themselves against physical and psychological abuse.

The story was assigned to producer Nicola de Chaud, who, with Ruda Landman, did the interviews and dramatisations to supplement the undercover footage, which, she said, had moral challenges: 'We were trying to show that the dignity of elderly people was being trampled on, but we had footage of them at their most defenceless, being shoved around while naked in the shower.' It created a dilemma for her in the final edit, with each shot having to be carefully considered as she painstakingly structured the story.

'Elder Abuse' was broadcast in January 2000, the first live broadcast of the new millennium. Ruda and Derek, looking fresh and relaxed after one of those lovely long breaks the viewers hate, walked onto a brand-new set. They'd already had their first fight, said Derek, arguing over whether it was the fifth or sixth set in the 12 years they'd been on air. This one had a news feel to it: an L-shaped desk with space for guests, who could remain out of view while Ruda and Derek did the 'cold start' to introduce the line-up for the evening.

M-Net had been toying with the idea of *Carte Blanche* going live with news every night, so the set was chosen with that in mind, although it never happened. That night, the third chair was occupied by Manu Padayachee, appropriately dressed in red shirt and tie, to report back on a story called 'Cape of Flames', about devastating fires on the Cape Peninsula. After that, it was on to:

Ruda: 'A sobering look at an element of life no-one can escape, old age ...'

Derek: 'A story we have worked on for more than a year ...'

Ruda: '... the possibility exists for each one of us ... that time when we can no longer look after ourselves, when we have to rely on others.'

And so began a hard-to-watch story of neglect and abuse. A sweet-faced woman named Alice, aged 81, her face creased by time, said she'd been fed dog pellets, had her mail torn up, been denied access to a phone, and been hit. She'd lost control of her financial affairs and been forced to sign an amended will that benefited her abuser, a close relative with whom she'd been living. And there was toothless Hester from Bloemfontein, who'd been living with her grandson in a shack. He'd starved her, locked her up and raped her, until finally she'd been rescued by neighbours who'd heard her cry out. 'I am waiting for my days on earth to end because I don't have any family to help me – to look after me, to love me.'

And things weren't much better at those institutions 'we look to in the hope they will provide the care that we can't', said Ruda, standing in a depressing room that spoke of substandard hygiene. She interviewed Mabel, a matron at a home in Pinetown, who'd embarked on her own investigation after finding unexplained bruises on some of the elderly residents. Mabel had hidden in a room adjacent to that of a woman who'd had a stroke. At one in the morning, the frail woman had complained to a carer that her paralysed arm and leg were falling out of bed. Mabel said the woman was slapped four times. Earlier, when the same woman had asked a nurse to switch off the main light and leave the door open, she was told to shut up; the light was left on and the door closed. Another woman was sprayed with carpet cleaner when she asked for a bath. Because there was no footage, Nicola did dramatisations, using her grandmother Mavis and her great-aunt Dolly, both in their eighties, and who gamely pretended to be slapped around, pushed and shoved.

There were no dramatisations needed at Sunset Lodge, where hidden-camera footage showed 87-year-old Henry, who suffered from Alzheimer's, sitting on a plastic chair in the shower, his back to the camera. The nurse standing in front of him rapped him repeatedly on the head with her knuckles, for no apparent reason. She said 'knock-knock' as she did it. Then she put a towel over his head. It was not dramatic violence, but subtle cruelty and disrespect.

Another woman, clearly unable to stand unaided, bent to sit on a shower chair with wheels. But the nurse who'd led her in hadn't properly positioned the chair and the decrepit woman crashed to the ground and lay there, helpless. A wider shot revealed that there was a man in the same shower, even though the home had separate facilities for men and women. The nurse left the woman flailing, with the parting sentence: 'Wash that thing yourself – it stinks.'

Once Odette had identified the worst incidents of abuse on the tapes, Nicola organised for Gabriel to fly up to Johannesburg to watch what had been going on under his nose. He was appalled, saying it was standard procedure to check for injuries, or to call for assistance, if anyone fell in the shower. As for the physical abuse doled out by his staff: 'Being slapped on the face is very wrong. At that age your skin is as thin as paper. The man can also not defend himself; arthritis has left his hands disabled.'

A lot of the abuse didn't leave marks: it was taunting and callous. Basic requests were treated with disdain. Clothes were thrown at people unable to dress themselves. When a woman asked the nurse to please get her out of the chair she was sitting in because she was in pain, 'I DON'T LIFT!' was shouted back at her.

There was an interview with Melissa, a volunteer who visited elderly people in a home in her neighbourhood. One day she'd arrived to find that one of her favourites, Elizabeth, wasn't in her bed, and was told she'd been taken to the bathroom. An hour later, Elizabeth still wasn't back, so Melissa went hunting for her and found her tied to the loo with a draw sheet. She'd fallen asleep and was blue with cold: it would be another cameo role for Nicola's Aunty Dolly.

Carte Blanche couldn't show the Sunset Lodge footage without first consulting the relatives of those being abused, so researchers tracked down some of them. Daughter Avril had thought her mother Nancy was being well cared for. But she wept when she saw Nancy's tiny frame being smacked and pulled roughly off her bed for daring to lie down when she should've been sitting in her chair. 'My mom was once such a dignified person ...'

In an on-camera link, Ruda pointed out that legislation passed in 1998 made it compulsory to report abuse, or face a fine or a five-year prison sentence.

Back in the studio, presenter Manu Padayachee interviewed the Commissioner for Elder Abuse from the Human Rights Commission (HRC). Tom Manthata appealed to communities to record and monitor abuses, and to report these to his office. But Manu had in his possession a 12-page letter that had been sent to Manthata's office, alleging abuse at a particular institution. The writer had received a letter from the HRC saying that the complaint did not 'constitute a violation of human rights'. Manthata looked embarrassed. 'Well that was before the Act was passed,' he said, referring to the 1998 amendment to the Aged Persons Act of 1967.

It was a damning and devastating story and had massive repercussions. The programme was shown to the parliamentary portfolio committee for Welfare, at the insistence of Social Development minister Zola Skweyiya, who appointed an independent commission. Ruda and Nicola interviewed him for a follow-up programme and were impressed by his commitment: 'It was appalling and cannot be tolerated ... the beating of helpless old people is a bad reflection on our society and our country as a whole,' he said.

Viewers flooded *Carte Blanche* with emails, faxes and calls, some describing other incidents of abuse, some wanting to help, but many just expressing their outrage. The disciplinary hearing for the Sunset Lodge staff members implicated in the video became a media event. Four nurses were called to appear, but only one turned up, a lone figure surrounded by dozens of protestors, including bikers, with grannies riding pillion, revving their engines in an intimidating way. A trade unionist representing two of the nurses said a court order should have been obtained for the video evidence to be used, but in the end they were all dismissed. There were big changes at Sunset Lodge, with new staff and a new matron, and many old-age homes installed permanent CCTV cameras.

The commission appointed by Skweyiya went around the country listening to cheerless testimony from thousands of elderly people. New

119

regulations would introduce minimum standards for old-age homes, introduce a national register on the abuse of the elderly, and make management at old-age homes responsible for checking on the treatment of residents.

But in 2010, *Carte Blanche* received more video footage, picked up on CCTV cameras, this time at a home in Johannesburg. An 82-year-old man was assaulted by two nurses and had a stroke a day later, his face black and blue; an elderly woman was beaten so that her skull cracked and she was barely conscious when paramedics got to her. But rather than being proactive in exposing and expelling the abusers, the home involved was defensive and combative, clearly wanting to limit bad publicity.

The laws might have changed, but attitudes had not.

Hurry up, Aubrey de Grey.

Thoko of Ikageng – 2001

Six months later, the story of Thoko Adonis restored faith in humanity. Every morning, this 60-year-old resident of Ikageng township, near Potchefstroom, got up with a purpose. Ikageng means 'make something of yourself' in Tswana, and Thoko certainly had. She rose at five, kneeled at the foot of her bed, asked God to give her strength for the day ahead, and then began cooking soft porridge. She cared for more than 30 elderly people in her neighbourhood, despite having neither resources nor facilities, nor even a salary. 'I do this because nobody else cares,' she told Ruda. She also did it because she'd heard a voice telling her to put her love on a tray and carry it out to people. Blinking behind her tortoiseshell glasses, she said that instead of worrying about the world, the voice had told her to try to change it. She lived in a modest house with her 33-year-old son Mongezi, the youngest of her four boys.

Once she'd carted her pots of porridge off to feed bedridden people in shacks, it was back home to fetch a tin bath and a gas cylinder and off she'd go again, bath on her head. She'd boil up some water and lovingly wash people like Lydia Mofojane, who'd had a stroke and lived alone.

The bath would be followed by a massage with Thoko's healing hands.

Carol Albertyn Christie, who produced the story, remembers it as a 'quiet' one, a small but important story of self-sacrifice, the kind to end the *Carte Blanche* 'emigration' hour. Thoko's dream was to start an old-age home in Ikageng, or a daycare centre. Following the show, Billie O'Hara received floods of offers of help for Thoko, offers which translated into goods – even a specially constructed cart so she could wheel around her bath and gas cylinder. Cash donations were made to the newly established 'Thoko Project'. She was delighted ... her prayers had been answered. She would be able to employ helpers to reach more vulnerable pensioners. But, ironically, the funds she received may have contributed to what happened four months later.

In February 2001, Thoko, the light of Ikageng, was killed, her throat slit from ear to ear. Her body was apparently discovered by her son when he came home one evening.

Saddened, Carol and Ruda paid tribute to her in a follow-up story. A small group of old people gathered outside Thoko's house, holding vigil, quietly singing and praying for the person who'd enriched their lives. Inside the house, her four sons were struggling to comprehend why someone so loved in the community had been taken so violently. Nothing had been stolen, and there had been no forced entry. In her book *Off Camera*, Ruda wrote that 'her death was a riddle which left me helpless and depressed'.

Even more depressing was a newspaper headline a few months later: 'Son on trial for slaying Ikageng's "Good Samaritan"'. Her son, Mongezi, with whom she'd lived, and who'd discovered the body, had apparently wanted to get his hands on the donations she'd received for her project.

Carol and Billie still get tearful when anyone mentions Thoko Adonis.

Carte Blanche Babies: Gabriel, Pippie and Georgina

The story of Gabriel Proost is one of George Mazarakis's all-time *Carte Blanche* favourites and has been repeated in various guises since it was first broadcast in 2005. Two-year-old Gabriel was found completely lifeless in the swimming pool of his Johannesburg home. For his 'normally paranoid about pool safety' parents, Rikkie and Louise, their worst nightmare had become a reality. In the process of selling their home, they had been preparing for a show day when they let Gabriel out of their sight for ten minutes. He'd apparently spent seven of those submerged in the pool. Even though it looked hopeless, an estate agent who'd arrived at the house administered rudimentary CPR and didn't stop until paramedic David da Silva got there. Da Silva said later that the only thing in Gabriel's favour was this 'bystander CPR'. In his ten years on the job, he'd never attended an emergency where anybody had survived pre-hospital cardiac arrest without CPR. Gabriel was flown by helicopter to Garden City Clinic in Brixton.

Carte Blanche's Africa editor at the time, Bernadette Maguire, had been at Rhodes University with Rikkie Proost and had been contacted by a mutual friend. She'd heard that Gabriel was undergoing controversial treatment that could save his life. If his life was saved, it would be an amazing story.

At the hospital, Bernadette found Gabriel in intensive care, surrounded by ice packs, and with tubes up his nose and down his throat. On the Glasgow Coma Scale, used to measure conscious states, his condition was between three and five, which meant a ten per cent chance of recovery. Things were not looking good.

The Garden City team, led by paediatrician Miles Bartlett, was hoping Gabriel hadn't suffered neurological damage. When the brain is deprived of oxygen – as it is in a drowning – some brain cells die within minutes, while others are programmed to die. But they can be saved by hypothermic treatment. This so-called brain freeze was first used in the 1950s, when doctors realised that in cases where blood supply to the brain was diminished, patients stood a better chance of recovery if the body could be cooled down to as low as 30°C. Although they'd found it to be beneficial, the risk of infection was so high that the treatment had been abandoned.

But things changed in 1999, when a Swedish woman named Anna Bagenholm, aged 29, had a skiing accident in Norway. She'd fallen head first onto a layer of ice over a frozen stream, landing on her back. The ice gave way and she came to rest in the freezing water, with only her feet and skis sticking out. She was unable to move, but was able to breathe because her face wasn't underwater. But after 40 minutes in the freezing water, she suffered cardiac arrest. Her heart stopped pumping and her blood stopped circulating. By the time she was rescued and flown to hospital, her body temperature had dropped to 13.7°C, the lowest ever recorded in someone with accidental hypothermia, and she looked absolutely dead. But because she'd been given CPR on the way to hospital, her brain had received some oxygen. Doctors connected her to a machine that warmed her blood outside her body and then put it back into her veins. Nine hours later, Anna Bagenholm started breathing again. It took months, but she made a full recovery, and the incident reignited interest in the therapeutic use of hypothermia to limit brain damage in cases of cardiac arrest.

In South Africa, Dr Miles Bartlett had pioneered the use of hypothermia involving child victims. He'd seen many children in Gabriel's condition. The little boy was sedated to protect his brain pressure from rising, and for 72 hours ice packs were used to lower his temperature to between 33 and 34°C, inducing controlled hypothermia.

At the hospital, Bernadette Maguire filmed what looked like a hopeless situation. Rikkie and Louise sat by Gabriel's bed, singing to him, holding his hands, while he lay there in a nappy, little legs splayed, not moving at all. Full of raw emotion, Louise recounted what had happened: 'I just heard Rikkie scream like he's never screamed before ... my name three times ... and then I just knew ...'

Rikkie: 'His face was blue, his eyes were wide open, just staring, and his tongue was hanging out his mouth ... just looking at this little face and shouting at him to come back to us and shouting at God to help me.'

A miracle was needed, and it came in the form of Dr Bartlett, who looked more like a rugby player than a paediatric ICU specialist. The induced hypothermia was decreasing the metabolism of Gabriel's brain, making it less dependent on oxygen. But there was a chance that he wouldn't wake up at all, or that, if he did, he might be brain-damaged. He was also being pumped full of massive amounts of blood pressure medication, from which he'd have to be weaned and his body warmed up to normal temperature again.

Then, on day seven, Gabriel started crying. His face scrunched up, his chin quivered and his lip went out. Louise and Rikkie had never been so delighted to see their son bewildered and in tears. He was still in a coma, but he was crying.

The following day, he was taken off the ventilator and began to breathe on his own. *Carte Blanche* decided to do the story.

Two weeks after drowning, Gabriel walked out of the hospital, a tiny figure pulling a suitcase on wheels. Initially, he was unable to talk, but by the time he visited the *Carte Blanche* studio as a guest, he'd regained his speech and was able to deliver a confident 'hello' into the microphone from his perch next to Ruda on yet another new *Carte Blanche* set – a big comfy tan couch, which now resides in the reception area of Combined Artistic Productions.

A few months later, there was a follow-up story entitled 'Gabriel's Gift'. Three-year-old Jack, one of triplets, had fallen into the filthy waters of Hartbeespoort Dam and was only found 20 minutes later. One of the adults present had done a CPR course the week before and kept pumping until the paramedics arrived, even though Jack looked long gone. He was then worked on for another two hours before being declared stable enough to be flown to Garden City Clinic. Jack's chances of survival were slimmer than Gabriel's – only one per cent. Nonetheless he was packed with ice blocks, in Dr Bartlett's primitive but proven method, and the team spent ten hours giving him fluids and blood pressure drugs in an attempt to get his circulatory system on the move again. Dr Bartlett was with him from six in the evening until four o'clock the next morning: 'I kind of said, okay, little Jack, do what you are going to do. I am getting tired.'

Little Jack survived the first week, still in an induced coma and connected to life support that decreased his brain's demand for oxygen and its metabolism. He was also on 11 antibiotics because of all the sewage he'd swallowed when he fell into the dam. He remained on a ventilator.

On day 15, Jack decided to give life a chance and was able to breathe on his own. But he had severe withdrawal symptoms from the drugs that had kept him under for so long. He developed water on the lungs and suffered a seizure. His parents thought it was the end – again.

But Jack turned out to be another of Miles's Miracles and on day 36 was well enough to leave hospital.

Since that time, there have been advances in the use of hypothermia. Dr Bartlett and his team no longer use the blue ice packs that saved Gabriel, but a thermo-wrap system. Cold water is pumped through the wrap, controlling the temperature. Around the world, therapeutic hypo-thermia has become a standard protocol when dealing with both adult and juvenile cardiac arrest patients. Overseas, the portable RhinoChill™ machine has been developed for paramedics, with special nasal catheters that spray rapidly evaporating coolant into the nose to bring down the temperature of the brain after cardiac arrest.

The Proosts now live in Australia. Gabriel is on his school swimming team and is a junior lifesaver. He has a well-worn DVD copy of the *Carte Blanche* story, 'Saving Gabriel'.

Pippie

The most inspirational story ever. God Bless you and your family.
Our love and admiration to Pippie, Anice and the phenomenal Dr Mia.
Pippie Kruger story killed me. Such courage & love & such lessons to all of us.
I am humbled by the story such uplifting work by our Doctors & all the supporting staff.

She could've become just another of the 15 000 South African children seriously injured by fire each year, a tragic statistic brought about by careless use of candles, paraffin stoves and open fires and worsened by a lack of immediate expert medical care. But Isabella 'Pippie' Kruger was born to the right parents, with the will and the means to save her life. She was to become a household name.

'These days, it takes me and Pippie two hours to go to the shops just to buy bread because everyone stops to talk to us,' laughed her mother

Anice, in November 2012. She'd brought Pippie to the *Carte Blanche* offices to say hello to the team. Pippie still looked far from normal, but was able to eat, smile and even laugh. She was a far cry from the sight that greeted plastic surgeon Dr Ridwan Mia in January 2012: 'She had 80% full-thickness burns. She was at least three or four times her body size because of all the swelling.'

The accident had happened on New Year's Eve at the Krugers' home in Ellisras, Limpopo. Pippie's father Erwin, a professional hunter, had been using firelighter gel to start a braai. The container had exploded in his hands and the burning gel had landed all over two-year-old Pippie, who'd been standing nearby. She'd literally melted in front of him, her skin bubbling before his eyes. 'And all I could see was her face in front of me ... fizzling and burning. But you get past that with God's help and the love of my wife and my family. You get through that,' he later recalled.

And thanks to modern medicine. When he first saw her, Dr Mia doubted that Pippie would survive. He could stabilise her burns, but what about sepsis, cardiac arrest, kidney failure and lung damage as a result of her injuries? Not to mention brain damage from the trauma. Pippie was to suffer all of those things in the weeks ahead.

All Anice wanted was for her daughter to look normal again. She started trawling the internet, and made contact with a professor at Harvard University who'd invented a method by which human skin cells could be cloned. There was a company in Boston, Genzyme-Sanofi, that specialised in growing layers of human skin, taking a small section of cells and culturing them into multiple sheets as thin as gossamer. The cost would be R750 000 – an astronomical sum. The procedure required a small sample from the transplant patient. The skin would be taken from Pippie's groin, the only part of her body that hadn't been burnt. (It had been covered with a nappy when she caught fire.) The money? The Krugers were confident that God would provide.

Carte Blanche researcher Amalia Christoforou, who'd produced the *Carte Blanche Medical* show in 2010, thought the skin cloning process would make a fascinating story, little realising that it would mushroom into a global media event and come to mean far more to her than just another clinical procedure.

In hospital, Pippie had had all the burnt tissue removed from her body and remained covered in oozing bandages from head to toe, her little feet and hands curled into claws where the skin had tightened as it healed. Her top teeth were covered in a tiny 'Hello Kitty' bite plate to stop her grinding, as she clenched in pain. She had, said a CNN report, experienced a level of suffering that would 'test the nerves of a soldier'.

Now she was to undergo a procedure never before done in Africa. Called 'cultured epidermal autograft', it had not yet been used outside the United States because the newly grown skin had to be administered within 30 hours of it leaving the laboratory. And even if the skin did make it to the patient on time, there was no guarantee it would work. It could tear or become infected.

At Garden City Clinic, Dr Mia and his colleagues were in constant contact with the American lab. Human tissue import and export permits had be obtained from the Department of Health. Pippie's tiny biopsies, sent three weeks earlier, were to be returned as 40 transparent sheets of skin, roughly the size of playing cards. Dr Mia had to know exactly what to do with them when they arrived.

Filming such a procedure can feel like an intrusion. Amalia felt almost guilty for asking, but was delighted when her request got the thumbs-up from Anice, Erwin and Dr Mia. On a June morning, she and presenter Chantal Rutter Dros and cameraman Dudley Saunders prepared to spend the day at the hospital.

First came a visit to Pippie's isolation room to film her before the op and to interview her parents. As a news reporter, Chantal had done several stories on people who'd been maimed and disfigured by fire, so she knew what to expect. Dudley was also a hardened newshound, used to being in the thick of things. But this time he hoped the artificial distance created by the camera would make filming easier. He had a daughter at home, also called Isabella, also three years old.

While they were scrubbing and putting on face masks, Anice Kruger, whom they'd never met, burst into the room, her hair streaked pink, Pippie's favourite colour. Chantal liked her immediately: she was a whirlwind of energy, excited that the big day had arrived and excited to have *Carte Blanche* there. Only 28, she'd spent the past six months by her daughter's bedside and knew as much, if not more, than some of the doctors. She was completely unaffected by the way Pippie looked and whipped back the sheets to reveal the full extent of her injuries to the camera. She expertly adjusted drips, massaged her daughter's skin, applied Vaseline to her scarred lips and acknowledged that this had become her home. All Pippie could do was gaze at them through long lashes that had somehow survived the fire, and give the occasional whimper. She'd lost her ability to talk.

But her parents certainly hadn't. Chantal conducted a frank and forthright interview with Anice and Erwin by Pippie's bedside. Yes, of course Erwin felt crippled by guilt over the incident that had brought untold suffering to his daughter and changed their lives forever, but they were strong and had faith that God would make things right again.

While they were doing the interview, 40 pieces of skin were on a 21-hour flight from Boston to Johannesburg. Once the consignment arrived at OR Tambo International Airport, a blue-light escort would be required to get it to the operating theatre. Dudley's assistant, JP, mounted small hands-free point-of-view cameras in the emergency vehicle that would be transporting the skin. Meanwhile, Dudley filmed Chantal's links: 'The countdown has begun at Garden City hospital – the skin has arrived from Boston, Massachusetts, and is on its way and should be here within the hour.'

There was a quick interview with a nervous-sounding Dr Ridwan Mia, who was conscious that the eyes of South Africa were upon him. After her parents, Dr Mia had become Pippie's favourite person. He's definitely the type any girl would want to bring home to meet mum – handsome, with impeccable dress sense and a gentle demeanour. The interview was cut short – the skin was on its way at breakneck speed from the airport, accompanied by a doctor from Genzyme-Sanofi. The pieces of skin would be viable for only a few more hours. Fortunately the trip took 18 minutes as opposed to the usual 45 – no wonder politicians love blue-light escorts.

Thankfully, the *Carte Blanche* film crew was the only one in the operating theatre, as it was small and cramped and hot – but apparently the perfect temperature for this life-changing surgery. Pippie was asleep, and nurses washed her body with a brown disinfectant that made her look like a little golden statue under the lights.

Shortly after 7pm the theatre door burst open and a cardboard box was wheeled in. Inside was a sturdy metal case with a glass door that had begun its journey in Boston. Conscious of the time remaining for the cells to stay alive, Dr Mia lost no time in flattening the translucent grafts against Pippie's open wounds, making sure they made contact with the blood vessels. He started with her thighs, then her chest, hands and arms, face and neck, even painstakingly covering the damaged areas on her hands and fingers.

Outside, Anice cradled her other child, one-year-old Arno. 'I trust Dr Mia with my life ... he will bring her back out,' she said.

Two hours later, Dr Mia and his team were done. Pippie was bandaged up like Tutankhamun and wheeled back to high care. The mood in the theatre was celebratory.

A week later, the bandages were changed. Ninety per cent of the skin graft had taken. New life in the form of blood vessels was clearly evident on her chest. Now the grafts needed to thicken and pigment.

Dudley and Chantal moved on to other stories, but Amalia kept in touch, knowing that viewers, who'd responded with such interest, would want a follow-up. Once the bandages were off, Pippie and Anice moved to a rehab hospital and later to a cottage in Joburg, to be close to the doctors and to physiotherapy. Pippie had to be put into boot splints to help her stand upright, had to have dry needles inserted into her muscles to enhance mobility, and had to learn to talk again, something Anice missed: 'I just want to sit and have a conversation with her again like before. I just want to hear her voice, and her telling me what's wrong and her telling me that she loves me.'

Amalia visited her at home to film her progress and was amazed to discover that the busy Dr Mia even made house calls. He was delighted with Pippie's progress, to see that she was responding to different stimuli, following her mother around the room, eating like a horse, grasping things. And one day she would grasp the enormity of what had happened to her.

In 2013 the 'Pippie se Gesiggie' Foundation, started by the Krugers, funded a skin transplant operation for five-year-old Celiwe Maseko, who'd suffered extensive third-degree burns.

Georgina: Making a Difference

Karolina Andropoulos: 'I lost a little girl called Georgina. I was terribly moved by, of course my daughter first, and by all the other children I had seen in state facilities both here and abroad.'

Few at *Carte Blanche* had ever met Georgina Wurr, the muse behind the Making a Difference campaign. She died on 5 April 2008, only seven years old, having suffered more than many adults do in a lifetime. She'd been diagnosed with neuroblastoma, a childhood cancer, in 2001, while living in Australia, and was treated at the Sydney Children's Hospital, but in 2006 returned to live in South Africa with her mother, Karolina Andropoulos, and older sister, Claudia.

Determined to find herself a positive focus after Georgina's death, Karolina decided to try to kick-start a project she'd seen work amazingly well at the Sydney Children's Hospital. That institution maintained its standard of excellence through a fundraising foundation, which formed financial partnerships with businesses and community groups. Such arrangements enabled state hospitals to afford the latest technology and treatments and to create a homely atmosphere for children and parents who spent weeks, sometimes months, there. Said Karolina: 'It was focused on creating a world, an opportunity for each and every child without discrimination, and it was a joyous environment.'

The paediatric departments at what was then Johannesburg General, now Charlotte Maxeke Academic Hospital, were not joyous places. After their return, Georgina had been treated at the hospital on occasion and the family had got to know Professor Peter Beale, the head of paediatric surgery, who'd operated on Georgina before she died. From discussions with him, Karolina became increasingly aware of how much the hospital could benefit from a project like the one at Sydney Children's. It seemed a perfect starting point. She began making tentative approaches to potential sponsors, but realised she needed high-powered media support to make the idea fly. *Carte Blanche* would be the perfect aircraft, but for that she'd need to bend the ear of George Mazarakis. A phone call to him went unanswered, so she engineered a meeting through a friend who was acquainted with Michelle, the wife of George's business partner, Jon Sparkes.

George reluctantly sat next to Karolina at a function hosted by Jon and Michelle – reluctantly, because saying no to someone who has just lost a child isn't easy. But Karolina, garrulous and glamorous, has a way about her and persuaded him to meet with Professor Beale, who took them on a tour of the children's wing at Charlotte Maxeke, where staff with the best intentions in the world were doing what they could for their tiny patients in dilapidated facilities and substandard conditions.

A few days later, George arrived at the weekly *Carte Blanche* editorial meeting with a plan. An editorial meeting is, in the words of Derek Watts, a bunfight between hot-headed producers, researchers and presenters, where tempers are raised and egos trashed in the name of finding and producing journalistically excellent and entertaining stories.

George is a small man with big ideas, which often meet with resistance because they seem out of reach: 'Guys ... we're turning 20 this year and to say thank you to our viewers and to the country, why don't we ask big business to help us raise money for sick children in a unique way?' The initial response ran along these lines: 'Can't we just concentrate on this Sunday's show, instead of spending time on something unachievable? Why would corporates give money to a TV show they usually run away from?'

George had all the answers: because most big companies have corporate social responsibilities that need to be met; because *Carte Blanche* was a well-known brand and could be entrusted with their money and could give them positive exposure on television.

The Sydney Hospital Foundation had raised A$100 million in its 20-year existence. What was to stop *Carte Blanche* marking its 20 years by raising a million for every year on air, not just at Charlotte Maxeke, but countrywide? The Making a Difference campaign was born.

The first task was to identify hospitals and their needs, and then, armed with their wish lists, to approach big business. *Carte Blanche*'s production manager at the time, the youthful but super-efficient Jo

Munnik, was tasked with making the initial contact with the heads of the major state hospitals. 'No, thank you,' was the response from Dora Nginza and Frere hospitals in the Eastern Cape; they didn't need help from a show that, in various stories over the years, had accused them of being responsible for neglect and suffering. But Charlotte Maxeke was obviously in, as were Steve Biko in Pretoria, Chris Hani Baragwanath in Soweto, Universitas in Bloemfontein and King Edward in Durban, albeit with some degree of cynicism. Although all were in dire straits, the campaign's acronym, MAD, seemed apt. Having become used to begging for proper equipment to help save little lives, it seemed amazing that a TV show was now saying 'write it all down and we'll see what we can do'.

Jo had never heard of a defibrillator or a digital hanging theatre, but after a few months she could've become a hospital equipment sales rep. She organised meetings with Professor Beale, his equivalent at Bara, Dr Graeme Pitcher, his successor, Dr Jerome Loveland, and Professor Ken Boffard at Charlotte Maxeke. They sat for hours with the *Carte Blanche* MAD team, explaining every piece of equipment, the extras needed to make sure it worked properly, and the staff training required to make it work. The doctors examined warranty plans and cost estimates, met with potential suppliers, facilitated meetings with hospital CEOs and promoted the campaign to colleagues. Some of the requests sounded basic and doable: new linen, the painting of wards, televisions, cots, ventilators and humidifiers. Others were far too expensive: a laparoscopic operating theatre, a full-body scanner, a cardiac heart-lung machine, a brand-new post-operative high-care ward, a surgical high-care unit, incubators, diathermy and sonar machines. While Jo went from hospital to hospital coordinating the wish lists, the chatty and charming *Carte Blanche* researcher Quereshini Naidoo, also a Radio 702 talk show host, began making tentative calls to the PAs of captains of industry and got a slender leg in the door. They set off for the first meeting, with KFC – Que in high heels and a business suit, George his usual smart self, but a little worried that he'd set the bar too high and was being downright forward. Half an hour later, after a meeting with KFC's S'thembile Shabangu, who, said George, immediately 'got' what they were trying to do, they had R1.2 million.

This donation laid the foundation: KFC had entrusted a television show with its money; from here they could move on.

Once the word was out, the campaign took off. Nedbank's Pinky Moholi was so taken with the idea that, as well as donating R1 million from the company coffers for five dialysis machines, she dug into her own pocket: 'I thought that I would donate R50 000 towards buying … an ECG machine, primarily because the focus is children. These are teaching hospitals for future doctors. If they don't have basic equipment, what kind of doctors will we produce?'

In just six weeks, the R20-million target had been reached.

Insurance tycoon Douw Steyn made a personal contribution of R1 million, while mining group Xstrata, MTN, Discovery Health, ABSA, Nestlé, IDC, Transnet, Standard Bank, McDonald's, Browns, Hollard and a string of others followed suit. Some of them increased the amounts as the success of the campaign became evident. Even members of the public chipped in, like the Grade One schoolboys of St Andrew's School in Bloemfontein, who raised R40 000. Everyone seemed inspired and motivated because of *Carte Blanche*'s involvement.

The initial requests for equipment expanded to include building reno-vations. Mining giant BHP Billiton, with a bit of arm-twisting from George, agreed to a staggering R20 million for a brand-new paediatric unit to replace the run-down, leaking and cockroach-infested build-ing at King Edward Hospital in Durban. Then came another R5 million towards equipment at Kimberley Hospital. The campaign was becoming massive.

The procurement of equipment became too big a job for Jo to do in addition to her production management tasks, so part-time staff were hired. Karen Brooks and Kathy Ferreira – neither of them the retiring sort – became procurement managers, and soon everyone at *Carte Blanche* was *au fait* with the most modern hospital equipment in the world, who made it, how it worked, how much it cost, and why it was taking so long to be delivered.

The millions had to be carefully managed; an investigative TV pro-gramme can't make mistakes with other people's dough. A registered trust was set up; lawyers Webber Wentzel and accountants Deloitte offered their services *pro bono*, making sure funds ended up where they should.

Karolina became patron of the 'Making a Difference' Trust and chief fundraiser, working without a salary, deciding what should be procured next and dealing with architects, builders, planners, plumbers and painters, as well as provincial and national health departments. Sometimes she found it completely overwhelming; at other times it seemed that anything was possible. Like the inclusion of two welfare organisations struggling to cope, with erratic funding, with increasing numbers of abandoned and orphaned children. The homes they ran needed equipment for skills development, containers for daycare and computer centres, vehicles to do community visits, swings and jungle gyms, and salaries for the staff.

A series of stories was done showing conditions at the hospitals and charities. At Bara, for example, 12 ventilated ICU beds were expected to serve 24 000 babies delivered every year; King Edward had no resuscitation room, minimal equipment, no isolation wards and no facilities for mothers. State hospitals generally were severely under-resourced and certainly not conducive to the recuperation of child patients.

As equipment was delivered and refurbishments were done, there were report-backs. A story showed a three-year-old who had been born at Bara with her bowels outside her tummy; she needed an operation, which was not possible until an ICU bed became available. A year later, the same hospital had a neonatal post-surgery recovery room and high-care ward, as well as an operating theatre complex with two theatres, able to treat efficiently babies with the same condition.

Every time there was a handover of a new ward or new equipment, the nurses burst into song, the sponsors into tears. And every time George Mazarakis watched a campaign story and saw delighted doctors beaming over state-of-the-art resuscitation units or incubators, he got emotional, amazed by the generosity of South Africans, horrified at what mothers and children and dedicated doctors and nurses had had to endure and proud that *Carte Blanche* had moved beyond its core function with such positive results.

Karolina was overrun with requests for help, particularly in neglected rural areas. Another charity was added: the 1000 Hills Community Helpers in rural KwaZulu-Natal, run by the indefatigable Dawn Leppan. There was a changing of the guard in the Eastern Cape Health department, and doctors there asked if Dora Nginza and Frere hospitals could benefit too. Karolina flew to Port Elizabeth and East London to meet with officials and to assess their needs: 'I think that we're all fairly aware that the Eastern Cape is an area that has many challenges, and we'd like to be part of the solution ... We'd need R15 million for starters, but just for starters ...'

At King Edward, she attended sod-turnings and site meetings, despaired when a geotechnical report said the project was doomed because of the fine marshy soil, and then rejoiced when clever engineers made a plan.

On a warm winter's day in Durban in June 2012, a brand-new hospital was handed over to the Department of Health, the first time that a television programme had done anything of this kind. The new BHP Billiton Centre of Excellence looked nothing like the gloomy building of old, with vibrant colours, natural light and ultra-modern facilities. At the ceremony, M-Net CEO Patricia van Rooyen called the Making a Difference campaign inspirational: 'For the first time in our country, a television programme has been the force behind real change. It is a beacon of hope ... and a testimonial to the passion, dedication and vision of a group of remarkable people ... a group of remarkable South Africans.'

And to the invisible force behind it, who will always be a child.

Karolina: 'I think Georgina is with us in spirit and represents the value ... of each and every child ever born.'

By the time of *Carte Blanche*'s 25th birthday, close to R100 million had been raised.

Mama Jackey: the Angel of Soweto 11

In 2001, *Carte Blanche* researcher Nikki Lindsay was looking for an inspiring story for that week's show. On the inside pages of the newspaper she happened upon an article on what sounded like a remarkable project, led by a visionary teacher named Jackey Maarohanye.

Mama Jackey had taken it upon herself, after some sage advice from Nelson Mandela, to source problem kids from various schools throughout Gauteng and to give them special tuition in unused classrooms at the Soweto College of Education over weekends. It was an unconventional and innovative set-up: Mama Jackey was the only teacher and she trained the older children to coach the younger ones, not only in school work, but in gardening, singing and character-building, with great emphasis on God and religion.

Not everything had gone smoothly. Mama Jackey was having problems with the provincial Education department. It had accused the Ithuteng Trust, the NGO she had set up ('*ithutheng*' is Sotho for 'never stop learning'), of being a bogus institution, without financial records, tutors or previous addresses. MEC Ignatius Jacobs had sent a report to President Thabo Mbeki, describing the learners as 'a violent lot', and saying that they were trashing the building they'd occupied.

The President's office instructed Jacobs to find an amicable solution. The Ithuteng kids had obtained a 100 per cent pass rate the previous year. According to Jackey, the department just couldn't stomach the fact that a 'school' without teachers was producing such fantastic results. The department was trying to tarnish the reputation of the Ithuteng Trust, she said, with allegations that could harm potential international funding.

Nikki thought Jackey sounded like a feisty character with her heart in the right place. She'd taken the Department of Education to court, and they'd been ordered to find suitable alternative classrooms for the kids of Ithuteng, failing which they could continue using the disputed college premises. MEC Jacobs was accused of showing 'disturbing hostility towards the education of the black child'.

Nikki passed the information on to producer Odette Schwegler, who'd been working on a series of dense and difficult investigative stories and was relieved to be assigned to something positive and uplifting.

On Sunday, 13 May 2001, *Carte Blanche* broadcast 'The Angel of Soweto'. Using archive footage to great effect, it told the story of a lost generation who'd grown up in turbulent townships in the Vaal Triangle and the East Rand, where they'd witnessed unspeakable acts, even seen their parents killed. To deal with their pain they'd turned to drugs, crime and prostitution. Just when everyone had given up on them, Mama Jackey had come along, as if sent from Heaven, and put them on the right path. In the two years since she'd started out, with a zero bank balance, she'd taken in 1 500 rough diamonds and turned them into gems.

Presenter Les Aupiais remembers the first shoot, under the trees at the makeshift Ithuteng School, listening to heartbreaking tales of abandonment, sexual abuse and violence.

One story stuck out: a teenager named Lindiwe, hair in long braids, dressed neatly in Ithuteng T-shirt and gray gabardine trousers, who recounted the trauma of her young life. Through tears that welled up and splashed down her cheeks, she spoke of the killing of her father, of seeing his 'headless body' staggering down the road in Thokoza.

Lindiwe was a fragile teenager, and, although the headless body sounded a bit over-dramatised, neither Odette nor Les felt inclined to challenge the account of a sobbing adolescent whose first language wasn't English and who'd been forced into prostitution after her father's murder. Les gave Lindiwe's hand a comforting squeeze.

Most of the children recounted similar litanies of horror, all quite believable in a country that had emerged from a violent and abusive past, and all validated by the Truth and Reconciliation Commission.

There was Lebogang Makheta; walking down a Soweto street, the eloquent but troubled teenager poured out his heart to Les and the crew. He'd arrived home one afternoon in the early 1990s to find his mother's body 'crushed by an Inkatha spear that cut across her stomach', and his father riddled with bullets. In a sorrowful voice, eyes downcast, Lebogang told of how his little sister had clung to his mother's body, crying '*Mama, tsoga ke lapile!*', Sotho for 'Mum, wake up, I'm hungry!'

The gruesome accounts were backed up by Jackey, who explained, also with wide, moist eyes, how she'd saved these wayward children from a life of crime and turned them into responsible citizens.

One thing that seemed slightly incongruous to Les was Jackey's outfit, a canary-yellow leather ensemble. Apart from the fact that it drove the sound operator mad because it creaked, as new leather does, it looked expensive. But, Les reasoned, who was she to begrudge a selfless angel a little splash on smart clothing? This was an extraordinary woman, who had gathered society's castoffs and turned them into model citizens.

Odette thought the outfit was an attempt on Jackey's part to look 'smart for TV'. After the interview, she asked her to change into something more practical for shooting the scenes with the kids at the school. She chose a navy tracksuit, and there were touching images of her mingling with her charges, wiping away tears as they sang, holding hands as they prayed, eyes tightly shut, gently swaying with emotion.

There was video footage of a march, in which Jackey had taken her young charges to a dam in Soweto to throw away their 'weapons', recalling Mandela's famous 1990 call to 'take your guns, your knives and your pangas and throw them into the sea'. There were mostly sticks on Jackey's march, but a gun could be seen lying in the shallow water.

She told Les she'd given up waiting for politicians to try to come up with initiatives to change the lives of delinquent youngsters: she was now appealing to the corporate sector. The story did just that; big sponsors – both local and international – stepped up. Here was a woman dealing with the horrors of the past in a practical way and showing everyone how to do it. Mama Jackey and 45 of the kids went to New York for special counselling courses; the UN presented them with inspirational leadership awards; they sang for former President Bill Clinton the day he moved into his offices in Harlem.

In the *Carte Blanche* Africa studio, which rebroadcast the story, presenter Doreen Morris congratulated Jackey on winning an international award for the 'most innovative NGO'.

Innovative it certainly was.

At the opening of Parliament in 2001, President Thabo Mbeki spoke of Jackey as an inspiration and called her school 'the dream of Africa'. Jackey and the Ithuteng kids touched the minds, spirits and souls of everyone they met. She had only praise for *Carte Blanche*, describing the initial story as 'a master key to even the tightest door. Everybody in the USA who watched that video was in tears, but the beauty about it is that it made people lend a hand to the entire body of the Ithuteng students.'

Former *Carte Blanche* story editors Joy Summers and Peta Krost remember also being moved to tears when the students arrived in a beat-up old bus to sing their gratitude in the parking lot outside the *Carte Blanche* offices. Another story was produced, entitled 'Angel of Soweto Returns from New York', and later the Ithuteng students were invited to sing live in the M-Net studio. Executive producer George Mazarakis, who'd come across many a chancer in his years at the SABC and six years at *Carte Blanche*, found her inspiring: a good woman doing good work. He invited the Ithuteng choir to sing at his church.

Graduation ceremonies at Ithuteng, with its 100 per cent pass rate, became big affairs. Joy, Odette and Ruda Landman attended some of the early ones as guests of honour; in later years, President Mbeki was a guest speaker and his wife Zanele handed out the prizes. He called Ithuteng an outstanding example of 'what can and must be done'. Yvonne Mokgoro, a Constitutional Court judge and chair of the South African Law Reform Commission, became patron of the Ithuteng Trust.

Ruda's first meeting with Jackey was at one of these early graduations. She wrote about it in her book, in a chapter called 'A Down-to-Earth

Angel', describing it as 'the most joyous occasion she'd ever witnessed'. Sponsors handed out bursaries, a car for the Trust, food and clothing. Then the mood changed and the orphaned students performed a play, with scenes that reflected where they had come from. There was glue-sniffing, mock rape and assaults, during which some students became so emotional they had to be helped off the stage.

There were more follow-up stories on *Carte Blanche*. Ruda and Odette tackled the rape issue, which was told through the eyes of teen rapists, who were supplied by Mama Jackey. As so often happens, the boys had themselves been victims, and had been raped by uncles, fathers and coaches. They were, Ruda concluded, 'speaking out for the sake of the community ... so that villains could be apprehended ... and that all of us who live in the wood can be safe once more.'

Jackey and her students became *Carte Blanche*'s 'pet project'. Combined Artistic Productions paid the fees for two of them, Thomas and Nosipho, who were interested in studying journalism. They even worked as interns in the office during their varsity breaks. When troubles continued with the Department of Education, George and Peta went and fought for Jackey and the kids.

The only discordant note was Jackey's outfits. Producer Bernadette Maguire, who could, and still can, sniff out a crook from a mile away, thought Jackey was just too slick, decked out to the nines in her Escada clothing. Something didn't ring true. And, as the years passed, Odette, who'd initially been bowled over by Jackey and the kids, became less enamoured of her. She felt she was constantly looking to promote herself, and that sometimes her courtship of the media seemed a little too vigorous.

But it was to be five years before Mama Jackey was exposed, before the Ithuteng Trust's gates were bolted and funding withdrawn.

The unravelling of the Angel of Soweto came gradually. In 2004, one of the students, named Fiona, arrived at the *Carte Blanche* offices, complaining to Peta that her school fees hadn't been paid. She also hinted that much of Ithuteng was founded on lies. George and Peta were astonished and weren't quite sure what to do. Jackey Maarohanye was a friend, trustworthy and believable. Then another bunch of students began complaining about the non-payment of fees. Some basic interviews were done, but most of those with gripes had been expelled from the school and seemed to have an axe to grind.

Carte Blanche researchers began investigating Ithuteng's finances, but, without a money trail, and with only unsubstantiated allegations, there seemed no solid evidence against Jackey.

While Odette went off to have the first of her four children, Peta organised for Ruda to do a follow-up interview with Jackey, who gave her a tour of the much-improved Itutheng facilities. Funds had been donated by the US National Basketball Association (NBA), and there was now a double-storey hostel with dozens of bunk beds, new linen, TV sets and even toiletries. It all looked rather too neat and unlived-in, but Jackey explained that the 200-odd abused and abandoned children who lived there were away 'on camp'. Ruda, believing the complaints against Jackey to be trumped up, asked about Lindiwe and Lebogang from the original story. They were doing well, Jackey said, and were studying at tertiary institutions. There seemed no reason to doubt her.

Then, out of the blue, in 2006, a distressed Jackey phoned George Mazarakis, saying she was on the run because her life was in danger. The police had threatened her, and if they found her they would probably kill her and say she had died in custody. She was hiding out at a friend's home in Johannesburg, too emotional to talk over the phone. Odette set off to meet her with cameraman Michael Yelseth and fellow producer Nicola de Chaud. Jackey was in hiding in Westcliff, an affluent and established suburb that still hints of old money. Her hidey-hole, set high on a hill, belonged to an elderly veteran of the struggle who'd provided refuge for scores of freedom fighters in the bad old days. A drawn-looking Jackey explained that a former student had set fire to the school and that a child had died. She said that the police were protecting the perpetrator and accusing her instead.

Nicola and Odette decided that, this time around, they needed to challenge Jackey's version of events. They contacted the police in Kliptown, supposedly the ones who were out to get her.

Dealing with the police is often an unrewarding experience, as journalists are frequently referred to a 'head office' often unfamiliar with the intricacies of individual cases. So Odette was surprised to have her call returned by a Captain Ellen Ndaba, the commander of the Kliptown station.

She said she knew nothing about threats against Jackey's life, but would be happy to meet with *Carte Blanche* to tell them a few other things about the Angel of Soweto. Intrigued, Nicola and Odette set off to meet the glamorous Captain Ndaba, who told them that Jackey was probably in hiding because there was a warrant out for her arrest for public violence and malicious damage to property. There had indeed been a fire at the school, in a rondavel, where children had been sleeping around a brazier. Although it seemed to have been a careless accident, Jackey had accused an expelled student of arson and then tampered with the scene, planting a 'memorial garden' before police could do their forensic work. And when they didn't arrest Jackey's 'suspect', she had staged a march, pitching up in combat gear and inciting, said Captain Ndaba, 'her hooligan students' to commit violence. Hence the arrest warrant.

Then came a bombshell: checking her elaborate hairdo in a mirror on her desk, Captain Ndaba said, actually, nothing about Ithuteng was true. Everyone in Soweto knew that. The students were just good actors, coached in drama by their director, Jackey Maarohanye. And she could get hold of a bunch of them, right then and there, who could tell Nicola and Odette all about Jackey's tricks. Which she did. Odette immediately recognised Lebogang, whose mother had been 'crushed by an Inkatha spear'. She didn't let on; it had been five years since that interview. But one by one the students told a completely different story. They said they weren't orphans at all and that their heart-wrenching stories had been part of an elaborate hoax.

Lebogang told them how he'd been instructed to fool the blonde lady from *Carte Blanche* (Les Aupiais) in an interview in 2001: 'Before ... Mama Jackey told me that I ... whatever they ask me, I must say it the way she wrote down because it would help us get sponsors and so forth.' He said he'd admitted to being a drug addict and a gangster in order to get his education paid for.

'What about your dead mother?' squeaked a disbelieving Odette. He grinned sheepishly and said it had all been a lie. His mother was very much alive. As for the hostel, built with NBA money, that was just a dummy set up to bring in funds. It was shown off to potential donors and only the chosen few were allowed to sleep there on occasion. That's why students had been huddled in the rondavel trying to keep warm on the night of the fire.

In September 2006, NBA players and coaches visited Ithuteng and attended a memorial service for the child who died in the fire, naming in his honour a new dining room funded by the US Embassy. A page on the NBA website, called 'Basketball without Borders', documented the occasion: 'An emotional and uplifting day was enjoyed by all in attendance. This was the third visit to Ithuteng Trust by the NBA as part of the Basketball without Borders camp.' The website showed a picture of two huge players praying next to some sobbing children. They too were being duped.

But in contacting *Carte Blanche* for help, Jackey had become the architect of her own demise. Once he'd heard the allegations, an outraged George Mazarakis told Nicola and Odette to pursue them with vigour, which they did, with help from researchers Amalia Christoforou and Julie Maritz. For two months they delved deep into the lies buried in Ithuteng's foundations.

In the meantime, a documentary called *Ithuteng*, produced by two young Americans, was winning awards in the US for its 'gut-wrenching portrayal of perseverance in the face of great agony and strife'. The film had received backing from big names like Ben Affleck, Ashton Kutcher and Bono. Oprah had seen it and had donated a million dollars to Ithuteng. She even had Jackey on her show. 'I think Mama Jackey is a living angel on earth,' said Winfrey, as Jackey ran onto the set from the audience, arms outstretched as if she was about to take off. They embraced like long-lost sisters.

But back in Johannesburg, the truth was emerging from what Odette calls the most challenging investigation since the 'Elder Abuse' story. All the sources were flawed: they had lied so exquisitely and convincingly before, so who was to say they weren't lying now? They'd only found a conscience because Jackey had defaulted on their college fees. If *Carte*

Blanche didn't get the story 100 per cent correct this time round, many lives would be ruined. Everything the students said had to be verified by as many witnesses as possible.

Amalia and Julie contacted other students, recording and verifying their stories. One of them was Lindiwe, who'd seen the 'headless body of her father whose head was chopped off'. She'd been one of Ithuteng's shining stars, a leader and a model student.

She'd moved on and had made a success of her life and was working across the road from the *Carte Blanche* offices, at MultiChoice. Interviewed in her flat, she giggled apologetically and said her father was alive and well – always had been. They'd all been actors, she said; their lines had been scripted. She'd never, as she'd claimed in the first *Carte Blanche* story, done sex work, or been abused. 'To me it was just drama. It was just acting,' said Lindiwe.

And the director and scriptwriter was Jackey Maarohanye.

Carte Blanche hired a bus to collect about 30 former students from three locations in and around Soweto and gather them together in the M-Net studio to speak to an incredulous Ruda. The story that emerged had similarities to the Mandela United Football Club scandal of the late 1980s, in which township youths had acted as Winnie Mandela's bodyguards and had obeyed her every command. Some of the Ithuteng boys said they'd been Jackey's henchmen, intimidating and beating up people at her behest and telling lies to raise funds. A teenager named Simphiwe said he'd laid charges of assault and kidnapping after being put in the boot of her car, taken to Ithuteng and beaten with a pipe.

As for being the only school in Africa to achieve a 100 per cent pass rate in the past seven years, that wasn't true either. The Ithuteng graduations had been a farce. Jackey hadn't even asked them if they'd passed or not.

Carte Blanche, its viewers, Oprah Winfrey and three presidents (Mandela, Mbeki and Clinton) had been duped. The only way for *Carte Blanche* to recover was to tell the truth, tell it fast and tell it well.

Auditor Chris Nel was called in to analyse Ithuteng's financial statements and to work out what percentage of the donations had actually been spent on bursaries. Suspicions were that Ithuteng was Jackey's own personal trust fund. Odette phoned her, told her there had been allegations against her, and requested a list of the graduates she'd funded at tertiary institutions. There was an awkward silence, but she reluctantly agreed to ask her daughter, who was clearly part of this 'family business', as it was all getting too much for her. The list never arrived.

Students were interviewed with their parents, who admitted to sometimes being completely confused. Lebogang's mother, Phyllis Makheta, said she'd only found out that her son was an 'orphan' when she'd attended a play at Ithuteng: 'I don't fully understand English properly, but I did ask them – even Jackey – why these children are crying and saying they are orphans, but we are here? She said, "Don't worry, it is a drama."'

Another drama was about to begin. It was time to confront Jackey – a much slimmer Jackey, looking like a million dollars, black camisole peeping from beneath a smart cream trouser suit, and hair immaculately braided. But Odette, Ruda and cameraman Mike Yelseth knew that this confrontation wasn't going to be pretty.

Jackey said the children had turned against her and were spreading lies. She tried to avoid Ruda's questions, and denied scripting lines for the teenagers. No, she had no idea why Lindiwe had said this. And she knew nothing about Lebogang's background: 'I don't, Ruda. I don't. I really do not.'

Mike, on camera, saw a tell-tale sign – a pulse beating furiously at Jackey's throat. And he remembers Ruda, who'd once been Jackey's biggest champion, allowing her to get away with absolutely nothing. Jackey got defensive: none of this could be proved; she couldn't discuss any of the other students with Ruda, because charges had been laid and they were the subject of a court case. It was the same Jackey who'd once been more than willing to discuss anything on camera. But, in Mike's words, 'Ruda kept her shit together.'

What about the money? Chris Nel, whose association with CAP goes back 25 years, in examining the financial records, had established that spending on bursaries, at 54 per cent in 2001, had dropped to six per cent by 2004. And tertiary institutions attended by students revealed that money paid by donors hadn't reached them. But cash of R850 000 had flowed into Ithuteng's coffers in 2003, a figure that reached R2.5 million in 2004 and R1.9 million in 2005.

Carte Blanche researchers could not find a single student who had graduated from a tertiary institution on an Ithuteng bursary. When Ruda asked Jackey for the promised list in the interview, she got snippy and said *Carte Blanche* should do its own investigations.

What about the phoney 100 per cent matric pass rate? *Carte Blanche* had checked with the Gauteng Department of Education. Ithuteng was registered with them only in 2005. Of the 36 who had written matric, 22 had passed and none of them had received an exemption. To her knowledge, said Jackey, everyone had passed.

She'd even sent her own son, the now-infamous Molemo 'Jub-Jub' Maarohanye, to New York as one of the 'orphans'. Included in the group was the similarly privately-educated daughter of Justice Yvonne Mokgoro, the Ithuteng patron. But now Mokgoro, the patron of a non-existent trust and also a Constitutional Court judge, said she'd had no idea the children were disadvantaged, or that the 100 per cent pass rate, something Jackey publicly held up as the greatest measure of her success, was a misrepresentation.

Ruda asked Jackey about the hostels that the students said were just for show.

Ruda: 'How many of the students live in the hostels?'
Jackey: 'About 140.'
Ruda: 'Permanent.'
Jackey: 'Permanent, 140.'
Ruda: 'Now?'
Jackey: 'As it is now.'

Carte Blanche set up surveillance outside the Ithuteng hostels. There was no movement at all. Not one child came or went. In the strangely chosen words of the private investigator they'd hired: 'The gates at Ithuteng are as quiet as the gates of Heaven.'

In studio on 19 November 2006, Derek Watts said: 'over more than 18 years of *Carte Blanche* we've brought you heart-warming stories of wonderful people who've uplifted communities and left us in awe of the power of the human spirit ... one of those featured the larger-than-life

Mama Jackey, who had turned around troubled lives at her school, Ithuteng ... now it is time to bring you the latest chapter in the life and times of Mama Jackey. But this one is not so easy to tell ...'

The broadcast unleashed a storm, with headlines like: 'Angel of Soweto a fraud, TV show claims'; 'Trust Head Caught Out as Liar'; 'Mama Jackey No Angel'; and 'Bill Clinton, Oprah Winfrey and Nelson Mandela ...

Zapiro cartoon for Independent Newspapers, 22 February 2007

request copies of the explosive exposé ...'

But Jackey hit back, telling everyone that it was an elaborate smear campaign. The board of Ithuteng released a statement, saying that the broadcast was one-sided and that *Carte Blanche* had taken the word of thugs. But board chairman Joseph Kanagka distanced himself from the statement and resigned, saying it was bogus and had been released by Jackey's daughter.

In 2007, Jackey Maarohanye was acquitted of kidnapping and assaulting a journalist from the *Sowetan*, who'd gone to the school to investigate the missing funding. But in the same year she was found guilty of kidnapping student Simphiwe Ncoguthu and was fined R8 000. During her trial, dressed in combat fatigues, she said there were only two 'real women' in South Africa: Winnie Madikizela-Mandela and herself.

For their work in unmasking Mama Jackey, Odette and Nicola won the broadcast category of the CNN African Journalist of the Year awards. The judges said: 'The story showed that we as journalists can be taken in like anybody else, and the programme makers were bold enough to show this and reveal the real situation.'

In 2009, Ithuteng closed its doors.

In 2012, Jackey's son, Jub-Jub, a hip-hop artist, was sentenced to 25 years in jail for killing four Soweto teenagers in a drug-fuelled drag race. A headline in the *Saturday Star* read: 'Mama Jackey's son didn't stand a chance with the example set before him.'

ABOVE: First broadcast, 1988: Bill Faure (left) with Ruda and Derek on the original *Carte Blanche* set.

LEFT: 'Rick Lomba – minutes before he was killed by a tiger in Luanda, 1994'.

ABOVE: Diana Lucas and Derek Watts on a US helicopter over the Persian Gulf bound for the aircraft carrier USS *George Washington*, 1998.

LEFT: Derek becomes involved in an altercation outside the All Blacks' dressing room, Wellington, 1998.

LEFT: Surrounding a recovering Pippie Kruger and her mother are, from top (left to right), Peter Griffiths (interactive editor), Jon Sparkes, Amalia Christoforou, Chantal Rutter Dros; middle (left to right) Mari Truter (PA), Chwayitisa Futshane (researcher), Anice and Pippie Kruger; and bottom (left and right), Karolina Andropoulos and Sasha Schwendenwein (researcher).

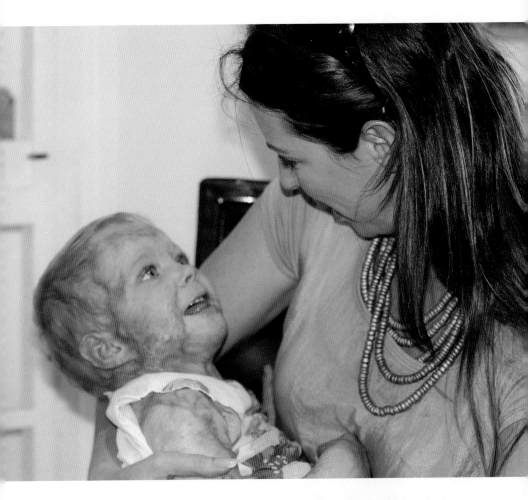

ABOVE: *Carte Blanche* presenter Chantal Rutter Dros with Pippie Kruger, 2012.

RIGHT: Georgina Wurr, 2001–2008, the silent force behind the *Carte Blanche* 'Making a Difference' campaign.

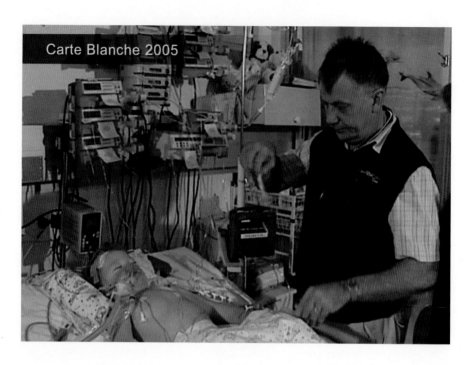

ABOVE: Dr Miles Bartlett with his tiny patient, Gabriel Proost, at Garden City Clinic.

ABOVE: Executive producer George Mazarakis and patron of the *Carte Blanche* 'Making A Difference' Trust Karolina Andropoulos receive the Inyathelo Philanthropy Award in 2010.

ABOVE: Mark Shuttleworth prepares to go into space, 2002. *(Photo: Getty/Gallo)*

ABOVE: Devi interviewing former hostages Bruno Pelizzari and Debbie Calitz after their release by Somali pirates, 2012.

LEFT: Producer Liz Fish did a series of stories proving that inferior fish was being sold at higher prices and that threatened species were being renamed as not endangered.

(Photo: Tony Weaver 2013)

ABOVE: Derek and crew waiting for Braam the builder to arrive to sort out the 'faulty' Mini, 2012.

ABOVE: Researcher Susan Comrie with producer Joy Summers, 2013. *(Photo: Ivan Naude)*

ABOVE: *Carte Blanche* presenters, 1988 – 2013. (Photo: Ivan Naude)

ABOVE: *Carte Blanche* staffers, 2013. (Photo: Ivan Naude)

i-spy 12

Caller: 'I wish to complain about the conduct of Devi Sankaree Govender. She has been watching me have sex.'

Carte Blanche *journalist Amalia Christoforou*: 'Watching you have sex? Where?'

Caller: 'In my bedroom, where else would I be doing such a thing?'

Amalia: 'How did she get into your bedroom?'

Caller: 'You know how, you have implanted a camera into my foot. Now she watches everything that I do.'

The use of spy cameras, pioneered by CBS's *60 Minutes* for sting operations to record corrupt politicians or businesspeople, is now a common tool of TV journalism and certainly a very entertaining one. Sometimes criticised as an unjustified, overly aggressive and unethical technique, it can lead to flights of fancy. 'Are you recording me?' is the paranoid question often asked before a simple information session. But some of *Carte Blanche*'s most watched and most entertaining stories have been the product of clever surveillance by its journalists.

In Sheep's Clothing – 2008

Farmer (on hidden camera): '... a sheep? Female, or male or what?'

Policeman: 'I don't mind, meat is meat.'

Farmer: 'Meat is meat and a man must eat!'

The call that eventually led to this on-camera exchange came in to the

Carte Blanche office one morning in May 2008 from Hammanskraal, a rural town north of Pretoria, home to cattle, casinos and, as was soon to be discovered, corrupt cops. Caller Mariaan Nel said the Hammanskraal farming community had finally had enough of being treated like mobile ATMs by the local police. Bribes, she said, were usually extracted in exchange for turning a blind eye to the employment of Zimbabwean and Mozambican labourers without legal paperwork. But sometimes, even when the paperwork was in order, workers were arrested anyway and only released if the boss coughed up.

Accomplished producer Odette Schwegler, who began her *Carte Blanche* life as a researcher in the days when there was one computer and everyone took turns to use it, accepted the commission with alacrity. Mariaan helped her set up a meeting with complainants in Hammanskraal, where everyone confirmed the modus operandi: employers were targeted via their labourers, and the ringleader of this extortion racket was a certain Captain Makhene.

Proving the existence of corruption was going to be difficult. As is often the case, people are happy to 'tell on' someone over the phone, or off the record, but are less enthusiastic when it comes to showing their faces on camera. Mariaan and Odette persevered. Finally, a Hammanskraal door manufacturer, the incongruously named Marco Di Polo, came forward. He said 30 or 40 policemen had descended on his smallholding some weeks before and arrested him and his workers. Despite proving that they were South African, with valid identity documents, they were released only after Marco paid R2 500. He had no doubt it was a bribe when one of the policemen bent down to put the cash in his sock. Marco and his workers agreed to be interviewed on camera; they'd laid a complaint with the police anyway. But how to catch the offending cops red-handed?

Odette put the story on the back burner while she and fellow producer, Nicola de Chaud researched an important follow-up story. May 2008 had seen the outbreak of xenophobic violence that forced thousands of foreigners in South Africa to flee for their lives. More than 60 people had been killed, and government had promised a re-integration plan for victims who'd had to flee to makeshift refugee camps. Now the camps were closing, but those still in them were too nervous to return to the hostile township communities they'd fled from in the first place. It was not typical *Carte Blanche* fodder, but the programme had extensively covered the attacks.

Then, one morning in early June, came a breakthrough from Hammanskraal. A stock auctioneer-cum-farmer named Stephan Smith was stopped by police while driving with three Zimbabwean employees – all in the country illegally. He was given a choice of being fined R25 000, or paying an 'on-the-spot' cash fine of R10 000. Smith told the officer he didn't have that kind of money, but offered him a sheep instead. The officer was Captain Makhene. He said a sheep would do it for him and made an arrangement to pick up the animal.

There followed a tale of police raids that appeared to have little to do with illegal immigrants and everything to do with making money, and that ultimately led to action being taken against a man who turned out to be the head of crime intelligence at Hammanskraal police station. Captain Richard Makhene was about to make his spectacular debut in the first of three *Carte Blanche* stories in which he would feature. But there were a few hitches.

Odette and Nicola enlisted a fresh and enthusiastic Rhodes University graduate named Peter Neilsen to watch and wait for Makhene. Spy camerawork can be a tedious process. Will the subject pitch up when he says he will? And if he doesn't, will the camera battery run out? Will a dog run in front of the camera and obscure the shot at a crucial moment? Will it record sound? Will the sound be audible?

The date set for Captain Makhene to collect the sheep came and went. Now it became an ethical issue. Was it right for *Carte Blanche* to ask Stephan Smith to remind Makhene to collect the sheep, or could that be regarded as entrapment? After much debate, it was eventually decided for Smith to make one phone call to see if Makhene was still keen. He was, but Odette and Nicola decided that if he didn't turn up this time, they'd have to settle for a story without the on-camera evidence. Makhene agreed to collect the sheep the following Saturday. And so, while most Hammanskraal farmers were watching the Springboks play Wales at Loftus, Peter Neilsen set up the spy camera at Stephan Smith's

Livestock Auctioneers. The camera was positioned in a pot plant to take a wide shot of the area near the sheep pens where they expected the policeman to park and load up his booty. When a police car was spotted coming down the driveway, Peter switched on the camera, turned on Stephan's microphone and hid in the bathroom, where he recorded sound on a second camera. Ten minutes later it was in the bag – that infamous shot of a sheep being loaded into the back of a police vehicle.

The rest of the shoot, in Odette's words, 'had fairy dust sprinkled on it'. There are those occasions when everything in a story clicks into place without extra shoot days, when the perpetrators are there when you arrive to confront them, and when the interviewees are graduates from case-study school.

Presenter Devi Sankaree Govender joined the crew when the day came to confront the 'sheep uncle', as she later began calling him. When Odette first told her they'd managed to catch a police officer accepting a sheep as a bribe, it took a while to sink in. Huh?

For some reason, the Hammanskraal station commander didn't refer Odette to SAPS headquarters when she requested an interview that would focus on illegal immigrants and corruption. He was happy to oblige and brought along his head of communications, who also happened to be head of crime intelligence – Captain Makhene. Devi remembered his wallet lying on the table in front of him, so full the press stud wouldn't close.

Devi began by asking the station commander why he hadn't followed up on complaints of bribery laid against his officers. The superintendent said this was because the complaints hadn't been in writing.

Her next question was more direct: 'What if I tell you that I have evidence that Captain Makhene takes bribes?' She then confronted Makhene with the news that he'd been caught on camera stuffing a live sheep into the back of his police vehicle. A wide-eyed Makhene insisted that he'd paid for the sheep and that he had a receipt to prove it. He clearly hadn't studied the receipt, because on it was written 'gratis'.

Odette suspected that farm workers were being held in the cells downstairs. Devi asked if they could go there. Amazingly, the station commander agreed, and he and a nervous-looking Makhene accompanied the crew. The camera focused on a Zimbabwean man, whom they'd never met before, who said he was there for not giving a policeman his 'cheque'. Devi asked who the policeman was, and, in a moment that sealed the shoot, a thin finger came through the bars and pointed at Captain Makhene.

The story won for the team a Taco Kuiper Award for Investigative Journalism for 'a local story that told a national tale: that of petty police corruption with large-scale consequences ... And they have done it with great skill, using secret filming to great effect, nailing the culprits on camera, confronting them with their deeds and presenting it all in a precise, well-structured narrative.'

Captain Makhene was suspended from the police pending his corruption trial, but it wasn't the last sight of him for *Carte Blanche* viewers. In 2011 he featured again in a story about the illegal sale of state-owned land at Haakdoringlaagte, near the Wallmansthal military base. But, in March 2012, Makhene's moneymaking schemes came to an end. After a trial during which Odette took the stand and the sheep footage was used as evidence, he was convicted of taking a bribe and given a seven-year sentence.

When Will They Ever Learn?

Another story that used hidden cameras to great effect was produced by Victoria Cullinan in 2001. It came in the wake of revelations that education officials in Mpumalanga had artificially boosted the 1998 matric results. At a news conference in January 1999, Education MEC David Mabuza had proudly announced a 20 per cent increase in the pass rate, from 52 to 72 per cent. But the inflated figures had raised suspicion, and a subsequent investigation revealed massive fraud. In a scandal that rocked the nation, 26 officials were charged, among them director general Faith Sithole, who was fired. Worst of all, 7 000 matriculants, who'd believed they'd passed, were told they had failed.

Craig Padayachee came in as the new MEC for Education and vowed to clean up the rotten department. Two years later, in an interview with

Derek, he said Mpumalanga could now take pride in its security systems. Staff showed *Carte Blanche* how every step of the process was now monitored, from cameras watching the safe where papers were kept to tamper-proof envelopes. One of the people on the guided tour of the department's offices in Middelburg was Joyce Khumalo, assistant director of the Systems section, where the final exam marks ended up. She explained to Derek how marks were captured and verified and said it was 'very foolproof'.

But there followed an exchange between two people sitting in a car, one of them with his back to the camera, face obscured. The other was clearly the same Joyce Khumalo.

Andre: 'So what subjects can you change, increase?'

Joyce: 'You will tell me ... if you say, Joyce, I want an increase by 10 per cent, I can work on that.'

Andre: 'You have to physically type it in?'

Joyce: 'I am in the IT section ... you just have to open the system a little bit.'

Andre (not his real name), for whom Joyce was offering to 'open the system', was the headmaster of a private school and he was secretly recording her. She told him that for R9 000 she could inflate the results of his entire class – 112 matrics – for a mere R80 a head.

The negotiations that led to this deal had started over the phone, some months back. Joyce and Andre had been discussing marks and pupils who were registering, when suddenly out it popped: she was able to change the marks of external papers. 'I can change them up or down,' she said, '... even a 90 per cent pass rate.'

Andre couldn't believe his ears. But what if someone compared the marks and saw that they didn't add up? That wasn't a problem, said Joyce, because the marks would be going straight to her.

At first, Andre was so shocked he didn't know how to respond. But Joyce kept calling, and then made what sounded very much like a veiled threat. She told him she could also drop marks if she felt like it. According to government regulations, unless private schools obtained a 50 per cent pass rate, they could be closed down.

At this point, Andre contacted *Carte Blanche*. He was nervous, but, like Walter Niedinger, who'd set up the Randfontein police (see Chapter 8), he simply couldn't sit back and watch this happening. Victoria and Derek persuaded him to begin recording his phone conversations with Joyce. And so he arranged to meet her to pay half the amount (R4 500). *Joyce*: 'I wouldn't want you to pay me in full, you give me half and then in January when the schools open you pay me the money when you register.'

Andre: 'OK, I will probably be there around 12:30, 12:45.'

Joyce: 'Let's make it 13:00.'

And so Victoria and researcher Desmond Thompson set up a hidden camera in Andre's car in downtown Middelburg. They then moved to a nearby restaurant, and Andre waited for Joyce. She arrived shortly before one o'clock and got straight down to business. She would be sending Andre the previous year's results from all the schools in Mpumalanga, so that he could decide where he wanted to slot in, percentage-wise. But, before any of this happened, Andre had to hand over the boodle. He gave her a cheque, asked her to sign the back of it and write down her ID number, which she did, thereby leaving a trail of evidence. Clearly she'd done this before without any comeback.

On 11 September 2001, Desmond and Victoria set off for Witbank to check Joyce's credentials with the Mpumalanga police. They discovered that, two years previously, she'd been charged with fraud, for allegedly raking in thousands from beauty contestants and businesspeople by promising them incentives in the Miss South Africa competition, of which she'd falsely claimed to be a co-director. It was a simple enough check for *Carte Blanche* to do, but not, it seemed, for the Education department, where she was now employed in a position of trust. Armed with this new information, Victoria and Desmond headed back to Johannesburg to plan the rest of the shoot. On the way back they heard news on the radio that, for a while, overshadowed the satisfaction they felt about their investigation coming together.

The twin towers of New York's World Trade Center had been obliterated in a terrorist attack.

But it was to be two months before 'Exam Scam' was ready for broadcast.

155

An interview with Joyce's boss, Joe Molai, the director of examinations, was set up, ostensibly to discuss what security arrangements were in place for the current crop of matrics busy writing their exams. Mike Yelseth, gifted with what Victoria describes as 'a great sense of occasion', was the cameraman.

Joe assured Derek that his staff members were trustworthy: it would be foolhardy, after the 1998 scandal, for anyone to try anything. Joe was about to be disappointed.

Derek asked if he could show Joe and Joyce, who, fortuitously, had just shown them around, some hidden camera footage.

Wonderful as it is when a story comes together so perfectly, Victoria felt distinctly uncomfortable – she never relished the 'cringe moment'. Joyce walked in, looking bemused, and she and Joe began watching. It took a while, but slowly it dawned on Joyce that she was watching a video of her transaction with Andre. Joe clicked at roughly the same time and his glasses nearly flew off his face as he did a double take. Victoria remembers a pulse pounding so rapidly in Joyce's throat that she worried she was going to have a heart attack. Mike resisted the urge to zoom in on her from the two-shot because he guessed that Joe would turn to look at Joyce for an explanation. She collected herself in seconds and said that she'd actually been 'setting up' Andre because she'd suspected irregularities at his school. But it was top secret and she couldn't disclose who she was working with. Joe looked at her in astonishment. Derek pointed out the small matter of a cashed cheque with her name and ID number on the back of it. Ah, that, she said, was for 'someone else.'

Joe convened an emergency meeting with the MEC, but Joyce wasn't going to hang around to hear her fate. Mike was outside filming an establishing shot of the building, when Victoria spotted Joyce hurriedly leaving the building with her bags, a pathetic figure. It was the perfect parting shot and spoke volumes.

Two days later, windows at Andre's school were smashed. But, he said, it was a small price to pay for achieving justice for the youth of South Africa.

Security Robbers - 2002

In 2002, producer Hayley Levin, whose pilot father, Scully, is renowned for dangerous, daring aviation feats, showed similar chutzpah when she engineered a story that involved installing a series of spy cameras in a house supposedly protected by several security companies.

The idea was sparked during a research editorial meeting, when executive producer George Mazarakis said it would be interesting to see exactly what security guards did upon entering premises after being alerted to a break-in – how could absent residents be sure they didn't get double-robbed? Hayley enlisted help from private investigator David Jones, who had assisted in the 'Turning Back the Clocks' story (see Chapter 8). He agreed to let *Carte Blanche* use his house in the south of Johannesburg. The team rigged cameras in the main bedroom, living area and kitchen, and David took out short-term contracts with several security companies. Because the house didn't have an alarm, David told the companies that he needed guards to do drive-by checks and to respond to emergencies. Over four days, he and Hayley staged a series of robberies: they ransacked the house, pulled clothes out of cupboards in the main bedroom, dumped a box full of Ruda Landman's sponsored jewellery on the floor, left CDs lying around in the lounge and unplugged TVs and DVD players as if they'd been disturbed. They then turned on the camera recorder, concealed by a trapdoor in the ceiling, left the front door ajar and took cover in bushes nearby before phoning to report a break-in. What followed was the ultimate inside job.

The programme was a damning look at the multi-billion-rand security industry, which is quick to cash in on public fear, but not good at providing value for money. The Private Security Industry Regulatory Authority (PSIRA), which is meant to play a watchdog role, stands accused of inefficiency and being unable to enforce its own rules. In 2009, another *Carte Blanche* investigation demonstrated how easy it was to obtain a Level B PSIRA certificate, which allows guards to carry firearms without doing any training at all. So it is up to security companies to vet their own guards, but many don't even bother to check if they have criminal records because they are PSIRA-registered.

Carte Blanche was keen to find out if there were guards who would use an attempted break-in as a window of opportunity. Hayley and David used a stopwatch to time the responses to their break-in calls. But what happened once the guards arrived was so shocking that their less-than-speedy response times seemed irrelevant.

Two guards, from a company called Burglar Alert, entered the house and, on discovering that no one was home, made a beeline for the bedroom, where they casually pocketed a few items from the jewellery case. Then they walked around the house and were heard to say they wished it was dark so they could steal appliances without being seen.

Guard 1: 'If it was night-time, we would have emptied the house.'

Guard 2: 'I don't even have a radio, and there's a portable radio.'

Without knowing what they'd got on tape, Hayley and David set up the same scenario for another company, Walkerville Security. Fortunately Ruda had plenty of jewellery, because once again the guards were like magpies. One helped himself to a brooch, then a bottle of whisky. The other pocketed a cellphone lying on a table.

As soon as they'd left, Hayley and David would go and retrieve the tape and prepare for the next sting. Their faith in the industry was restored when guards from Chubb arrived within five minutes of being called out, secured the area and did all the right things, as did the guards from P&P Security.

But some security guards made themselves right at home. It would've been comic had it not been such a travesty. Hayley's call to SOS ProTecSure in central Joburg saw three guards pitch up after 45 minutes. One of them, Jannie, an area supervisor, began rummaging through the cupboards in the main bedroom. He selected a folder of documents, paged through it, looking for who-knows-what, then burrowed deeper in the cupboard and found a funny mask attached to a wig, which took his fancy. He put it on, drew his gun and went off to the other room to scare his colleagues with a hilarious 'hands up!' It was clearly all in a day's work, for they fell about laughing and didn't turn a hair when Jannie opened the fridge and helped himself to a sausage and swigged Coke straight from a two-litre bottle.

Hayley was delighted when she got back to the office to view the footage: she had the basis for a highly entertaining and damning story with some real 'gotcha' moments. But now the security robbers had to be confronted.

She and presenter Les Aupiais set off to find Daniel and Isaac, the two guards from Burglar Alert. They established that the pair were on duty outside a shopping centre in Lenasia. Hayley remembers Les feeling uncomfortable about doing the interviews – like a teacher going off to scold naughty boys. And that's exactly how they looked. The confrontations made for uncomfortable viewing because the subjects were so clearly guilty.

At first they denied taking anything from the house. When shown the video evidence, Daniel said, OK, it was him, but that he hadn't taken anything, in spite of being shown clearly pocketing items of jewellery. The other guard, Isaac, blamed the owners: 'I didn't want to take those things. Maybe I can say I can blame the owner of the house for forcing us to go there many times to go inside the house and check. Maybe it's where I get tempted by those things.'

Les began worrying that Isaac might have a point. But, reasoned Hayley, how could they plead entrapment when nobody had talked them into stealing and when they'd been hired to secure the house?

Next stop was Walkerville Security, where the footage was shown to the owners, in the presence of the two guards, William and Martin. They were played a rather revealing conversation about a DVD player and how to unplug it.

William: 'The wires are far at the back.'

Martin: 'You are failing, friend.'

William: 'Well, it's up to you, friend. If you get into trouble, I was never involved.'

William: 'You see the problem here? When they broke into the house, somebody saw them. So how are we going to leave without somebody seeing us? At least if there were bushes nearby, we could take it and hide it.'

William: 'The CDs – you can take them, there's no problem.'

Despite being faced with hard evidence, most of the company bosses did neat, choreographed sidesteps and backflips along the lines of 'we don't train them, we just send them out', 'we rely on the Security Officers' Board', 'I can't be responsible for something he does in his individual capacity', 'They're all PSIRA-trained and we just hire them', and, said one, 'We don't get any complaints. It's the first we've ever had.' As Les pointed out, this was hardly surprising: homeowners could be robbed and robbed again in a double whammy, and how would anyone know?

Hungry Jannie, the supervisor, got all red-faced when he saw himself trawling through the cupboard and larking about with the mask, but said he'd merely been looking for 'suspicious' items. And when Les asked him why he had raided the fridge, he responded: 'I didn't really raid the fridge. If I raided it, there will be nothing left.'

His boss, Akkie, said Jannie had been off duty at the time, even though he'd been with two other guards, in uniform and carrying a gun. 'If he's off duty and swears at somebody in the street, I can't take responsibility for that,' was his reasoning.

It was a *Carte Blanche* classic, and the viewers loved it. But Hayley hadn't thought of the consequences and described the ramifications as 'hectic'. Some of the offending security companies weren't pleased to have their guards exposed as thieves during prime-time viewing and began harassing David Jones. He was followed home, forced off the road and threatened with a sawn-off shotgun. An entertaining look at what happens in your own home when you're not there had turned nasty. The lesson learnt was, next time, to hire a house from an uninvolved third party.

Casino Con – 2001

This was another Hayley Levin gem with unintended consequences, and it would have Hayley and Derek Watts 'poeping in their broeks'. It began, as many *Carte Blanche* stories do, with a phone call. Two viewers in Kempton Park believed they'd been ripped off by someone who claimed to have a gambling formula and gave courses on how to win on the slot machines. However, months had gone by and the callers, Ivan and Chris, hadn't won even a rand, despite parting with more than 100 000.

Although it didn't sound like earth-shattering stuff, and was clearly motivated by greed, Hayley thought it would be a funny consumer story. She spent weeks with Ivan and Chris, and they found a bunch of outraged people who believed they'd also been scammed. They'd even started a support group to unite against the alleged rogues.

Dennis Geldenhuys and his wife Katrien had advertised in the classifieds that they had a foolproof way to beat the slots. For a fee, they were prepared to share this with a select group of people. The formula involved learning how to read the signs on a machine that would indicate when a jackpot payout was imminent. For instance, 20 minutes after a 'double-double-double' had appeared on a certain machine, there could be a payout. But it never happened for Ivan and Chris ... or for anyone, other than Dennis and Katrien.

Clearly, Dennis had a winning sales pitch, so Hayley sent an undercover cameraman, wearing specs rigged with a miniature camera, to meet up with him. Dennis, neatly dressed in shirt and tie, seemed a grandfatherly figure – until he opened his mouth. 'My product is not a quick fix ... because quick fixes are scams ... bullshit! Put in quality time, boet, and you are going to have a ball of a time ... they will never take your money again. Never! And never is a very long time. '

By 'quality time' he meant paying R5 000 for course material and spending hours memorising the 'grip signs'. After that came the advanced course, then a specialised weekend away at his game farm, then a series of computer courses with information on 'selected' slot machines and the date of the next jackpot. It just required being at the right machine at the right time. And, said Dennis, if someone happened to be busy on that particular machine, you simply went to reception and got the person called away to an emergency. He didn't disclose how you would know the person's name in order to do this. Perhaps that was one of the 'signs'.

For R150 000, said Dennis, this information was available only to a chosen few. But he was prepared to share it with the undercover cameraman, whom he'd never met. 'I gotta know how big is your need – how big is your greed!'

It was all a lot of nonsense, computer programmers, technicians and the Gauteng Gambling Board told Derek: it was impossible to predict when a machine would pay out.

It was time to confront Dennis, who was clearly a gambling con artist. Derek always causes a bit of a stir wherever he goes, and the staff at Dennis's Kempton Park offices were all a-twitter when the *Carte Blanche* crew arrived. But Dennis, sucking casually on a sweet, was as cool as an ice lolly. He said it was the first complaint he'd ever had about his gambling courses.

Derek: 'Do you know that a lot of people are upset and want their money back? They feel they've been cheated.'

Dennis: 'To be quite frank, you know more than I.'

If there were complaints, said Dennis, it was because people were not following his system 'stringently correct'. He then introduced *Carte Blanche* to some very happy members of his slot-playing club, who swore by his abilities: 'Dennis will take you to a machine and a machine will pay out.' So Dennis agreed to take Derek to a casino to demonstrate his skills. But while Hayley and Derek were awaiting this demonstration, Dennis was hatching plans of another kind entirely.

After the story was broadcast, *Carte Blanche* received a phone call from private investigator Mike Bolhuis, saying Dennis wanted to hire him to 'take care' of Derek, Hayley and all those who had maligned him on the programme. Bolhuis is an interesting character – a sort of Dutch Johnny Bravo without the beefcake – who has, over time, probably taken care of quite a few people. But he wasn't keen to break Derek's knees or to inflict damage on Hayley.

Hayley was in a state, so she and George Mazarakis went to Pretoria to talk to Bolhuis at his extraordinary house, complete with rolling manicured lawns and exotic birds and fish. He met them scantily clad, fresh from a jog, and took them to his lounge, which was possibly his interrogation room, because the focal point was a glass tank filled with venomous vipers. When they managed to tear their eyes away and concentrate, Bolhuis assured them that Dennis meant business and that they needed to get the police involved. So they set up a sting.

On 24 June 2001, three weeks after the 'Jackpot Junkie' story had aired, Ruda was in studio next to Derek, introducing the next instalment, entitled 'Casino Con': 'One for a good smack, two for a thorough beating and three to put him in hospital. That was the code when he hired his hitmen. But it didn't quite work out that way ...' Derek continued: 'Bad enough to catch a con family in the act as we did a month ago around so-called courses for gambling, but the story didn't end there ...'

Taking a Gamble

The story opened with grainy spycam visuals of Dennis and Katrien Geldenhuys and their son, Joggie, in Mike Bolhuis's office. Also present was Mike's henchman, who was actually a policeman, Superintendent Du Plessis. The spy camera, which was hidden in an African mask on a shelf behind Mike's chair, had been set up by *Carte Blanche* researcher Seamus Reynolds, who waited outside with a broadcast camera. Dennis had his hit list of names, with numbers one to three next to each name.
Mike: '*Wie is die mense wat die ergste pak moet kry Dennis, in jou opinie?*'
Dennis: 'The guy that must get the worst hiding is Eddie West and Chris Viljoen ... let him know his days are numbered ... Pam as a woman must be nicely sorted out.'
Mike: 'Were these people on that "Carter" Blanche?'
Dennis: 'They were the informants for *Carte Blanche*.'

Of the 18 people on the list, Dennis felt that some needed to be punished more than others. Joggie explained the grading system: 'Number one is just a straight smack, number two is a really good beating, and number three is hospital.'

There was even a cheque for R100 000 so that Mike could get started straight away. But before Derek and Hayley got a 'really good beating', Superintendent Du Plessis revealed himself: 'Right, *mense, ek het slegte nuus vir julle* ... we are here on the orders of the Attorney General, who knows the whole story ...'

At this point two more policemen walked into the room, followed by Seamus, who filmed a disbelieving Dennis. The latter briefly covered his face with his hands as Superintendent Du Plessis continued: '... for conspiring to commit serious offences, serious assault ...' He read them their rights and they were carted off to the Kameeldrift police station to be charged under the organised crime laws.

Derek still dines out on the story of the nice old man with the gambling formula who once put a price on his head.

toxic somalia 13

Bruno and Debbie – 2012

*This story really touched my heart and I can't get Bruno & Debbie out of
my mind ...*
This was the worst Carte Blanche *interview ever, there was no compassion
shown and inappropriate questions were asked ...*
*Devi has no tact. She should NEVER have asked the rape question ...
shame on you* Carte Blanche *...*
... It is no-one's business to know whether such things happened to them ...
*Baie goeie onderhoud, net jammer die persoonlike vraag oor verkragting. Dit
was onnodig ...*

On 26 October 2010, Bruno Pelizzari and Debbie Calitz became the first
South Africans to be captured by Somali pirates. Twenty months later,
after protracted negotiations and the payment of a not-to-be-mentioned
ransom, they were released and became world news.

Durban-based producer Nicky Troll, who'd been following the story since the couple was first captured, lost no time in contacting Vera
Hecht, Bruno's sister, to secure a one-on-one interview on their return
to South Africa. Vera, a Durban book-keeper, who describes herself as 'a
basic working-class South African', had found herself thrust into a world
she never knew existed after her brother and his girlfriend were taken

165

captive while sailing off the Tanzanian coast, on their way to Richards Bay. Suddenly, she was taking calls from a pirate negotiator named Ali, trying to raise an impossible ransom of US$10 million and meeting with officials from the Department of International Relations and Cooperation. *Carte Blanche* had introduced her to Mark Courtney, a South African-based ransom negotiator, who'd allayed her fears that Bruno and Debbie might be killed. They were, he insisted, a commodity to be kept alive. He also gave her insight into Ali, who was now phoning several times a week at any time of the day or night, pressing her to raise the ransom:

Ali (phone recording): 'These people are very angry. What I am telling them now? Tell me something to tell them now; they are listening.'

Vera: 'Please, we'll show you that we will ... that the money is growing. Please don't hurt them! Please don't hurt them.'

Ali: 'I am sorry for you, but now the situation is like this. These people have said, and I am saying, that you have to pay us this amount of money.'

Ali, said Mark, was a professional negotiator working for more than one band of pirates and was accomplished at psychological warfare.

Part of the negotiation process was to establish proof of life by giving the kidnappers questions only the hostages could answer. With Mark coaching her, Vera had established Ali's bona fides by dictating questions for Bruno and Debbie relating to names of pets and colours of vehicles they'd owned in the past. Ali had phoned back with the correct answers.

With some of the money raised through an SOS campaign, Vera paid for a representative from the National Somali Community Board of South Africa to travel to Somalia to negotiate on her behalf, which seemed to get the ball rolling. The final negotiations involved both the South African and Italian governments – Bruno being an Italian citizen. Now, post-release, Vera was faced with a bunch of pushy journalists – whom she'd once relied on for publicity – pressing her for interviews and information. Producer Nicky, who'd stayed in touch with Vera over the months Bruno and Debbie were held hostage, was one of those phoning every day.

One of the drawbacks of broadcasting on a Sunday night is that if news breaks on a Monday or Tuesday, the story can look a little tired by week's end if every other TV show in town has already had a go at it. What Nicky had to do was to get a South African exclusive on-camera interview with the couple.

Mercifully, Bruno and Debbie were alive and relatively well, having spent 20 months being shunted blindfolded between prison quarters and pirate groups in and around Mogadishu.

They were first flown to Italy to be reunited with family there, including Bruno's and Vera's elderly mother. *YOU* magazine had secured an interview with them in Italy and had paid for two of Debbie's children to fly over for a reunion and a photo shoot. Nicky wasn't concerned; *Carte Blanche* would broadcast before *YOU* hit the shelves and, apart from a satellite interview with CNN's Christiane Amanpour, the only local television coverage would be a stage-managed news conference at OR Tambo International Airport on Wednesday 27 June, with the Minister of International Relations and Cooperation, Maite Nkoana-Mashabane. The *Carte Blanche* interview was set for Friday midday. Vera had delivered and Nicky's persistence had paid off.

Devi Sankaree Govender, who had presented the *Carte Blanche* story on the couple's disappearance in 2010, joined Nicky for the shoot at a fancy Joburg hotel that had agreed to serve Bruno a bunny chow for lunch – something he'd apparently longed for while in captivity. In terms of payment, lunch is about as far as *Carte Blanche* will go. Paying for an interview calls into question the veracity of the information: will the paid source tell the truth, or tell the reporter what they want to hear? In a pre-interview chat with Devi, Vera, Bruno and Debbie said that what they didn't want to be asked were questions that could endanger other hostages, like details of the ransom paid. In the interview, Debbie explained how they'd been stripped, paraded and examined by their captors. So Devi had no qualms about asking the question: 'We know that you were physically assaulted ... but sexually?'

At that point, Bruno grabbed Debbie's hand. He said: 'Let's not talk ... I'd rather not answer that.'

At lunch after the interview, while Bruno ate his bunny chow and spoke of his plans to complete a spiritual voyage to India, Debbie took a call from a *YOU* magazine journalist, telling her that she hadn't told *Carte Blanche* 'everything'. A week later, *YOU*'s front cover screamed: 'Debbie & Bruno tell-all hostage interview: I WAS RAPED IN PIRATE HELL'.

But by this time some viewers had already vented their feelings about what they thought was a callous, uncaring interview, threatening NEVER EVER AGAIN to watch *Carte Blanche* and almost issuing a fatwa on Devi. Bruno and Debbie had no problem with the interview and a complaint to the Broadcasting Complaints Commission was quashed.

There was no reaction from the thousands of Somalis living in exile in South Africa, having fled a country which, for centuries, has been a crossroads of commerce. Today, any trade associated with Somalia is perceived as bargaining for people's lives and property. There's no doubt that a ransom, rumoured to be in the region of US$500 000, was paid to secure the release of Bruno and Debbie. Vera refused to provide details, on the instruction of the Department of International Relations and Cooperation. Money is an issue that has since caused a rift between Vera and Debbie and her family, who imply that millions donated for the couple's release has disappeared. Vera was even accused of stashing a million rand in cash in her piano, instead of donating it to a trust set up to rehabilitate the pair following their release. Vera has described Debbie and her family as 'totally delusional'.

In November 2012, Bruno and Debbie, now living apart, travelled to the Netherlands together to testify in the trial of five suspected pirates, arrested after firing on a Dutch navy frigate patrolling the Gulf of Aden. Sixteen Iranian fishermen hostages were found on the pirate boat. Some of the pirates were identified as part of the band that took the South African couple hostage. Bruno and Debbie described the trip to face their kidnappers as 'the closing of a chapter'.

Mogadishu – 1993

Ruda Landman calls Somalia her 'glance into the abyss'. It was mid-November 1993 and she was about to turn 40 in a country in the grip of a civil war. It was a month after the so-called Battle of Mogadishu, in which two US Army Black Hawk helicopters had been downed during an unsuccessful attempt to capture warlords loyal to Mohammed Farah Aidid, the self-proclaimed Somali president, who was accused of trying to control the country by diverting food aid. The story that Ruda, producer Victoria Cullinan and cameraman Mike Yelseth went to do was about how foreign journalists operated in such a hostile environment. There were no commercial flights to what Victoria described as 'an insanely anarchic country'. So they latched onto South African cameraman Tony Wasserman, who was working for US network NBC with his producer Sue Burt, and hitched a lift on a UN plane from Nairobi.

Tony was, said Victoria 'the classic war-savvy cameraman', who, fuelled by adrenaline, had covered conflicts around the world for 18 years. But he regarded Mogadishu as one of his toughest assignments. Here the danger began soon after leaving the rudimentary airport, teeming with military planes and UN soldiers. From the outset, Ruda made it clear she wasn't even going to attempt to be brave ... she would stay in the shadow of Tony and his minders. He'd been in and out of Somalia several times that year, and within minutes of arriving had hooked up with his 'fixers', men from the same clan without whom no foreign journalist could operate safely in the unpredictable country. Some of them would travel ahead with the equipment, because journalists and camera kit in one car were too tempting a target for bandits. Victoria didn't trust their 'guards' for a minute; they were chewing khat, a mild stimulant said to cause excitement and euphoria, and seemed motivated only by the dollar.

They all piled into the vehicles and hurtled at breakneck speed on the treacherous road into Mogadishu. It was nicknamed 'Mad Max territory', because the alleyways and low walls concealed snipers and bandits. Eventually they reached the relative safety of the Al Sahafi Hotel. Sahafi means 'press', and this was the hangout of the international press corps. There was hot water, air conditioning, generators, high walls and armed guards. When things got too dangerous in the city, the roof of the Sahafi provided a perfect view of the hostile world outside. There were satellite and transmitter dishes for phones and for feeding pictures.

Looking down onto the bullet-ridden buildings of the city and into the crowds, the scene was peaceful, but, as Tony said, it could change in seconds. He described an incident some months previously in which six Somalis working for CNN had been killed a few metres from the hotel while journalists watched helplessly from the roof. In the footage Tony was heard saying: '... be fucking careful, they are shooting straight at us ... somebody's hit!' The Sahafi had become a target and the journalists had to be airlifted off the roof. But the only way to make contact with the UN compound outside Mogadishu had been a satellite link via the Pentagon. Hours later, a chopper had arrived and lifted the journalists to safety.

Now Tony was back, this time to cover Mohamed Farrah Aidid's first public appearance in six months. Aidid had been on the UN's most-wanted list and was vehemently opposed to the presence of foreign troops in Somalia. His presence at the Mogadishu Stadium would make world headlines. Ruda felt unsafe; every male over the age of 15 seemed armed to the teeth, and Victoria was terrified that something would happen to Ruda and she'd have explain it to everyone back home. They tunnelled their way through the teeming crowds behind Tony, joined a crowd of journalists and tried to ignore the guns and ammunition slung over shoulders. Aidid, an unassuming man with a bald head and colourful shirt, told thousands of supporters what they'd expected: 'We do not need foreign intervention!' Tony got his story, *Carte Blanche* got theirs and the team beat a hasty retreat. Before they left, they had to get an exit permit from the US military base. It was boiling hot, so they stopped to get a cold drink from one of the army shops. Victoria opened a freezer and found it packed with bottles of Champagne. So they celebrated Ruda's fortieth with Moët and left Mogadishu to Tony and the diehard newshounds.

In Somali culture, it's said that on the day you are born, the day you will die is written in the book of life. Mohamed Farrah Aidid suffered a fatal heart attack in 1996 after being wounded in fighting in Mogadishu. Tony Wasserman collapsed and died of a heart attack in a London street in 1999.

Ilaria Alpi

For 33-year-old Italian journalist Ilaria Alpi, 20 March 1994 was written in her book of life. She had been staying at the Sahafi Hotel and reporting on the withdrawal of foreign troops from Somalia when she stumbled onto another story. It involved the fishing industry. The Italian government had, through a company called Shifco, provided boats to develop commercial fishing in Somalia. But Ilaria Alpi had been tipped off that although the boats were sailing back and forth between Europe and the Horn of Africa, their cargo wasn't fish. It was toxic waste, to be dumped on Somalia's unpatrolled coastline. In the last interview she ever did, Alpi asked a warlord if she could film one of the boats donated by her government, a boat she knew had recently arrived in the northern Somali port of Bosaso.

Ilaria: 'Where is the boat? Can I see it?'

Boqor Moussa (warlord): 'Why do you want to see it? Are you a spy or something?'

Ilaria: 'If I don't see it, I can't report it.'

Within hours of the interview, Ilaria Alpi and her cameraman Miran Hrovatin were murdered on the streets of Mogadishu. Gunmen cut in front of their vehicle and opened fire. Ilaria's bloodstained notebook was handed to an Italian resident of Mogadishu who happened to be on the scene, a man known only by his first name: Giancarlo.

In 2012, *Carte Blanche* broadcast a special report entitled 'Toxic Somalia'. Investigative journalist Paul Moreira took up the story that Ilaria Alpi had been unable to complete. He visited a fishing village where mysterious containers had been washed ashore, where children were born with deformities, and where most of the fish had died. Locals told him of men in protective clothing who'd arrived some years previously and sealed the barrels on the beach. But more barrels had washed up since. Eventually they would rust and break open, releasing their contents.

The documentary moved to a harbour town called Hobyo. Here the men had long stopped fishing; piracy was now their livelihood. A pirate called Fahrat (he even had one leg) confirmed that there was 'smoking

171

toxic waste' all the way up the coast and that foreign ships had destroyed almost all the fishing. So the former fishermen had become modern-day pirates. Anchored off Hobyo was a Korean supertanker seized several months earlier. 'There are two types of pirates. The small ones who attack ships to survive and then there are others who empty our sea of fish and pollute it with their chemical waste,' one of the pirates told Moreira. Before venturing into piracy, they'd proclaimed themselves the nation's coast guards, protecting their seas and shoreline from toxic waste and illegal fishing. But these days they were just pirates – and the scourge of East Africa.

In Mogadishu, Paul and his cameraman visited a children's hospital, where doctors had been struggling for years to deal with an outbreak of genetic deformities, symptomatic of exposure to dangerous chemicals. Cases of children born with urethras poking out of their legs and other urogenital problems had increased threefold in the past 20 years. Moreira's conclusion was that the inexplicable outbreak coincided with the start of the civil war in Somalia.

In Italy, an investigation into Ilaria Alpi's murder eventually uncovered a complex network involved in the illegal trafficking of toxic waste and arms to Somalia. Each ship would transport 10 000 tons of waste at US$100 a ton – so a single load was worth US$1 million. Giancarlo Marocchino, the man who took Ilaria's notebook at the scene of her killing, turned out to be a shipping agent in Mogadishu. It's alleged he knew the warlords and had secured authorisation to dump toxic waste in exchange for giving them weapons.

In October 2010, the first Somali pirates to be tried in Europe were jailed for five years by a Rotterdam court for attacking a Turkish cargo ship.

But none of the Italian industrialists suspected of dumping toxic waste on East Africa's beaches has even been bothered by investigators. And no one has ever been arrested for the murder of Ilaria Alpi.

The Pirates of Puntland – 2009

Nothing about Puntland is normal, according to intrepid Australian newsmen Wayne Harley and Andrew Fowler, who produced an extraordinary story on Somalia, at a time when piracy was on the increase, but access to the region riskier than ever. In November 2008, a British journalist and a Spanish photographer were abducted in Puntland – an autonomous territory in northern Somalia – and spent 40 days in a cave before being released.

The story, also aired as a 'special' on *Carte Blanche*, had made the bureaucrats at the Australian Broadcasting Corporation (ABC) nervous: 'You've got one week in the place and that's it,' the corporate desk jockey back in Sydney had told Harley. And the budget was tight: about US$25 000 to cover their expenses in Somalia, as well as time in London and Paris to speak to shipping experts and the French navy. The two wondered if their bosses were thinking that they wouldn't make it back and that the less money they took, the less would be lost.

Puntlanders often joke that their country is the promised land: God gave it to them because no one else wanted it. The only flights to this arid region on the northeastern Somali coast were in clapped-out Soviet-era turboprops.

And so Harley and Andrew found themselves bouncing along in a bug-infested plane, on the way to Bosaso, Puntland's main seaport. Andrew had the window seat, which he soon realised was a big mistake. The air vent was above him, and when the fan was finally turned on to counter the sweltering heat, a mass of cockroaches vented straight into his hair.

One comforting thing about this trip was a friendship Harley had struck up with Issah Farah, a member of Puntland's new government, who had studied in Melbourne. Farah met the two journalists at the airport, accompanied by a posse of bodyguards, to ensure that they didn't end up in a cave too. And the Puntland president, it seemed, was as nervous as the ABC bureaucrats. He insisted on providing them with a mobile anti-aircraft gun from his own security detail.

First stop was the local prison, where they found a hundred tinpot buccaneers jammed in a cell for attacking foreign fishing vessels. Through the bars, they told a sorry tale of a livelihood stolen from beneath their noses, of watching while Western trawlers with huge nets scooped up everything in the sea, even taking the stones off the seabed.

So they retaliated, and intermittent skirmishes gradually became a well-orchestrated campaign. But nowadays they were no longer seen as heroes in Puntland, because their attacks, as the Minister of Ports explained to Harley and Fowler, had become indiscriminate and had stopped all foreign vessels from coming into Bosaso harbour. He'd personally made sure that several of the fishermen had been arrested.

But there had been no action against foreign trawlers – that would need a well-resourced coast guard. A local fish factory owner confirmed there'd been a whopping 96 per cent reduction in the local catch. Out at sea, the world's navies were ignoring the foreign fish thieves, too, and concentrating on the pirates. None more so than the French navy, which was particularly aggressive in its dealings with the pirates. Andrew spoke fluent French and had extensive contacts within the military in Paris, so managed to get them aboard a warship, under the command of Vice Admiral Gerard Valin. He showed the two Australians video footage of French commandos delivering a ransom of US$600 000 to pirates on board a luxury yacht they'd seized.

After the hostages had been released, the pirates had fled in a speedboat with their booty. Then six helicopters, flown by French special forces, had swooped onto the beach where the pirates had landed and were making off in a 4x4 to deliver the ransom to their headquarters. A sniper on board one of the choppers delivered, as the vice admiral put it, 'a very precise shot to stop the engine'. Out bundled the pirates with AK-47s at the ready, but with six helicopters hovering above them, they decided hands-up was the best option.

The French had won a notable victory. It was the first time any of the more than US$50 million paid out to Somali pirates had been recovered. In heavily accented English, Vice Admiral Valin gallantly declared: 'I could have killed them all, but I did not.'

On their last day in Puntland, Andrew and Harley went back to the Bosaso jail, which was on high alert because there'd been an attempted breakout. The pirate inmates had shown great ingenuity; using a spoon, they had dug out a network of tunnels, almost engineering the collapse of the entire building. Now the spoon had been confiscated, the holes blocked and they had nothing to do but plaster the walls with tragic graffiti – crude images of lobsters and sharks – reminding them of the livelihoods they had lost.

They were, the documentary concluded, victims of the failed state of Somalia and the world's indifference to the problems of a blighted country.

mark, musk and madiba 14

Nelson Mandela: 'It's such an encouragement that a man of your status should take part in this project.'

Mark Shuttleworth: 'Madiba, looking at Africa from space is truly inspirational and there's much work to be done, but much hope for the future.'

This polite exchange took place in May 2002, with Nelson Mandela in the *Carte Blanche* studio and Mark Shuttleworth floating high above the Earth's atmosphere. Also in studio was Michelle Foster, a 14-year-old cancer sufferer. Some months earlier, on a Reach for a Dream outing, she'd told the former president that she wanted to be an astronomer when she grew up. Thinking she'd said 'astronaut', Mandela invited her to the studio with him to chat to Mark Shuttleworth, who'd gone from cyberspace to outer space. And there Michelle and Madiba sat with Derek Watts, linked up via satellite to Africa's first cosmonaut. But the teenager had things other than celestial navigation on her mind: 'I was wondering whether you'd like to marry me?'

Mark was slightly taken aback, but recovered, saying he was honoured by the question.

'So what's it like to be the world's most eligible bachelor?' asked Derek later.

'I am a cranky guy to live with, not a catch,' he laughed, showing that famous toothy gap.

Shuttleworth first captured headlines in 1999, after selling his company, Thawte Consulting, to American competitor Verisign. From the garage of his parents' modest home, he'd burned the midnight oil, doing business in internet security, providing digital certificates for websites the world over. After hitting the jackpot, he gave over a million rands to each of his 63 employees – about the same amount he would make in interest every day from the R3.5-billion deal. 'Part of this is about creating a South African dream – an economic dream ... a belief that if you start in the right places and take risks, you'll win ... it's the belief that it's possible.'

Carte Blanche followed Mark all the way, from that first laid-back meeting in his shorts and slops in Cape Town – soon after he'd bought his only luxury, a sports car – to London the following year, where, in polo shirt and chinos, he travelled in black cabs and his own Bombardier jet. He might be rich and call himself cranky, but he came across as Mr Nice Guy.

The day after the studio link-up with Madiba, mission control in Moscow phoned Michelle at her home in Pinetown. Africa's billionaire cosmonaut was on the line from the International Space Station (ISS), 350 km above the Earth, to continue their conversation. 'You haven't answered my question yet,' she said to him and when he stammered that he needed to know her better, she told him he'd better hurry up. The next time Mark phoned Michelle was from terra firma, but the cancer had spread to her lungs and she was on oxygen, too weak to talk to him. Three weeks after her visit to the *Carte Blanche* studio, she died.

'Afronaut mourns his "bride"' was a BBC headline. It was a wonderful sidebar to a South African success story: a man who'd concluded one of the biggest deals in internet history and become the second civilian in space, only too aware that fortune doesn't smile on everyone.

Sophia Phirippides, who'd produced the 'Internet Billionaire' story, heard about the intended mission from the horse's mouth. She'd been on a harrowing shoot about the police and post-traumatic stress disorder, and was feeling down, when her phone rang. It was Mark Shuttleworth.

He was in Russia and he had some uplifting news for her: he was going into space and was offering Sophia and *Carte Blanche* an exclusive.
Sophia is seldom lost for words, but this time she was, momentarily. Her
first thoughts were: 'Amazing ... an exclusive ... and I've always wanted
to go to Russia!' Then 'shit ... how are we going to find the budget to get
cameraman, producer and presenter there?'

No problem, said Mark; he had his own cameraman, Peter Ribton, and
would happily give *Carte Blanche* whatever footage was needed.

Big-picture thinking has always been a hallmark of George Mazarakis's
editorship. He had no qualms about giving Sophia the go-ahead, and so
began a series of stories – '2001 Space Odyssey', 'Shuttleworth's Shuttle
Stalls', 'Spaceman' and Shuttle Countdown' – with footage fed by satellite via London to keep the story current and up to date.

Mark was doing his preparation at the Yuri Gagarin Cosmonaut
Training Centre at Star City, the heart of the Russian space programme,
where cosmonauts have trained since the 1960s. His was to be the 229th
manned orbital mission on the Soyuz-U, the passenger transportation
craft that would take them to the ISS, a habitable artificial satellite in
Earth orbit. Twice a year, three cosmonauts flew a new Soyuz up to
the station, spent some time there, then flew the old one back, most of
which burnt up in the atmosphere, leaving only the capsule for landing.

Although designed to land by parachute in the Kazakh desert, if
there was an emergency the capsule could end up anywhere between
the Arctic and Antarctic. And so Mark and his fellow cosmonauts –
Commander Yuri Gidzenko, a Russian fighter pilot on his third test flight
and NASA-trained Italian Roberto Vittori – prepared for all eventuali-
ties. They bobbed about in the Black Sea inside a cramped, hot capsule,
their pulse rates climbing from 60 to 180. A specially modified aircraft
took them high up and then plunged, so that they fell at speed, experiencing relative weightlessness for up to 30 seconds at a time. All of
this was filmed by Peter Ribton and sent back to Bernadette Maguire in
Joburg to pass on to Sophia and her co-producer and editor, Jonathan
Pienaar, to weave into yet another fascinating first-hand account of the
makings of a home-grown astronaut.

Apart from the survival training in Russia, they also went to NASA's

Johnson Space Center in Houston, Texas, where weightlessness was simulated in a gigantic swimming pool to accustom them to conditions aboard the ISS. And there was toilet training: peeing into a suction funnel meant not getting too close, or you'd never see it again. Because the air used to direct the waste into special containers was returned to the cabin, it had to be filtered to control the smell. The ins and outs of module domesticity also included the world's most expensive and complicated kettle, used to boil recycled water from condensation in the air conditioning units.

Mindful of criticism that his trip was a self-indulgent splurge and that the US$20 million cost (he later told Derek he'd beat them down to US$14 million) could have been better spent on feeding Africa's starving, Mark had insisted that he be not just a paying passenger, but a fully trained cosmonaut carrying out scientific experiments formulated by South African institutions. These were demands that had put an initial trip on hold, but he eventually got his way.

With Mark at Star City was his flight surgeon, Dr Wayne Derman, who helped prepare his body to cope with zero-gravity conditions, as well as two researchers from the Sports Science Institute of South Africa, who carried out tests on muscle wastage and the amount of energy needed to live and move in space. Mark would also be conducting stem cell and embryology experiments designed by South African researchers.

Blast-off was to be on 25 April 2002 from the launch facility at Baikonur, on the plains of Kazakhstan, and Mark's family was to fly in to watch the launch. Sophia interviewed them in Cape Town, as part of a series of stories *Carte Blanche* did on the preparations. The Durbanville house that had once been Thawte Consulting had made way for the shiny new offices of Mark's venture capital company. Mum Ronelle was a bundle of nerves and excitement: 'I think it's fantastic the way he's done what he wants to do. I would never ever have stood in his way or advised him not to go. The fact that I feel nervous has got absolutely nothing to do with the whole thing.'

T-minus six days: Derek flew to Moscow armed with a small, not-quite-suitable-for-broadcast camera and a satellite phone, which was to give him lots of stress. No producer ever willingly stays behind on a trip, but it seemed that, for this one, Sophia's yen to visit Russia would have to be a vicarious one. The times between launch and broadcast were too tight and she'd have to stay put in Joburg to prepare the story. Footage would be couriered to her and Jonathan during the week, and Derek would fly home with the rest of the tapes after the launch.

But now he was on his way to Star City, 30 kilometres outside Moscow, to meet up with Mark. In the Soviet era, Star City was a top-secret military zone, a closed, self-contained city, access to which was severely restricted. Now the status of the territory had changed from military to civilian and the cash-strapped Russian Federal Space Agency was attempting to make money from commercial space flights. Journalists were welcome, particularly ones with connections to a paying passenger who was about to become a Russian cosmonaut. Mark had spent months mastering the lingo. He'd had no choice. Every button on the spacecraft was labelled in Russian and all the radio comms were in Russian. Luckily, Mark said, 'big red button' was labelled 'big red button'.

Derek tested him: 'How do you say: "comrade, you're pressing the wrong big red button?"'

Mark: '... uh ... Товарищ [tovarish] ... uh ... вы нажимаете на ту [vuy nazhumaete na tu]... uh ... кнопку [knopku]... by which time we've already hit the ground!'

Derek asked Roberto and Yuri if they had confidence in their new comrade:

Roberto: 'He's a very young, talented gentleman, and I was surprised because he has handled many of the difficulties better than I could.'

Yuri: 'He's very effective, very flexible, he can understand anything.'

Now, after seven months of training, the trio was preparing to leave Star City. They were given a traditional Russian sendoff, which meant Champagne and vodka at 7am. In Russia, any occasion calls for a drink, as Mark had learned, no matter the hour.

Derek was to fly to Baikonur separately with the South African contingent. 'Be ready at 5:30, or we leave without you,' was the curt instruction from the military men in charge, who arrived two hours late, clutching big briefcases. They boarded a military plane, the kind with seating along the sides, foldout tables and an open section in the middle.

Soon after takeoff, the briefcases disgorged a mouthwatering smorgasbord: salami, caviar, rye bread, cheeses, pickles and, of course, vodka. Derek, who hadn't been able to find even a cup of coffee at the airport at Star City, waited for the come-hither sign. But the Russians laughed, joked and munched without so much as glancing his way. The South Africans had to make do with a packet of jelly snake sweeties which one of the researchers had in her bag. Not exactly caviar on rye.

Baikonur was a huge, grey Soviet-style establishment where rockets were launched and housed. There was nothing shiny or new about it and Derek, despite being focused on finding a snack, couldn't help wondering about safety. The last time a Soyuz mission had ended in disaster was way back in 1971, when the capsule had depressurised, killing the three-man crew. Mark, who was staying at the crumbling Cosmonaut Hotel complex, was upbeat and confident, and had no such thoughts in his mind. They might be in two-star surroundings, but the Soyuz was one of the most reliable spacecraft in use. Its technology hadn't changed since the 1960s, which was both reassuring and nerve-wracking, he said: 'I've dealt with a lot of software bugs in cutting-edge systems. I'm not sure I want to be flying to space on a cutting-edge system – although every Soyuz that flies is a brand-new Soyuz, handmade, and that's a bit terrifying. We won't know if it works until we press the big red button.'

T-minus five days: Mark walked Derek around the Baikonur gardens, where every cosmonaut plants a tree in the Avenue of Cosmonauts prior to liftoff. The first tree had been planted by the legendary Yuri Gagarin in 1961. Gagarin, the first man in space, died in a plane crash in 1968, aged 34.

There were still final preparations for these cosmonauts of 2002, like being spun around in a 'vomit chair' and being suspended upside down to get their bodies used to their blood shifting. However, said Mark, the intense work was over: 'I've noticed that they've very carefully and very deliberately not given us much to do in the way of new things to think about and complex problems to worry about.'

So Derek went off to visit a South African project at a muddy sheep farm in the Kazakh countryside. There, Dr Danie Barry from the

University of Stellenbosch was harvesting embryos and stem cells to be monitored in the zero-gravity environment of space. Mark was also going to be growing HIV crystals at the space station to see if they developed into three dimensions, making them easier to study on Earth.

T-minus four days: The cosmonauts had to be quarantined to avoid the risk of illness before launch. Mark spent hours with Derek in his room, talking non-stop about the technicalities of the mission and trying to help him with his satellite phone. On the Sunday before liftoff they managed, by some miracle, to get through to Ruda in the M-Net studio from the hotel room, cables everywhere, satellite dish in a suitcase outside. It all looked absurdly complex for the relatively simple goal of getting Derek's face and some images back to Johannesburg. He was sure it wasn't legal and that, if he was discovered, the Russian military simply wouldn't believe that all he was trying to do was to say: 'Hello South Africa, I made it to Russia and all is well for Mark's takeoff.'

But the important people all seemed to be in the pub, playing Russian billiards and table tennis. Derek is handy with a bat, and one afternoon he decided to take on some of the top brass who hadn't shared their picnic on the plane and who now seemed to be only on liquids. To Derek's annoyance, even though his opponent was practically sweating vodka, he just couldn't beat him. Shortly after the game, the man passed out on the floor, and his colleagues simply stepped over him. There was something about Russians, thought Derek, who also had a battle of wits going with the yellow-jacketed officer in charge of the launch. The man always seemed to be shooing Derek and his camera out of the way.

T-minus 48 hours: As the days before launch turned into hours, there was a flurry of traditional ceremonies: a traditional walk around the garden, a traditional haircut, a ritual screening of *White Sun of the Desert*, one of the most popular Russian films of all time. And although crowds could watch the rocket being hauled to the launch site by rail, it was tradition that none of the cosmonauts caught sight of it – like a bride and groom before their wedding day. In the edit, Sophia and Jonathan amusingly put captions on screen like 'Tradition No 4: Don't

Watch the Roll-out' and 'Tradition No 5: Place Coins on the Track', the latter a reference to the custom of placing coins on the track in front of the oncoming train. The squashed coins were considered good-luck charms.

T-minus 12 hours: Derek spent a few hours of the night before launch with Mark in his hotel room. Mark had received a parcel of photographs, wishes and prayers from home and was looking emotional. They stayed up chatting until well after midnight. Yellow Jacket burst in at one point, threatening to ground Mark if he didn't go to bed immediately: he had to be up at 3am for the first of a series of pre-takeoff enemas, and to complete a few more traditional ceremonies – Champagne breakfast with the crew, prayers and blessings from an Orthodox priest, vodka toasts and the traditional signing of their hotel room doors. Not to mention the traditional sit-down before the journey – 'Посидим на дорожку [posidim na dorozhku]' – to calm and focus the mind.

T-minus 6 hours: While Derek was the worse for wear the next morning, Mark, who'd bashed on his door before dawn, was a bundle of nervous energy. Cameraman Peter, in a sterile suit, wasn't required to film the enema, but was given special permission to film the cosmonauts putting on their heavy space gear, intended to keep them alive if the craft depressurised. Being a cosmonaut comes with celebrity status, and their suits were given the final going-over behind a glass window, with a crowd watching. But Derek was told by his *bête noire* to 'stand back', and was relegated to a corner where he couldn't see. He decided it was time to give Yellow Jacket an earful, after which, he said, their relationship improved. Clearly, you needed an argument to gain respect around here.

T-minus 3 hours: The final trip to the launch site, 20 km from the hotel, wasn't free of ceremony. Halfway there, the cosmonauts' bus stopped: they had to pee on the bus's wheel, just as Yuri Gagarin had done 41 years before: 'Tradition No 12: Take a Leak.'

T-minus 1 hour: It was a perfect day for liftoff. Commander Yuri Gidzenko, Flight Engineer Roberto Vittori and Second Engineer Mark Shuttleworth ascended the gantry of the Soyuz rocket. Derek felt emotional and, with his newfound freedom from Yellow Jacket's nagging, followed Mark to the steps with his little camera, blasts of white smoke shooting up around him. But he didn't go as close as Peter, who got scorched as the Soyuz lifted off. Derek's commentary ran: 'The Soyuz rises majestically upward with the power of 210 tonnes of thrust and the South African flag soars proudly into the heavens: a successful liftoff and the realisation of Mark's lifelong dream. It takes just two minutes to reach orbit, break the shackles of gravity and then everything starts to float.'

The first African was in space. It would take a day for the Soyuz to catch up with the International Space Station, and then undertake the extremely delicate docking procedure: two heavy craft orbiting the Earth at over 28 000 km per hour approaching each other at the gentle rate of 10 cm per second.

Derek, who'd been part of a unique experience, had no time to dwell on the intricacies of docking. He had to get a scheduled flight back to Johannesburg, where an anxious team was waiting. He arrived on the morning of Saturday 27 April with 14 hours of footage. It was Freedom Day, but Sophia and Jonathan Pienaar spent the next 34 hours imprisoned in their edit suite, cutting a 20-minute story for the following evening. Sophia had a rough script outline pasted on the wall and a jet-lagged Derek showed her where to find all the key moments. While Jonathan edited and designed graphics, Sophia managed some quite poetic scripting: 'Under the control of Commander Yuri Gidzenko, the Soyuz docked successfully ... Their destination reached, hatches were opened, and as is the tradition, the commander entered first to greet the ISS crew, who had been there for four months ... followed by Roberto and Mark. This is just the beginning of their space adventure.'

Sophia and Jonathan were wrecks by the time a wide-awake George Mazarakis arrived for the pre-viewing on Sunday morning. They'd not had time to review anything they'd edited. Sophia jokingly said that, like Lot's wife in the Bible, she and Jonathan had feared that, if they looked back, they'd turn into pillars of salt. George was reasonably impressed, but he's not the kind of executive who allows an impossible deadline to get in the way of good television. He'd heard President Thabo Mbeki talking to Mark on the International Space Station, and he wanted that in, too. So there was more stress for Sophia to find the footage at that late stage, but it was definitely an African Renaissance moment:

President Mbeki: 'The whole continent will be proud that at last we have one of our own people from Africa up in space, taking part in cutting-edge development with regard to science and technology.'

Mark: 'I'd like to say I wish you well on South Africa's Freedom Day; it's a very auspicious day and we're thinking of you down in South Africa up here in space.'

President Mbeki: 'What would you say about the liftoff and the journey to the space station?'

Mark: 'Mr President, I had moments of terror, moments of sheer upliftment and exhilaration. I have truly never seen anything as beautiful as the Earth from space, and I can't imagine anything that can surpass that.'

But the burning question on everyone's minds – even President Mbeki's – was what Mark was having for lunch. Mbeki asked: 'You can't eat T-bone steak up there, can you?' Mark let go of what looked like a tin of tuna and it gently floated towards the camera: 'Here comes a little bit of lunch – this one is pork with potatoes. I'll send that flying back in your general direction, with love.'

Sophia got most of the special moments in, but arrived at the final sound mix desperately late, with only two hours to broadcast time. Just as she thought she was home and dry, putting the last bits of sound to tape, the machine began playing up. Sophia tried to keep calm, but every time the sound dropped out, she felt her blood pressure rise. And, as the minutes ticked by, with the crew standing by in studio to play the *Carte Blanche* jingle, everyone started screaming at her, saying things like 'Where the **** are you? Derek and Ruda are already in studio!' and 'If you don't get the **** tape to the **** studio by seven you will never **** work for *Carte Blanche* again!'

But in true news broadcast style, the tape arrived with seconds to spare, and the story of Africa's first man in space made it to air on time. Sophia collapsed in a heap; Derek gave her a *matryoshka* doll to say thank you; Jonathan won two SAGE editing awards.

On 5 May, Mark Shuttleworth and his fellow cosmonauts made a dramatic landing in the desert of Kazhakstan, tightly rolled up inside the module, watching mountain ranges flying past, metal burning and blistering around them. As he was carried off on a stretcher, beaming from ear to ear, legs too wobbly to walk, his father Rick was there to meet him. There's a wonderful moment in the helicopter going back to Baikonur, where he shouts out in excitement, the context unclear: 'I just KNEW you'd love that, Dad ... I knew you'd think it was the BEST!'

Maybe he was talking about the launch, maybe the landing. But he could've been an eight-year-old talking about a new toy, not a 28-year-old space celebrity.

Elon Musk – 2005

It's great from a personal standpoint ... It doesn't do a great deal to advance the goal of humanity becoming a space-travelling civilisation ... which is my objective ...

Elon Musk had bigger ideas than becoming a mere space traveller and said he would've paid US$20 million *not* to have to spend six months in Russia learning to be a cosmonaut, nor would he go anywhere in a 'clunker' like the Soyuz.

But, like Mark Shuttleworth, this South African had made his money from online ventures. His first company, Zip2, produced online content-publishing software for news organisations, and was bought in 1999 for US$340 million. His next success stories were PayPal, the online money transfer payment system that was acquired by eBay for US$1.5 billion and then SpaceX, a space exploration company. Its first client was the US Department of Defense, and by 2008 SpaceX had signed a US$1.6 billion contract with NASA to deliver cargo to the ISS, replacing the function of the about-to-be-retired Space Shuttle. And he certainly wasn't stopping with cargo – putting passengers into outer space was next. Americans were gobsmacked: how had a young African with no background in rocketry come to represent their future access to space?

But in 2005, when *Carte Blanche* interviewed him, Elon was still the small guy throwing the punches at the big blokes – the commercial rocket industry. A picture on the wall of his Los Angeles office said it all: a classic shot of Muhammad Ali standing over a prone Sonny Liston. Elon was just 34, but already big companies like Arianespace and Lockheed Martin were watching him warily. Each time a satellite was launched, they charged up to US$80 million for the trip. But SpaceX promised to get payloads into space for a fraction of that. And since he was the 23rd richest man under 40 in the US, his competitors feared it wasn't just big talk. Musk's rocket, Falcon 1, was almost ready for launch and he was headline news all over the United States:

Derek: 'You haven't done too badly for a Pretoria High old boy.'

Elon: 'I think we are doing quite well, given that we are simply alleging at this point that we can put something in space.'

He didn't even need to work: he was the co-founder of Tesla Motors, which developed the first fully-electric sports car. He had a mansion in the affluent LA suburb of Bel Air, a million-dollar McLaren F1 sports car, executive jets and all sorts of smart toys. But he hadn't taken a holiday in years, intent instead on making space travel accessible to all, and on his real dream – creating an oasis settlement on Mars for space pioneers.

The interview with the young tycoon had been the idea of Namibian producer Linda de Jager, who was interested in tracing relatively unknown southern Africans who'd made it big abroad. *Carte Blanche* is a great platform for showcasing ingenuity and capturing the zeitgeist, but justifying the expense of an overseas trip always means finding a few other stories to pack into an already tight schedule. So, in ten days Linda and Derek visited Jane Fonda at her ranch in New Mexico, interviewed musician Trevor Rabin and another space expert, Dr Japie van Zyl, at that time NASA's director of astronomy and physics. In 2012, Van Zyl was to feature on *Carte Blanche* again as head of the Jet Propulsion

Laboratory, instrumental in launching and landing the space agency's Mars Rover, *Curiosity*. His space dreams had begun as a boy camping in the Namib Desert and looking up at 'moving stars' in the night sky. His father had explained to him that those were actually spacecraft, or satellites, launched from Florida in the US: 'I told him that is where I am going ... one day I am going to be working on those things.'

More than 40 years later, Japie van Zyl had helped put a spacecraft on Mars, a planet that reminded him a bit of Namibia. The Mars Rover could search for elements of life, such as water, and for energy sources, and it had the potential to unlock some of the secrets of the Red Planet. And that tied in with Elon Musk's ambitious declaration that 'SpaceX may be the company that builds the rocket that takes the first person to Mars'.

Elon's South African accent hadn't entirely left him, despite him having left the country in 1988 at the age of 17, primarily to avoid the army. And there was nothing regimental about SpaceX. Derek had visited the Lockheed Martin plant, with its tight security, some years before and was struck by the relaxed and non-corporate atmosphere at SpaceX. The office set-up was open-plan, with high ceilings and lots of light, and a door opening onto the street. Derek asked if Elon wasn't concerned about competitors snooping around. He laughed, saying that even if he gave them the blueprints, there wasn't much they could do.

His staff, 140 of them, looked like a bunch of free-thinkers; one of them told Derek he was treated better at work than at home. There was even a 24-hour canteen. While he might be new to the rocket business, Elon had cherry-picked the sharpest minds around – and the ones who wanted to work hard. So he made sure that their working environment was a pleasant one. He commented: 'I don't think there has ever been a group this talented in one place, in one company, developing a rocket – ever ... with rockets, you have to solve the problem of a particular level of difficulty, one person who can solve the problem is worth an infinite number of people who can't.'

With no bureaucracy and no delays, they'd built the Falcon 1 in three years, something which could easily have taken ten. On the factory floor, Derek stood in front of a Merlin engine, a maze of metal innards that had been designed from scratch, and which would lift Falcon 1 off the launch pad. Unlike other rockets, much of the Falcon would parachute into the ocean, to be fished out and reused. But there were plenty of people who expected Falcon to fail: the highway to space was littered with brave attempts at building cut-price rockets that had fizzled out, at a cost of millions of dollars. Elon had put US$100 million of his own on the line to break the mould of space travel, and was prepared to dig even deeper if the first attempt failed. He had enough capital to survive at least three consecutive failures, he said.

The first stage of the rocket was already on its way to the launch site on the remote Pacific island of Omelek, in the Marshall Islands. Falcon 1's maiden flight would carry the ashes of 26 people aloft for the first-ever space burial.

'I think there is going to be a serious pucker factor on launch day,' remarked Elon. It wasn't clear whether he was talking about his own sphincter, or about his competitors'. Probably his, because that first launch attempt had to be abandoned because of bad weather; the second attempt had to be scrapped because of a faulty valve. On 24 March 2006, Falcon 1 finally launched, but the main engine failed after 30 seconds.

Then there was no news from SpaceX headquarters for almost a year, but the high-tech team worked day and night because, as Elon told Derek in a follow-up story 18 months later, 'There are a hundred things that can happen. One of them is success.'

And that came on 20 March 2007 – liftoff for Elon and the SpaceX team. They had convinced key stakeholders that they had what it took – the little guy could get into space for a fraction of the price of the big boys. Falcon 1 was the test; the successor to the Space Shuttle would be the Falcon 9 rocket and the reusable Dragon capsule, both big enough to carry people into full orbit.

In May 2012, the SpaceX Dragon spacecraft docked with the International Space Station, the first time a commercial firm had launched and docked a vehicle at the ISS. One day it would be Mars, be-cause, sooner or later, said Elon Musk: 'we must expand life beyond this green and blue ball ... I would like to die on Mars, just not on impact.'

On 1 March 2013, SpaceX conducted its tenth launch, sending the fourth Dragon on a mission to resupply the ISS and marking the fifth flight of the Falcon 9.

Light years away from Pretoria Boys High ...

going, going, gone

(Doorbell rings)

Devi: 'Hi Rael, how are you?'

Rael (on intercom): 'Fine, thank you.'

Devi: 'It's Devi, *Carte Blanche*.'

Rael (on intercom): 'From where?'

Devi: 'Is that Rael Levitt?'

Rael (on intercom): 'Yes.'

Devi: 'It's Devi from *Carte Blanche*.'

Rael (on intercom, voice altered): 'Rael's not here. Let's check if he's here. Hold on.'

*Devi (*sotto voce *to camera)*: 'I'm actually quite excited because it's been a long time that we've been trying to get hold of Rael Levitt, and it looks like he's home.'

Rael (on intercom): 'Hello?'

Devi: 'Hi!'

Rael (on intercom): 'He's just gone out now, madam.'

Devi: 'Are you sure, because you said he was here?'

Rael (on intercom): 'No, he's not here.'

This rather bad impression of a Zimbabwean butler caused much hilarity for weeks after it was broadcast in 2012. Popular online retailer takealot.com adapted it for a radio ad in which a fictitious Rael Levitt changed his voice, then changed it back when he found out it was a delivery man. The payoff line: 'Get books like *Public Relations for Dummies* delivered to your door ... safe, secure online shopping.'

And a public relations disaster it certainly was. Auction Alliance, South Africa's largest auctioneers, and a company worth more than R5 billion, was embroiled in an embarrassing kickback scandal, but the CEO, Rael Levitt – described as 'bold and ambitious' in a website listing the country's top 500 companies – was ducking and diving.

It is an accepted fact that no one wants to see Devi Sankaree Govender on their doorstep, even if they are squeaky-clean. She's quick-witted, as snappy as a Jack Russell and renowned for catching out inventive shysters without losing her cool. But surely a man of Rael Levitt's stature was above playing cat and mouse with the media? Phone calls and emails went unanswered; a visit to his Johannesburg offices had him in the building one minute, and exiting via the underground parking the next, where he apparently cowered in the footwell of a colleague's car while a security guard half-heartedly chased Devi and the crew around the foyer upstairs. And so Devi, producer Kate Barry and cameraman Jonathan Crawford eventually found themselves on the doorstep of Levitt's luxury apartment in Sea Point. But Houdini had wriggled away.

The story began in September 2011, in the way that many stories do, with a whisper in the ear of executive producer George Mazarakis. The source told an extraordinary tale of kickbacks and collusion, of how Auction Alliance paid liquidators, attorneys and bank employees to pass business its way. It was a complex story to try and unravel. Kate began poring over the so-called Merobex accounts. Merobex seemed to be a company closely linked to the alleged scheme. Each name and number in these accounts told a story of someone whose properties had been liquidated. From the documents, she unearthed two potential case studies: MKB, a property group that had gone into liquidation in 2009 when Investec Bank pulled the plug on its loans, and another Investec client, Miko Rwayitare, a Rwandan telecoms billionaire who had died in 2007, leaving behind a R100-million sandstone mansion in Sandhurst modelled on the Union Buildings.

Over the next two months, Kate began meeting with a variety of people who knew a lot, but would say only a little. She established that Merobex had been paid hefty commissions on the sales of MKB and Miko Rwayitare's properties. The burning question was: why? What had Merobex done to deserve this kind of commission? Neither Jonathan Killik from MKB, nor attorney John Oosthuizen, the agent for Rwayitare's executors, could fathom it.

George's snitch told Kate of the existence of a file containing damning evidence – financial accounts and emails stretching back over a decade, and all relating to cash kickbacks paid by Auction Alliance. But the former employee who was in possession of the file had yet to be persuaded to share its contents.

On 10 December 2011, the Auction Alliance story took an unexpected twist with what has become known as the 'Quoin Rock Debacle'. The 194-odd-hectare Quoin Rock wine estate, in the foothills of the Simonsberg near Stellenbosch, had belonged to South Africa's biggest tax dodger, Dave King, and had gone under the hammer in an effort by SARS to recoup some of his R2.7 billion debt. Valued at R120 million, the Quoin Rock Wine Estate and Manor was billed as the most high-profile auction event of the year. The showman himself, Rael Levitt, extolled the virtues of this splendid property, jokingly telling people he was part of the 'Cape Town mafia'. As usual, there was food, drink, music and live video streaming on the internet. The bidders were few but moneyed, among them Wendy Appelbaum, one of Africa's richest women. Levitt opened the bidding at R75 million, but there were no takers. A bid of R30 million came from the floor. Appelbaum raised it to R35 million. The original bidder raised his to R40 million; Appelbaum counter-bid R45 million, then R55 million. What happened next has been replayed over and over. It's a major squirm moment:

Rael Levitt: 'Our bid is at R55 million ... we've got to the price of an apartment in Clifton ... the bid is at 55 now. The bid is yours now at R55 million ... at R60 million against you. At R60 million ...'

But there was no genuine bidder at R60 million; Wendy Appelbaum had realised this and stopped bidding. The person who'd pushed the price up to R60 million was Deon Leygonie, an Auction Alliance employee. Levitt panicked: his ghost bidder was in for R60 million. The only thing he could do to save the situation was backtrack to Wendy's last bid. He recovered in a flash: 'There we go ladies and gentlemen ... we're all done now. Is that your bid, sir? No? What was our last bid here? Apologies, last bid is at R55 million. At R55 million it is your bid, ma'am ... going, going, gone! It's sold at R55 million!'

While Wendy Appelbaum questioned the integrity of the auction, Rael hatched a plan over lunch with a friend, Israeli businessman Ariel Gerbi. Rael would register Ariel as the bidder, creating the impression that Deon Leygonie had been acting on his behalf. But Appelbaum was having none of it. She cancelled the sale and called for an investigation. Rael was dismissive: she had been 'confused' by the difference between a proxy bidder and a 'vendor' bidder: 'She saw a proxy bidder – and saw someone who she thought did not have the means to buy the farms. But the "proxy bidder" was indeed bidding on behalf of a bidder who has huge and significant means, someone who is extremely prosperous.'

Substitute 'proxy' for 'ghost'. Auction Alliance insiders would later reveal that this was common practice. Rael Levitt would allegedly send ghost bidders to every auction to get the prices up. Then they would stop bidding and wait for the real bidders to take the bait. Levitt himself later admitted to the Consumer Commission that he lied about the proxy bidder.

The Quoin Rock incident wasn't *Carte Blanche*'s focus, although it made an interesting sidebar about the ethics of Auction Alliance and auction houses in general.

Kate began 2012 raring to go, emailing the office as soon as it opened after the Christmas break. She proposed an investigation into the racketeering surrounding the auction business, and particularly the kickbacks paid by auctioneers to bankers and liquidators once assets were sold. However, she worried that George Mazarakis might feel the story was too sensitive, and that certain parties might try to stop the investigation if they knew *Carte Blanche* was involved.

The newspapers were full of the Quoin Rock auction, so Kate decided to phone Wendy Appelbaum anyway, on the off chance that she might have information on the kickback side of Auction Alliance's business. Appelbaum said she had lots of information, but seemed a bit TV-shy.

She asked Kate to email her and said she'd give it some thought. In the email, Kate told her of the existence of the damning file about the goings-on at Auction Alliance, and that *Carte Blanche* was hoping to get access to it.

The next day Fiona Forde, a freelance journalist working for *The Star*, was onto the same story and had contacted the very same source, who arranged for her to see the file, apparently intimating that *Carte Blanche* had been 'sitting' on the details since September. Television is a much slower beast than print, and finding sources prepared to appear on camera, even with their identities hidden, takes some persuading. One of Rael Levitt's former employees was so nervous that Kate had to agree to use a different voice in the voiceover. It would mean writing down every word she said, then getting an actor to read them, with the same pauses and intonations, in the final audio mix. She had found an auctioneer called 'Mickey' who could corroborate the system of kickbacks prevalent in the industry, but he was so terrified of reprisals that he would only be interviewed in his lawyer's office, with his face masked.

At this point the historical evidence contained in the legendary file was sent to Kate, and she, with the help of researcher Susan Comrie – formidable with figures and doggedly determined – began scrutinising ledgers and journals from the previous decade.

What was clear was that lots of money was changing hands in return for obtaining business. If liquidators or bankers delivered big estates for auction, a big cash cheque would follow, or a car, or an overseas trip. Kate and Susan plugged away, getting hold of documents that revealed, for example, a 33 per cent commission paid to an ABSA employee for an insolvent estate and several payments to an Investec employee for delivering estates that could be auctioned by Rael. There was even an all-expenses paid trip to Disneyland for 'the whole family'. The payments were noted as 'referral commissions' – euphemism for kickbacks.

Auctioneer 'Mickey' had told them that unless kickbacks were paid, bank staff wouldn't pass work to the auction houses. Everyone in the industry knew that: 'When the liquidator phones you up, he says: "How much are you going to give back?" And the going rate is between 30 and 40 per cent and they want it in cash, and there's no way to record it.'

Eventually Kate had enough on-camera evidence to ask Rael for an interview. He agreed to meet at 11am at his plush Johannesburg offices. But, as the net closed in, he hired the services of a company called Luxury Brands, owned by Jeremy Nel and Annette Cowley-Nel, to do some urgently needed PR. Kate received a text message from Jeremy Nel the afternoon before the much-awaited interview, for which Devi had been booked and briefed. (Bringing a presenter in for these complicated shoots requires much last-minute reading and preparation.) The text read: 'Apologies, but we need to postpone tomorrow's interview due to sensitivities involved. Please contact me to reschedule at a mutual convenience. Sincere apologies, Jeremy.'

There followed a legal letter, resorting to the over-used and frequently misunderstood 'sub judice' excuse, to which Kate responded in an email to Jeremy:

Wed 2012/02/08 09:07 AM

Dear Jeremy

We have received a lawyer's letter raising concerns regarding the *Carte Blanche* interview with Rael Levitt scheduled for tomorrow at 11am at Auction Alliance offices in Johannesburg.

We do not intend to discuss any issues that are sub judice. Our interview will focus on the following:
1. The Quoin Rock auction
2. Proxy bidders/ghost bidders
3. Liquidations + referrals
4. Valuations of properties
5. Placing of reserve prices
6. General issues about relationships between 3rd parties and Auction Alliance.

Please note that the presenter will make the interview their own, and may go beyond issues surrounding Wendy Appelbaum. As the interview was confirmed yesterday, crew and presenter have already been booked for tomorrow.

The interview was rescheduled: Rael was in, said Jeremy:

Hi Kate.
Rael is a keen participant and is in no way trying to dodge the interview, and will be available on Friday. It's just that he needs to get clarity on one or two issues.
Kind regards, Jeremy

Then, out of the blue, Derek Watts, who had nothing to do with the story, got a call from Investec's Ciaran Whelan, wanting to know if *Carte Blanche* was 'investigating Investec'. Although Derek is the public face of *Carte Blanche*, he plays no part in editorial decisions – contrary to popular belief. He advised Whelan to make contact with the office, and Whelan offered to 'provide any information we can to assist with your research'. But Investec declined an interview, instead asking for questions to be emailed and then responding in a 15-page bound book, excluding the addenda. It was a TV journalist's nightmare.

Fiona Forde managed to get an interview with Rael in his Johannesburg offices that week. But, after being confronted with evidence of cash kickbacks, he brought the interview to an abrupt end and bolted back to Cape Town. Realising that his empire was crumbling, he quickly cancelled the *Carte Blanche* interview: 'Dear Kate. Due to circumstances beyond Rael's control he will not be able to attend the interview on Friday. Sincere apologies, Jeremy.'

Carte Blanche lawyers Dario Milo and Emma Sadleir got involved. They were eager to avoid an interdict, which is costly, time-consuming and often dependent on which side of bed the presiding judge has emerged:

Interview with Mr Rael Levitt – Auction Alliance (Pty) Limited

We act for Electronic Media Network Ltd and Combined Artistic Productions

CC, the producer of the Carte Blanche television programme ('our client'). We record that our client has been particularly accommodating of your client and has gone to great lengths to ensure that your client is given an opportunity to respond to the allegations contained in the programme. We are instructed that the interview was re-scheduled for Friday 10 February 2012, but that your client has once again cancelled the interview.

In the circumstances, we urge your client to reconsider his decision and to provide our client with an interview.

Yours faithfully

WEBBER WENTZEL

Dario Milo / Emma Sadleir

In the meantime, Fiona Forde and Independent Newspapers had been unable to avoid an interdict. Before the Western Cape High Court, Advocate Brian Pincus, for Auction Alliance, argued that it was vital that his client be allowed 'a fair chance' to reply to the 'very serious allegations' being made. Independent Newspapers replied that they needed to publish because another media company was scheduled to 'telecast' the story that Sunday – meaning *Carte Blanche*. But Pincus said his client had not done any interviews with the 'other media company'. Not for lack of trying, Advocate.

Independent Newspapers published on Saturday 18 February a story headlined 'Auction House implicated in kickback scandal'. It detailed a paper trail dating back more than 13 years and told how Levitt had ordered the company's accounting systems to be manipulated in order to keep auditors out of the loop. The report mentioned that two Investec staffers had been paid hefty commissions to ensure that auction business flowed to Auction Alliance, and that attorneys were on the take, too, with payouts of up to R500 000 in cash.

The report was followed by a lengthy statement from Auction Alliance, clearly part of the out-of-court settlement struck after the High Court application was withdrawn, saying the allegations against the company emanated from 'disgruntled ex-employees' now working for competitors. It denied unethical and corrupt business practices.

George Mazarakis was relieved; the heat was off, the story was out there, and *Carte Blanche* would go to air the following Sunday. Kate and Devi made a last-ditch attempt to get Rael on camera and attended one of his auctions in Pretoria. But, surprise, surprise, he'd pulled out of all auctions that week. Finally, at the eleventh hour – always nerve-wracking when a story is in the final throes of production – came a statement from Rael, saying he'd appointed an 'independent auditor to investigate allegations' and that there would be 'no further statements until the investigation had been concluded'.

The *Carte Blanche* story aired on 26 February and all hell broke loose at Auction Alliance. A newspaper article is one thing; 20 minutes of investigative television is entirely different. Less than 24 hours after broadcast, Rael Levitt resigned and three days later went into self-imposed exile in Israel until May of that year.

Banks launched internal investigations and stopped doing business with Auction Alliance, which eventually closed its doors. Investec appointed forensic auditors, who released a report saying: 'there is no indication that an employee allegedly received any amounts from Auction Alliance, unless such payment was made in cash.' Which was exactly what all *Carte Blanche*'s sources had said: payments had been made in cash.

Auction Alliance has yet to release the independent audit it commissioned. An impeccable source says it's dynamite.

Carte Blanche viewers had plenty to say: the liquidation industry was as crooked as they come and kickbacks were normal business:

> @JennzaLynn: Hmmm, looks like it's down to crooked auctioneers and practices again #carteblanche expose them all!!!
> @Touch_Dis: In the same manner that you pursued Auction Alliance, please for the sake of unsuspecting victims, hang them!!

Later that year, Kate and Susan were back on the auction beat.

Car Auction – November 2012

This story came to *Carte Blanche* via Paul O'Sullivan, the private investigator who compiled a dossier on the corrupt relationship between
Glenn Agliotti and Jackie Selebi. Not known as Mr Nice Guy, O'Sullivan
has a habit of sending threatening messages to those he's investigating,
or those connected to them, but his research is thorough and his reach
wide. He'd been conducting an investigation on behalf of a company
called Auction Operation, which suspected underhand dealings between
a rival auctioneer, Park Village Auctions, and an employee of Nedbank.
It seemed hard to believe. Surely auctioneers had learned a lesson from
the downfall of Auction Alliance?

A whistle-blower stepped forward, a former Park Village employee
named Firdouz. 'Beware of those with an axe to grind' is one of the basic rules of journalism, and Firdouz certainly did have. She'd been fired
from Park Village for alleged theft, and was now working for Auction
Operation. But her story was plausible. She knew of a Nedbank Motor
Finance Corporation employee who regularly supplied repossessed cars
to Park Village to be auctioned. At every auction, she said, cars would
be withdrawn and sold to him. His name was Hendrik Broodryk, alias
'Buyer 170'.

Kate found a strong case study: first-time car owner and Nedbank
client Mbulelo Dili, with the looks of a movie star. He'd bought a BMW
for over R200 000, which had been financed by Nedbank. But after he
was retrenched and defaulted on his payments, the car was repossessed.
To his horror, it was then sold at auction for R35 000 and he was left
owing Nedbank six times that amount. When the car was repossessed,
the inspection sheet showed it was classified as a 'runner' – the engine
and gearbox were in working order. But Hendrik Broodryk had reclas-
sified it as a 'non-runner' and bought it in his wife Brenda's name.
Brenda had then traded it in for R60 000 and another dealer had sold it
for R120 000.

Firdouz would agree to be interviewed on camera only if her identity
was hidden. She feared reprisals from Park Village Auctions, saying they
were a powerful family with a lot to lose. And so, swathed in scarves

200

and a baseball cap and looking a bit like a young boy, she chatted to presenter Derek Watts for two hours.

But, the next day, when she heard that Clive Lazarus from Park Village had called her a 'thief' during his interview, she was enraged and asked to be re-interviewed, this time hiding nothing. She said Buyer 170, or Hendrik and Brenda Broodryk, had bought four or five cars a week this way from Park Village Auctions. All of them were classified as 'non-runners' at the auction, but all were in perfect working order. They were then sold to other dealers for cash. The question was whether or not the auctioneers were in on this fairly lucrative scheme. Definitely, said Firdouz; she'd personally picked up cash on behalf of Park Village Auctions from car dealers and had dropped off the money at Hendrik's house.

When Susan and Kate had asked Clive Lazarus of Park Village Auctions for an interview, his lawyer sent a letter, using the sub judice excuse, although nothing had as yet reached the courts. After this was pointed out to them, it was agreed that Clive would be sent questions in writing. But Kate suggested that Derek and the crew personally deliver the questions to Clive at his office. As it happened, he was in, and, although he didn't look delighted to see the crew, he read the questions over and agreed to answer some of them. He looked tired and drawn, but his answers were emphatic. When vehicles were withdrawn from an auction it was on the bank's instructions. And he didn't know what happened to them after that.

Derek: 'Clive, a lot of these vehicles were bought by Buyer 170?'

Clive: 'Well, then it went on the auction process. If it did get withdrawn, I can't say to you it was withdrawn and bought by 170. How can it be withdrawn and bought by 170?'

Derek: 'Well, the investigators have proof of that.'

Clive: 'That it was bought and withdrawn by Buyer 170?'

Derek: 'And do you know who Buyer 170 is?'

Clive: 'Well, I've worked that out recently ... it was Hendrik's wife.'

Time to track down the clearly car-mad Broodryks: Hendrik said 'talk to my lawyers', and so did Brenda, who wasn't interested in explaining to Derek how she'd come to buy and sell so many cars in so few years.

Derek: 'Hi Brenda, Derek.'

Brenda Broodryk: 'I know who you are.'

Derek: 'How're you doing? Alright?'

Brenda: 'Okay, and you?'

Derek: 'Now, look, some serious allegations are against you?'

Brenda: 'I know, but you'll have to speak to my lawyer.'

Derek asked Clive if he knew Brenda at all. Yes ... no ... yes ...

Clive: 'I've never even seen her. I met her on one occasion when, I think, she fetched him from a Christmas party, approximately two years ago.'

Derek: 'But surely over the years you realised that Hendrik's wife was Buyer 170?'

Clive: 'No, I wouldn't know who the buyers are.'

Derek: 'But how do you feel now that you do know?'

Clive: 'I'm shattered that this actually came out. I'm actually shattered ...'

Clive was shattered, Hendrik Broodryk resigned, and Nedbank wrote off Mbulelo's outstanding debt of R228 000 and refunded him R42 000 for the payments he'd made on the car.

fat cats 16

M-Net to air testimony of Aurora directors ...
Carte Blanche *gets access to Aurora court hearings ...*
Aurora Inquiry to be recorded by Carte Blanche *...*
Dario Milo of Webber Wentzel ... said the ruling represented 'an
important precedent for the broadcast media and a victory for the
public's right to know ...'

It was to set a legal precedent and introduce *Carte Blanche* viewers to the 'mafia managers' of Aurora Empowerment System: Khulubuse Zuma, Zondwa Mandela, Thulani Ngubane and the father-and-son team of Solly and Fazel Bhana. Although they'd dominated the headlines, they'd generally managed to avoid interviews and to evade the cameras.

The occasion at which they were to testify – and at which *Carte Blanche* went to great legal lengths to be allowed to film – concerned the liquidation of Pamodzi Gold East Rand, which went belly-up in 2009. Liquidators appointed Aurora to run Pamodzi's once-profitable gold mines, Grootvlei and Orkney. It resulted in one of the most shameful episodes in South Africa's mining history, up there with Brett Kebble and Randgold, Central Rand Gold and Marikana.

Aurora had no experience in mining, and no capital, but had bid R605 million for the two Pamodzi mines and signed a management contract with the liquidators, led by Enver Motala. Over the years, Motala had used his political clout and empowerment status to establish one of the wealthiest liquidation practices in the country. Squeaky-clean he was not. The final story, presented by Bongani Bingwa, would be a dramatic example of the abuse of the institution of insolvency by the politically connected at the expense of thousands of workers, the mining industry and the economy.

Motala had put the deal together for Aurora's well-placed directors, who included President Jacob Zuma's nephew, Nelson Mandela's grandson and the President's lawyer, Michael Hulley, who was in a non-executive role. They had the right fundraising connections and displayed all the outward trappings of affluence and influence.

Gold mines need money, lots of it: workers need to be paid, as do suppliers like Eskom and Rand Water, equipment has to be maintained, and underground water treated with chemicals. Initially, there was a lucrative deal on the cards with a Malaysian investment company, but it collapsed. The investor, Dato Raja Shah, visited South Africa in late 2009. *Bongani*: 'What he wanted in exchange for substantial amounts of cash was transparency and good corporate governance ... Dato Raja Shah wasn't even allowed to see the bank statements ...'

When an unnamed source handed him the documents and he noticed six-figure cash transactions from Aurora's accounts, he allegedly got on a plane and flew out of the country, leaving Aurora R390 million short of the money they needed to run the mine. In a stinging letter to Motala, Shah complained of Aurora's 'woeful corporate governance, lack of transparency of financial affairs and integrity of management staff'.

Then, in August 2010, came good news: as Khulubuse Zuma and Zondwa Mandela looked on, Michael Hulley told journalists that Aurora had done a deal with a Swiss investment group. The future of Orkney and Grootvlei was rosy. 'I think you will see a different impetus, a greater responsibility ...' said Hulley.

Carte Blanche's first Aurora story had been broadcast some months before this announcement. It had been produced by Adam Welz, son of *Noseweek* editor Martin Welz, and not a regular *Carte Blanche* contributor. But, while investigating the pollution of water sources near Springs, Adam had stumbled onto another story: unpaid workers trying to save their livelihoods from their greedy bosses.

While waiting for its billion-rand investor, Aurora had been left with only one real source of cash to run Grootvlei and Orkney: the sale of the gold mined and smelted there. For six months after Aurora took over the mines, enough gold was produced to generate revenues of R112 million.

But miners at Grootvlei told Adam that profits weren't filtering back to the company and that they were being paid irregularly, sometimes receiving nothing for months on end. He filmed the conditions in which they were living: water and electricity supplies were intermittent and they had to rely on food parcels from their trade unions. One miner said: 'I feel like a beggar. I feel humiliated. I do appreciate the gesture, but I feel as if I now have to beg for food to be able to look after my family. I did work for my money.'

The workers suspected that Aurora didn't give a damn about them and were far more interested in stripping the assets and looting. There were rumours of trucks loaded with gold ore being sent to mystery destinations on the East Rand, with the contents sold through the back door, and with the mine seeing none of the proceeds. 'Never!' said the glib-tongued Thulani Ngubane, Aurora's 'commercial' director: 'Whatever is being said, it's not true; it's not true.'

There was no sign of the promised 'Swiss' investor.

Newspaper reports about Khulubuse Zuma's lavish lifestyle – splashing out on luxury cars, quad bikes, Johnnie Walker Gold Label and Cuban cigars – did nothing to placate the miners. Their unease gave way to strikes and violent clashes. At Orkney, miners were arrested trying to stop trucks laden with assets from leaving the premises. At Grootvlei, managers were trapped inside the administration offices, workers baying for their blood outside. Adam filmed police firing rubber bullets at striking workers, giving the bosses a chance to flee.

In a follow-up story a week later, he spoke to shaft foreman Jock Botha, whose job it was to prevent the flooding of the mine's tunnels by keeping the pumps going. Jock was, in effect, the last man standing, like the Dutch boy with his finger in the dyke. He took Adam 780 metres below the surface to the hot, humid and noisy pump station at the heart of the mine. This was the last underground pump station of the Eastern Basin – a huge underground area that had been mined since the late 19th century and on top of which the towns of the East Rand rested.

In the summer months, Grootvlei pumped enough water to fill 2 000 suburban swimming pools – ten giant pumps drove acidic water up four columns. Once the water reached the surface, it had to be purified before being released into surrounding streams and wetlands like Marievale, a world-famous bird sanctuary. But treating water meant spending money on chemicals like lime, to neutralise the acidity. Jock was doing all he could to stop Grootvlei from drowning, but could hardly be expected to prevent an ecological disaster as well. Adam asked Thulani Ngubane about the pollution. He was vague about the process, but, as always, managed to include some spin:

> We are spending money buying all the chemicals, iron, and we also ... we've been buying a um, the uh, the uh, what is the other chemical ... ? The Blue Scorpions could go there tomorrow, they will come back smiling and say ... Aurora Empowerment Systems have done the best ever project on that water ...

Actually, no one was smiling, or saying that Aurora was the best at anything. Adam couldn't get straight answers from the departments of Mineral Resources or Water Affairs either. By law, a mining house is meant to pay for the cleanup once the mineral wealth has been extracted from the ground.

Directives had been issued to mines on the West Rand, where toxic water had been seen bubbling out of rural boreholes. But what about the East Rand, where the nephew of the President and the grandson of Mandela were messing up? There'd been rumours that it had taken only one phone call to Eskom from Khulubuse Zuma to get the power switched back on at Grootvlei, despite the fact that Aurora's bill eventually topped R50 million.

Adam despaired, relocated to New York and got married. The print media continued to follow the looting of Grootvlei, a story that symbolised all that has gone wrong with post-apartheid South Africa – that don't-give-a-damn unaccountable greed that easily forgets history and disregards the future.

Producer Joy Summers, passionate about water issues, began a series of stories on acid mine drainage. All over the Witwatersrand, gold mines were reaching the end of their economic lives. Inside their shafts, levels of underground water contaminated with heavy metals were steadily rising, poisoning the good water. On the East Rand, Grootvlei was pivotal. If Jock stopped pumping, it would be only a matter of time before the toxic water started rising and bubbled to the surface somewhere near the Wimpy in Nigel.

Two stories, 'Yellow Boy Rising' and 'Sinking Solutions', looked at an impending disaster of epic proportions. Could Gauteng, the country's economic hub, one day drown in the poisonous legacy of what had made it rich? Dirty gold's sulphuric soup?

In a story called 'Aurora 3', Joy revisited miners at Grootvlei and Orkney who'd chucked in the towel, realising payday would never come. They'd watched scrap-metal dealers and other shady characters remove – under cover of darkness – headgear, winders, pipes and water pumps. Mines that had once produced 500 kilograms of gold a month had been reduced to skeletons.

What made them particularly furious, said Wellington, a worker at Orkney, was Jacob Zuma's silence: '... he is like a dead person. He is the President because of us, but his nephew is destroying us.'

Around the time that Khulubuse Zuma donated R1 million to the ANC's coffers, Marius Ferreira, a fitter and turner at Grootvlei, who had spent countless hours underground ensuring that the water pumps were working, took his own life. He hadn't been paid for months, and after he'd lost his house and his car he felt he'd lost his dignity too. On his deathbed he told his wife: 'You know, Bokkie, I took ant poison.'

Finally, in April 2011, the Aurora directors were called to account. But they told a specially convened parliamentary portfolio committee on mineral resources that they'd paid over 80 per cent of their workers, which prompted a lyrical line from Gideon du Plessis of the Solidarity trade union: 'There are people who are crying, there are people who are dying because we deal with people who are lying ...'

Looking on from his seat on the benches was Pamodzi's lead liquidator, Enver Motala, with his hawk-like nose, his eyes shadowed by dark rings. He said nothing, but plenty was said about him.

Solly Phetoe (COSATU): 'Enver Motala is not acting in the interests of the workers; he is acting in the interests of the real serious super-exploiters ... the Aurora directors.'

A month later, in May 2011, Enver Motala was given the boot by the Master of the High Court. Apart from the fact that he'd awarded a contract to an undercapitalised and clueless company, it turned out he also had 93 fraud convictions related to 93 purchases he'd made on a stolen credit card. And he'd changed his name to disguise the convictions.

It was a defining moment: with Motala out of the way, the remaining liquidators terminated Aurora's mandate and called for an inquiry into what had happened to Pamodzi's assets. R260 million had been paid out to the directors and their creditors from ten bank accounts. The now-looted mines had never been paid for and the workers were owed R20 million. The looting had apparently been aided and abetted by Aurora's financial 'advisors', Solly and Fazel Bhana.

Joy and Susan Comrie, who co-produced the story, were approached by a group of informants who told them of the extent of the Bhanas' involvement. But perhaps the directors were quite happy with the arrangement, because financial records showed that between October and December 2010, Zondwa Mandela was paid R450 000, and Thulani Ngubane R380 000. And Khulubuse Zuma didn't look like he'd missed many dinners – unlike the mineworkers who'd been forced to rely on charitable handouts.

In a series of meetings that stretched over seven hours, the informants told Susan and Joy that the Bhanas were pulling the strings. Father and son had effectively seized control of the mines and anything of value there. Joy sent a cameraman to Grootvlei to try to film their comings and goings. Mine manager Herbie Trouw hadn't seen them in a while, but could confirm that they'd certainly been there: 'My personal impression was that they were never here to mine; they were here to see what they could get out of it for their own benefit, like seeing what they could strip and put into their own pockets.' And chief gold smelter Douw van Niekerk said he'd watched Solly Bhana's brother load up assets: 'They sent in trucks. And they loaded scrap and cables ... Mohammed and them.'

Susan and Joy established that, over five months in 2011, one or other of the Bhanas took from Grootvlei gold worth more than R4 million. But the informants, who were intimately involved with the goings-on at Aurora, couldn't appear on camera, or even be quoted. And the only television appearances Solly Bhana ever seemed to make were with one of his prize racehorses.

Susan and Joy went to see the liquidators to try and find a way to film the impending Section 417 and 418 inquiries into the affairs of Aurora, where the directors and the Bhanas would be grilled by the liquidators. These two sections of the Companies Act allow liquidators to try to find the whereabouts of assets and how to retrieve them for creditors – in this case, R1.7 billion worth. But such inquiries were traditionally always held in camera. The only way to get access would be through an application to the Master of the High Court. The presence of the media is generally seen as inhibiting to witnesses and as interfering with the object of the inquiry. If the application was successful, it would be a ground-breaking ruling.

Such applications need money, a team of lawyers and, in this case, the go-ahead from M-Net, which would have to pay the legal fees. CEO Patricia van Rooyen, supportive of investigative journalism, gave the thumbs-up and *Carte Blanche*'s legal team drafted a 380-page court application. Hence the headlines in August 2011: 'M-Net's current affairs programme *Carte Blanche* applies for testimony of the Aurora directors to be heard in public ...'; '*Carte Blanche* applies for Aurora access'; '*Carte Blanche* seeks access to Aurora case'.

It was common knowledge, said the *Carte Blanche* application, that Aurora had failed to pay its workers, had failed to register with SARS, had contravened labour laws, was responsible for widespread pollution, had stripped mines of their assets for their own profit, and had been given special treatment by liquidators and others. And there was that constitutional right to freedom of expression: 'This freedom entails a right on the part of the public to receive information about matters of public interest and to form and express opinions on a wide range of matters.'

One thing the public wasn't allowed to receive information on was the identity of the sources called to testify against their former bosses.

They still hoped for their jobs back one day and couldn't be shown spilling the beans on camera. So the application was restricted to the testimony of the directors and financial advisors only. There were some stringent conditions, among them that the story be broadcast after the commission had sat and that the commissioners be allowed to view the programme in advance. There would be no chance of a breaking news story, but it would give Joy and Susan time to pull together, from hours and hours of testimony, a definitive piece on a mining scandal, a scandal that prompted tweets like these from viewers:

> Your GREED is sickening!! #Bhana #Mandela #Zuma You deserve the karma coming your way! While the miners starve! Disgusting!
> Let's hope the liquidators take the directors of #Aurora down in a big way ...
> All that Aurora money and Solly Bhana can't even get decent teeth ...

It wasn't so much Solly Bhana's missing teeth; it was more that he and Fazel came across as rogues of the first order.

Permission for filming was granted, in what *Carte Blanche* lawyers called 'an important milestone in the expansion of the broadcast media into previously non-public areas of legal proceedings'. Two cameras were allowed, but *Carte Blanche* was strictly forbidden from moving them around. Susan and/or Joy spent day upon day listening to lies, obfuscation and excuses. Finally, it was the turn of the Bhanas – the elusive father and son whom everyone at the mine seemed to fear. They were rather like villains in a B-grade movie.

John Walker (liquidator's attorney): 'What happened to the gold?'

Solly Bhana: 'I don't know where they sold it.'

John Walker: 'Would it surprise you to know that Mr van Niekerk said that all the gold was taken either by Mr Chammas, or Achmed Bhana, or someone, on your instruction?'

Solly Bhana: 'I don't know! I'm telling you – I wasn't ... I wasn't involved. If I go out with gold and the police stop me, what is going to happen to me? I wouldn't travel with gold for any price of money.'

Advocate Wayne Gibbs (commissioner): 'Why would everybody try to implicate you?'

Solly Bhana: 'I would love to know – really I would love to know.'

The inquiry began in July and was then delayed for months because everyone kept finding reasons not to appear. A novel one from Khulubuse was that his size, coupled with the stress of testifying, could induce a heart attack. The next day it was all over the press: 'Khulubuse – too fat to testify'; 'Zuma nephew too fat'; 'I'm too fat to come to court'.

Joy and Susan were worried that the leak could be attributed to them, the only journalists there. But they'd kept to their side of the bargain – the cameras had been switched off when Khulubuse made that comment. But they were switched on for other choice exchanges, such as one concerning the whereabouts of the mining assets, the stripping of which he said he'd never authorised. However, the Bhanas had been a law unto themselves.

Khulubuse: 'They were taking decisions on their own ... I would be told stories ... The media told me everything that was going on in my company.'

In a wistful voice, he said he longed for his old quiet life, before the stress of being a Randlord.

Khulubuse: 'I was living a very good life before this.'

Advocate Adrian Kruger (advocate for liquidators): 'An anonymous life?'

Khulubuse: 'Before, it was very nice. From that day when I had to answer journalists and this and that and everything changed.'

Zondwa Mandela, the Aurora CEO, didn't appear at all, despite summons after summons. That was because all the documents pertaining to Aurora had been 'stolen from his car'. In a voice recording of his testimony, he pleaded ignorance about the company's financial affairs, saying that the bank statements hadn't been under his control.

The other director, Thulani Ngubane, seemed equally vague. He hadn't known that large amounts of money had been paid to Aurora's 'investors' – Fazel Bhana, Solly Bhana, his wife, his two daughters, aunties, uncles, cousins ...

It seemed that, to stay afloat, Aurora had been taking short-term loans from family and friends. But lavish returns were promised, and loaning money to Aurora appeared to have been profitable business. Solly's son-in-law put in R300 000 and got out over R4 million.

Advocate Kruger: 'Did you ever ask your fellow directors, "But, guys, do we have sufficient money to repay the investors?"'

Thulani: 'It never crossed my mind that time.'

Advocate Kruger: 'It never crossed your mind?'

Thulani: 'That time ... that time ... that time ... But now it is crossing my mind.'

Solly Bhana himself was astonished to learn that about R800 000 had been deposited in his account in one month alone. His mouth dropped open.

Solly: 'All to Solly Bhana?'

John Walker (liquidator's attorney): 'All to Solly Bhana.'

Solly: 'There were so many transactions of Aurora.'

Advocate Gibbs: 'I am not talking about Aurora's transactions; I am talking about your personal transactions. Did you receive the money or not?'

Solly: 'I don't remember.'

Nor was son Fazel's memory more reliable. When asked if there were any investors apart from the Bhana family, he just shook his head in a tranquillised sort of way and said he couldn't remember.

These snippets were gems, but to find them and get to grips with the complexities of who'd helped themselves to what, Susan and Joy had to go through thousands of pages of transcripts. Once the final testimonies had been heard, they read for days, nights and weekends, pages of mind-numbing detail, knowing they couldn't start editing until they'd whittled it down to 20 minutes of airtime ... 30 at a push.

Bongani Bingwa, who came in after the hard slog to present the story and do the interviews, said working with them was a privilege: Joy was dramatic and meticulous, Susan calm and considered. Once he'd got to grips with the facts, he felt as involved and as outraged for the workers who'd tried so hard to protect their mine: 'In the shadow of a gold processing plant once worth R150 million, a crude gold smelting process is under way. These men ... are panning gold from the ore they find under the concrete and inside the corners of this plant that once produced up to 500 kg of gold per month. Now the ounces they eke out are profit-shared to pay security ... who watched helplessly as Aurora wrecked an asset and shattered thousands of lives.'

The liquidators issued summonses to all the Aurora directors under the Companies Act for acting recklessly with the intention to defraud creditors. They also filed an action for looting and stripping mines of their assets. The trial has been set for 2015.

While Grootvlei looks set for demolition, Orkney was taken over by a Chinese company that planned to have the mine up and running again by October 2013.

carte blanche extras 17

Caller to Carte Blanche: 'It has got quite bad – they are electronically harassing me with laser beams. I have pictures of lasers coming through my ceiling.'

Carte Blanche *journalist Wynand Grobler*: 'Right ...'

Caller: 'I've also had brain scans – my husband couldn't understand what the hell was happening to me. He sent me to psychologists and psychiatrists and they can't diagnose my problem because it's not a problem. I am flippen well being attacked by lasers ... and the stuff they are using against me is not the same stuff they used against me a year ago, it's more sophisticated.'

Wynand: 'What area are you in?'

Caller: 'Dainfern ... I have tissue burn, I sleep under thick duvets ... these weapons are able to go through brick ... why they are attacking me is because I've become a perceived threat. They live here, they don't work, they drive around in fancy cars ... and they suspected I was giving the police information ... '

Wynand: 'Right ...'

Caller: 'And it's getting more and more sophisticated ... every restaurant I go to they are there, or they phone. They trace my every flippen move ... men arrive and talk to the waiters. They put poison in my coffee, they tell terrible lies about me ... they want to kill me ... They are gang-stalking me with electronic weapons.'

Wynand: 'Golly ...'

Caller: 'So what I have for you is pictures of laser beams on my ceiling and in my house and I've got pictures of my burns and injuries. I've been to the police. Initially they said it sounded far-fetched. My husband, he's not being attacked, they are very clever ... if my husband moves near me they pull away their little laser beams ... and he cannot fathom what's going on with me. It's at night when he's sleeping that the worst of the harassment takes place. On YouTube you will see other people in the world have filmed electronic harassment. So go and do some research.'

Wynand: 'OK, I will familiarise myself with this and then I'll be in touch if I think it's a story.'

Caller: 'And if I do go on TV I would like to stay anonymous. That's the best way to deal with it. But I want to expose this whole lot of crap.'

Far-fetched it might sound, but the use of electromagnetic weaponry is well documented. Microwave devices emit low-frequency radiation that can cause an intense burning sensation, or evoke a sense of anxiety or paranoia in certain individuals. Whether this caller was being deliberately targeted, or had simply read up on the issue and imagined the symptoms, was never established. But dozens of viewers have complained to *Carte Blanche* about the environmental health hazards of our electronic age. And many people across the world are hypersensitive to power lines, cellphones, radar and transmitting stations. But they are frequently dismissed by corporations, which cite conflicting studies and the absence of long-term research.

In 2010, M-Net commissioned a season of *Carte Blanche Medical* and *Carte Blanche Consumer* programming, spin-offs of the Sunday show that would be broadcast on weeknights at 7pm. It provided an outlet for those medical and consumer stories that the eclectic Sunday slot couldn't always accommodate, but which were popular with viewers ... like electromagnetic sensitivity, a topic that was both consumer and medical.

Migraines, Maladies and Masts – 2010

The main case study in this story, produced by Nicola de Chaud and Odette Schwegler, was Tracey-Lee Dorny, from Craigavon, in northern Johannesburg – not far from Dainfern, from where the electronically harassed caller had phoned. Tracey was a businesswoman specialising in events and hospitality. But soon she was being labelled a crank.

Craigavon is a cluster and townhouse haven, where high-end property buyers flock to enjoy a secure lock-up-and-go lifestyle. All of them need technology to connect them to the 21st century – just not in their back-yards. Tracey-Lee woke one morning in August 2009 to find a wireless broadband mast had been erected 30 metres from the master bedroom of her luxury home. Within a few weeks, she began experiencing unusual symptoms: headaches, nausea, rashes, burning, itching and stinging ...

Then her son Keegan began suffering from nausea, vomiting and headaches. Tracey lined his room with insulation foil, to no avail. He got a rash and suffered heart palpitations. So they moved out. Immediately, the complications subsided. She canvassed the rest of her old neighbour-hood and compiled a database of complaints from 45 other residents:

Woman 1: 'All my body is itchy and it is burning. I am scratching and I can't even sleep.'

Woman 2: 'Itchy skin, bloodshot eyes, headaches, inability to concen-trate, I'd get an inflamed sensation down the one side of my body.'

Man: 'Like hot flushes, headaches ...'

Boy: 'I haven't really been able to sleep properly.'

Woman 3: 'My stomach is burning inside. I feel like I can vomit. And I've got a headache.'

Odette and Nicola found Tracey and the Craigavon residents totally believable, but the difficulty with the story was balancing the mountain of contradictory international research. They were mindful that science could be manipulated to prove or disprove just about anything and often depended on who was funding the research. A fact sheet from the World Health Organization (WHO) stated that there were no proven adverse health effects from masts, but its website carried studies showing a range of disturbances. Bongani Bingwa, who presented the story, interviewed

216

a neuroscientist in Sweden by phone, who called the proliferation of masts in residential areas 'the largest full-scale human experiment ever'. The science was inconclusive, but Tracey and other Craigavon residents were clear about what they were feeling.

The mast had been installed by business wireless solutions company iBurst. CEO Jannie van Zyl said radiation coming from the tower was much lower than recommended by the International Council on Non-Ionizing Radiation Protection, whose guidelines the WHO followed. Bongani asked him about research suggesting that it was time these public guidelines were revised because symptoms were being experienced within and below the recommended levels.

Jannie van Zyl: '... There are many, many more studies that say that no correlation can be found.'

Bongani Bingwa: 'We can play this ping-pong. I can say this study, I can say that study ...'

Jannie van Zyl: 'I've got slightly more studies than you ...'

'Mine's-bigger-than-yours' Jannie believed that something else must have been causing the Craigavon health complications. The residents were just blaming whatever was new in the environment – like iBurst's big, in-your-face tower. So Jannie decided to trick the residents, even though they were essentially *his* customers. In November, he told them he would switch off the mast for a trial period.

But just before the *Carte Blanche Medical* broadcast in February 2010, he phoned Nicola and Odette to say that, in fact, he'd switched off the mast six weeks before the November meeting, but residents had continued to experience symptoms, which had proved his theory that it was all in their minds. Then, clearly conducting his own private little experiment, he said he'd switched the mast back on in December. Nicola asked for the log records. He said he'd need his technical experts to analyse them first. She said she'd find an independent expert. But the logs weren't forthcoming, which made Nicola and Odette doubt him. If the mast had been switched off, why hadn't he said so during the interview?

Jannie van Zyl resigned in May 2010, for unrelated reasons; the new iBurst CEO, Thami Mtshali, said he certainly wasn't going to fight with clients, and had the mast taken down – an unusual approach in a cut-throat, multi-billion-rand industry where coverage is king.

In December 2010, Tracey-Lee Dorny moved back home after 18 months in exile. 'Well, I honestly stood up on that balcony and I just sobbed; I absolutely cried my eyes out,' she said.

Olive Oil

Mediterranean blood flows thick at *Carte Blanche*, and long before TV chefs were slathering it over just about everything, the quality of olive oil was considered worthy consumer news. These days it's a hot topic, and there's even a book called *Extra Virginity: The Sublime and Scandalous World of Olive Oil*, by US journalist Tom Mueller. But in 2001, when most South Africans were still wedded to their mayo and shop-bought dressings, producer Hein Ungerer and presenter Les Aupiais reported on a scam involving this liquid gold, with its unmistakeable aroma and taste.

The trail of the bogus olive oil began with an investigation by a member of the SA Olive Growers' Association, Guido Costa, whose family had been producing olive oil since 1904. He was suspicious of several varieties of oil being sold in supermarkets with exotic names like Aphrodite and Antico Frantoio, which, to his trained palate, tasted like doctored sunflower oil, with none of the nutty nuances of the real thing.

Hein sent samples for testing to the University of the Free State, where an expert in oil analysis, Professor Lodewyk Kock, said Aphrodite was neither desirable nor rapturous, as the Ancient Greek name implied. In fact, it contained a dye called Lipo Green LT, used in petrochemical solvents for cleaning motor engines. It was definitely not for human consumption, said Lodewyk.

A *Carte Blanche* camera crew accompanied the police on several busts, uncovering a bottling plant and 'extra virgin, cold-pressed, bottled in Italy labels' that certainly didn't match the oil in their containers. Dodgy distributors were adding olive flavouring and copper colouring to sunflower oil and selling it as the real thing. Rather than in olive oil, which is rich in anti-oxidants and good fats, it seemed that scores of health-conscious consumers had been tossing their lettuce in tinted sunflower oil.

By the time of the next *Carte Blanche* olive oil story, in 2010, South Africa had cleaned up its act and was winning awards for producing some of the best olive oils in the world. But producer Sophia Phirippides, a self-proclaimed olive oil goddess of Greek extraction, hadn't noticed. Every time she ordered olive oil with her salad at local restaurants, she could detect none of the robust flavours of the real thing. When she asked for the original container, it had either been turfed, decanted into another bottle, or she was presented with refined olive pomace oil – made from olive mulch, and which many believe should only be used for things like soap. Eventually, Sophia's teenage children refused to eat out with her because they feared another embarrassing olive oil episode. Sophia got hold of Guido Costa, who agreed with her that there were still retailers and restaurants who were deceiving the public. He suspected them of blending good oil with inferior and then marketing it as extra virgin and charging the equivalent price: a contravention of international trade standards.

The *Carte Blanche* office had become used to Sophia banging on about olive oil, but knew it would be a massive undertaking for a 10-minute story – the standard length of a Sunday night insert. The new *Carte Blanche Consumer* show would be the perfect vehicle.

Sophia, accompanied by a spy camera, and sometimes by her partner, Jonathan Pienaar, who'd become, by default, an olive oil aficionado, began eating a salad a day in three areas of Johannesburg with a high concentration of restaurants that claimed to use olive oil as an essential ingredient. Her opening line to the waiters was 'I feel like a salad ... do you have olive oil?' After it had arrived – 'Are you SURE this is olive oil?'

She would decant the offending olive oil into a sample bottle and re-searcher Wynand Grobler or Jonathan would film her sealing it – to pre-clude accusations of tampering. Wynand would catalogue the samples and send them off to Professor Kock at the University of the Free State.

The results revealed that, of the samples taken from 24 restaurants, ten of them were vegetable oils like canola or soya and the remaining

14 were pomace. Sophia felt vindicated, and she and presenter Devi Sankaree Govender set off to do some filming. The *Carte Blanche* team blindfolded members of the public, and then got them to sample seed oil, an olive oil blend, extra virgin olive oil and olive pomace oil. Impressively, over half of these Johannesburg shoppers were able to distinguish olive oil from the rest. And how would they feel if they were given something else in a restaurant?

Man 9: 'Well, obviously I'd be upset.'

Woman 5: 'That's a lie ... that's dishonest!'

Woman 3: 'And I would assume – especially if it is served with something like a bread or balsamic vinegar. Yes, I would expect it to be olive oil.'

Man 11: 'There is a huge difference, absolutely – in price – between the original real olive oil and of course it is a health benefit as well.'

Results in hand, Sophia and Devi challenged the restaurant owners. Confrontations are never easy, but Devi has perfected the art. She has a true sense of occasion and knows exactly when to turn on the heat with a degree of humour. But, as it turned out, even Sandton restaurateurs weren't shy to admit that they filled the olive oil bottles on their tables with any old thing, bringing out containers from the kitchen in what made for hilarious exchanges.

Devi: 'When people ask for olive oil, you are giving them this?'

Man 12 (manager): 'Portuguese seasoning, yes.'

Devi: 'So what does that mean? I'm sitting here at Nelson Mandela Square and you're serving that – masquerading as olive oil. Come on, that's not on. That's not on ... I mean, look at your clientele.'

Man 12: 'Yes ...'

Devi: 'This is not a takeaway; it's a fancy-shmancy restaurant.'

Some blamed their suppliers, showing Devi and Sophia invoices that passed off pomace as olive oil, but which had cost them far less. The team produced the results of tests Lodewyk Kock had done on what the owner maintained was olive oil:

Man 13: I'm saying it is olive oil, you are saying it is not olive oil. But on the bottle it says, "olive oil". Now my suppliers supply it as olive oil. There is no commitment where I say that you will be supplied the best extra virgin olive oil at R200 a bottle, do you understand?

Devi and Sophia didn't understand. If they were paying R75 for a salad and asked for a bit of olive oil with it, that's what they wanted: pure, unadulterated olive oil, not a mixture of who-knows-what.

The story was an indictment of the food industry and a classic *Carte Blanche* consumer story – directed at the high end of the market, but also intended to bring awareness to less-discerning restaurant patrons. Sophia has no doubt that the great olive oil con hasn't stopped. But when waiters see her coming, they rush off to the kitchen to get that 'special' bottle of cold-pressed extra virgin.

Fish Fraud

It used to be an endless source of amusement at *Carte Blanche* that Cape Town producer Liz Fish seemed so obsessed with the ocean: her company, Flying Fish Productions, had produced for *Carte Blanche* stories on shipwrecks, E-coli on our beaches, the state of marine and coastal management, intrepid adventurers rowing across the Atlantic and several award-winning stories on the fraudulent labelling of fish. As Derek Watts once put it after yet another fishy story: 'A powerful message to the industry, we need more passionate consumers ... and our producer Liz Fish is also very committed to her marine family.'

It was a story that truly showed her commitment, and that had her traipsing from wholesaler to wholesaler and eating plenty of fish. She'd read an American study in which students had done DNA tests on fish and discovered that a high proportion were misnamed as unrelated species, to hide the identities of protected fish, or to pass off cheap fish as something more expensive. 'Red snapper' was a name used all over the world to market anything from tilapia to hake.

Liz decided to find out what was happening in South African waters. She'd once produced a feature on Charles Clover's book (and subsequent documentary) *End of the Line*, which warns that by the middle of the 21st century most of the world's commercial stocks of wild fish could be wiped out. Bluefin tuna has been hunted to the brink of extinction and, in some parts of the world, cod stocks have collapsed. If wholesalers and retailers continue to mislead consumers, one day there will be nothing but jellyfish and worms left in the ocean.

DNA testing is expensive, so Liz approached the University of Stellenbosch, which agreed to help, because no similar study had ever been done in South Africa. Marine biologist Dr Sophie von der Heyden and Jaco Barendse from the South African Sustainable Seafood Initiative (SASSI) began educating Liz in how to tell the difference between kob and kingklip, dorado and yellowtail. She had to learn all their common names and the Latin ones too, in case unscrupulous wholesalers tried to pull the scales over her eyes. She posed as a caterer and made her way around Cape Town's industrial areas. Soon all the seafood merchants knew Mrs Fish and her cooler box.

Over the next few months, Liz sourced, and Sophie tested, 178 portions of fish from 20 randomly selected outlets in Johannesburg and Cape Town. At wholesalers, she had to buy fish by the box, even though Sophie needed only one small piece for testing. Each box contained 40 pieces of fish, and soon Liz's freezer was groaning. Her husband Tony and their teenage children stoically ate fish morning, noon and night, but her friends were less loyal and began turning down dinner invitations because they knew all too well what would be on the menu.

At restaurants, Liz would ask endless questions of the waiters about the 'catch of the day', or the 'linefish', which she realised was never caught on the day nor at the end of a line. Some restaurants were selling fish flown in from as far afield as South America and East Asia as locally caught linefish. She would always leave with a takeaway for Sophie to test. Linefish served at a well-known seafood restaurant in Simon's Town, listed on the menu as wahoo – a prize game fish caught off the Kenyan coast – turned out to be king mackerel, an inferior-tasting fish caught in nets on the American side of the Atlantic.

The first round of DNA tests showed that 80 per cent of kob, and 30 per cent of kingklip, had been relabelled. Boxes labelled kob turned out to be gastora, part of the mackerel family, while some contained a variety of species. Shark was often labelled 'ocean fillet'.

But Liz had to be sure it hadn't happened accidentally, so once she'd found a wholesaler or retailer that had mislabelled fish, she returned and repeated the process – more fish for her freezer. She got cameraman Tim Wege to hang around in the back of the shop, wearing a camera hidden in a jacket to film the exchanges: 'Are you sure this is kob?'

The tests confirmed exactly what Liz had set out to prove: inferior fish was being sold at a higher price, defrauding consumers, who were also unknowingly buying threatened species that were renamed as non-endangered.

Although she had no-nonsense presenter Devi to confront the offenders, Liz was nervous and was sure the microphone in the boom pole she was carrying would pick up the sound of her thumping heart. The first wholesaler pleaded ignorance, saying they were frequently misled by suppliers. News travelled fast, and by the time *Carte Blanche* had arrived at the third wholesaler, its CEO had 'fish bibles' set out on his desk, and a 'fish expert' sitting in the wings. When Devi told him that only three of the kob samples they'd bought were correctly labelled, he fobbed her off, saying: 'They are all from the kob family, you are just splitting hairs.' But, as Sophie pointed out, that was like saying sheep and cows were the same.

When confronted about selling red-listed and inferior species, restaurateurs said they had no way of knowing what was what, once the heads and tails were off. But some of them had deliberately tried to mislead their patrons, renaming unsexy-sounding species like 'slime fish' and 'bullseye-snakehead' as the more palatable-sounding 'orange roughy' and 'cardinal' – neither of them sustainable choices.

For Liz, the most depressing part of all was visiting the National Regulator of Consumer Specifications (NRCS) – the government body meant to police and regulate the industry. They made it clear that whoever sold the fish was responsible for naming it – nothing to do with them. And, anyway, they didn't have the budget to do DNA tests.

But, after the first insert was aired, the NRCS tightened up on inspections, passing new regulations. One supplier said: 'It was a real wake-up call for the industry ... since the programme, NRCS have become a real pain in the backside, ensuring we use the Latin names as well as all the common names on labels.' However, without testing, consumers still had

no way of knowing if fish had been relabelled. But it heightened awareness; restaurants were put under enormous pressure from the public
and began insisting their suppliers did regular DNA tests to ensure the
authenticity of their fish. SASSI's FishMs line began receiving thousands
of inquiries about the conservation status of different species.

Sophie von der Heyden and Jaco Barendse co-authored a paper entitled 'Misleading the Masses: detection of mislabelled and substituted
fish products in South Africa'. Liz did a follow-up story called 'Making
Waves', investigating the traceability of fish and retailers selling illegally caught species in unregulated waters.

Her Latin name is Eliza Piscis.

Building Blunders

Stories like 'Olive Oil' and 'Fish Fraud' take time and resources and can
impact on public policy. But it's often the minor issues that have a major
effect on ordinary lives and get the average *Carte Blanche* viewer hot
under the collar. These stories require the common touch and a degree of
passion. *Carte Blanche Consumer* editor Wynand Grobler – the force behind exposés that probed the hidden costs charged by private hospitals,
and several car classics like the Boksburg showroom that rebuilt written-
off wrecks in its basement – thrives on seeking justice for the viewers
who flood his inbox with messages. But putting together a meaningful
and entertaining consumer story is far more difficult than a straight
narrative. Consumers, he's found out the hard way, sometimes add a
few untruths to their tales of woe, either to make things sound worse,
or because they haven't quite understood the terms and conditions of
an agreement. But once solid stories have been selected, there's nothing
more satisfying than seeing ripoff merchants getting their comeuppance
– be it over a paid-for-but-never-built log home, unsolicited printer
cartridges or a rock pool that ends up as nothing more than a dry hole
in the garden.

In 2011, *Carte Blanche* set up a 'war room', where consumers with
complaints were invited to state their cases to be followed up by the

team. It was a high-maintenance show because each step of the process had to be filmed reality-style and the cases carefully chosen. There were also fun topics, like which supermarket did the quickest online delivery, or offered the best value for a basket of shopping. These became serious when supermarket CEOs began questioning the research: was *Carte Blanche* comparing goods of a similar quality? Of course it was, but it was a reminder of how meticulous research has to be.

The key to a successful consumer story is viewer satisfaction, and that is often only achieved by catching the alleged baddie, not from listening to a string of unresolved complaints.

Producer Bernadette Maguire realised the importance of this kind of journalism in the early 1990s, while working on *Fair Deal* with Isabel Jones, one of South Africa's early consumer crusaders. The much-loved Jones had caught many a small-time crook in her day, but one had eluded her: Braam the builder. He'd been around for decades, advertising dream log homes, but usually delivering only a pile of planks and a string of excuses before disappearing with the deposit. He would pop up in another guise in another part of the country a few years later. This time, he was building 'Canadian' log homes in the Pretoria area and had a flashy website with some impressive-looking structures. But he'd conned too many people, and now there were even blogs about him. One entry read: *'Ons het 'n totaal van amper R900 000 aan Braam betaal ... Dit is nou Januarie 2012, ons huis moes in Julie 2011 klaar gewees het. Dit is n gemors ... GLO MY ASB, NIE EEN VAN DIE HUISE IS DEUR BRAAM VOLTOOI NIE.'*

It was clear that Braam wasn't just a slacker with good intentions; he'd been at it far too long. Bernadette was determined to catch him this time. They met up with Anne Germishuizen, who'd started the 'Beware of Braam' blog, and who'd paid for a wonky-looking, far-from-completed home, which engineers had declared structurally unsound and on which, they said, she'd need to spend a further R500 000. It was a double-storey, but Braam hadn't bothered to put in a staircase. To film the chaos inside, the *Carte Blanche* crew – Derek, Bernadette, cameramen Dudley and JP – had to use a long builder's ladder. The interior of the house revealed live wires, incomplete bathrooms, sagging ceilings, and fittings and rubble everywhere. Anne said that when she'd complained, Braam had told her he had 'ways of dealing with difficult people'.

Another unhappy client was Tony Visser, who'd been battling to get his money back from Braam for seven years. All he'd got for his R74 000 deposit was a pile of wooden poles that he now used for braaiing. He had two judgments against Braam, who'd pleaded insolvency yet continued to trade. Bernadette made an appointment to see him and the team drove out to his factory, but on arrival they were handed a letter referring them to Braam's lawyers – the same lawyers who wrote to *Carte Blanche* saying Braam would 'address the allegations levelled against it ... in the appropriate forum as and when the "need" arise [sic]'.

Braam was doing a runner again. So, together with Tony, the team hatched Plan B. Tony knew that Braam also reconditioned classic Minis, so he pretended to be interested in buying one and arranged a test drive. He'd only dealt with Braam over the phone, so there was no chance that he'd be recognised. The *Carte Blanche* crew would wait around the corner and then confront Braam during the test drive. But Braam was clearly a trusting sort and let Tony test the Mini on his own.

It was time for Plan C. Tony phoned Braam and told him that the Mini had broken down. Derek and the crew hid behind a wall, while Tony opened the bonnet at the side of the road and unplugged a connection. Braam arrived in his bakkie a few minutes later, and, as he was checking the Mini, Derek pounced: 'Braam, can we help?'

Braam did a good job of looking completely nonchalant, despite the presence of the two cameras and the lanky Mr Watts, who introduced him to Tony: 'Braam, do you remember this man ... Tony Visser ... you started building a house for him ...'

'Howzit, Tony!' Braam pumped his hand vigorously. Then Derek and Tony let rip, asking Braam why he was still trading with judgments against his company and his person, and reminding him of the 50 other people who'd accused him of taking their cash and not delivering.

Braam muttered something about his lawyers and said he did have some happy clients. Tony was outraged: 'You have got no one who is happy because this is the way you operate.'

Braam stood there, hands on hips with his mouth agape, then got into the Mini and tried to start it. It wouldn't, because of the disconnected wire. 'You broke my car!' he said to Tony, who explained about the wire, and then suddenly lost it: 'Screw you! I have been waiting for seven years!' At which point Braam got out of the car, slammed the door and said: 'Take it!'

Later that day, he gave Tony the papers and signed over the Mini to him. The last shot of the story was a big thumbs-up from Tony, before he chugged off in his newly acquired car.

It had been a dream confrontation and viewers knew it:

Special thank you to the producer, Bernadette, for the time and research she put into this episode. Hopefully this will deter other people from using Braam in the future.

Baie dankie Bernadette en al die ander wat hard hieraan gewerk het. Hou ons ander asb hier op die blog op hoogte.

Isabel Jones would've been delighted.

The Next 25

Bongani and Devi, who may well remain the faces of *Carte Blanche* in the next 25 years, can still walk around shopping centres near Soweto, Umlazi or Gugulethu in relative anonymity. But put them in Hyde Park, Gateway or The Pavilion and they're celebrities; Bongani is asked to pose with bored-looking children while their beaming mums take photographs, or someone takes a quick cellphone video in which Devi has to say hello to a loved one at home who missed out on meeting her. 'You look taller on TV,' she's usually told as she tears around the supermarket on a rare day off, before being asked for advice on the most effective household products. Eating out at a well-known steakhouse, Bongani is coerced into inspecting the kitchens for cleanliness; at fish shops, he's asked not what he would like to buy, but if he's checking for red-listed species. At restaurants, Devi can't help noticing, she and her family are given bigger portions than their fellow diners.

Research conducted within the black premium market in 2012 revealed

227

a growing identification with the *Carte Blanche* presenters as fearless watchdogs, keeping an eye on corruption within provincial and national government and in the corporate world. The overwhelming perception was that the show was well-researched and professional, that it equipped viewers for the week ahead and that it gave them commonality with white colleagues, with their own long-standing attachment to the brand.

@mojaklehoko: Gotta watch CARTE BLANCHE tonight. I NEED to know what's troubling my white friends.

As much as *Carte Blanche*'s past was driven by the personal narrative, so may its future be determined by cleverly conceived consumer stories and in-depth investigations like those into auctions and the Aurora scandal. By the time the show celebrates its 27th year on air, South Africa should, according to international deadlines, have migrated from analogue broadcasting to a digital platform. Although South Africa is likely to miss the globally agreed deadline of June 2015 to switch to digital television broadcasting, the eventual outcome will mean – apart from better picture quality – loads more choice. So, while an exciting broadcast environment beckons, with huge scope for the expansion of community radio and television, the challenge for all existing channels will be how to avoid diminishing audiences and revenue.

Carte Blanche will need to continue to uncover the good, the bad and the ugly, to satisfy emotional needs and to appeal to a common humanity, to viewers who care about their country and who can laugh and cry about it together on a Sunday night.

Auntie Boksburg must meet Mrs Dlamini.